THE RISE OF CHINA
THE IMPACT ON SEMI-PERIPHERY AND PERIPHERY COUNTRIES

Edited by

Li Xing
Steen Fryba Christensen

中国 - 世界

AALBORG **UNIVERSITY PRESS**

The Rise of China
The Impact on Semi-periphery and Periphery Countries
Edited by Li Xing Steen & Fryba Christensen

© Aalborg University Press, 2012

Layout: akila v/ Kirsten Bach Larsen
Cover: akila v/ Kirsten Bach Larsen
Printed by Toptryk Grafisk ApS, 2012
ISBN: 978-87-7112-017-2

Published by:
Aalborg University Press
Skjernvej 4A, 2nd floor
9220 Aalborg
Denmark
Phone: (+45) 99 40 71 40
Fax: (+45) 96 35 00 76
aauf@forlag.aau.dk
forlag.aau.dk

This book is financially supported by The Department of Culture and Global Studies, Aalborg University, Denmark.

Table of Contens

List of Tables and figures

Tables

Figures

Notes on Contributors

Eduardo Daniel Oviedo is Professor at National University of Rosario and Senior Researcher Fellow of National Scientific and Technical Researches Council, Argentina.

Elijah Nyaga Munyi is PhD candidate, Center for Comparative Integration Studies, Department of Culture and Global Studies, Aalborg University, Denmark.

Ignacio Frechero is PhD candidate and junior researcher, Center for Interdisciplinary Studies on International and Local Problems (CEIPIL), National University of the Center of Buenos Aires Province (UNICEN), Argentina.

Johanna Jansson is PhD candidate, International Development Studies, Department of Society and Globalization, Roskilde University, Denmark.

Jørgen Dige Pedersen is Associate Professor and senior researcher, Department of Political Science, Aarhus University, Denmark.

Li Xing is Associate Professor and senior researcher, Research Centre on Development and International Relations, Department of Culture and Global Studies, Aalborg University, Denmark.

Raúl Bernal-Meza is Professor of International Relations and senior researcher, the Universidad Nacional del Centro de la Provincia de Buenos Aires and Professor at the Universsdad de Buenos Aires, Argentina.

Steen Fryba Christensen is Associate Professor and senior researcher, Research Centre on Development and International Relations, Department of Culture and Global Studies, Aalborg University, Denmark.

Introduction

The Unanticipated Fall and Rise of China and the Capitalist World System

From a "Middle Kingdom" to a Peripheral State: a Holistic Conceptualization

In the early 15th century, during China's Ming Dynasty, under the command of Admiral Zheng He, the Chinese imperial fleet set out on seven voyages in the name of the "mandate of heaven" to explore and trade with the outside world. Even by today's standards, the size and magnificence of the fleet remains unprecedented in maritime history - 27,000 men aboard 317 ships. The Admiral's command ship, called "*treasure ship*", was a most impressive vessel: built of hardwood, 130 meters long and 50 meters wide (in contrast with Christopher Columbus's 28-metre long "*Santa Maria*"). The voyages were aimed at spreading the glory of the Chinese Empire and culture, and exercising "soft power" in modern terms. The objectives of these voyages were more political than economic, namely to display China's imperial power, to strengthen the traditional tribute system and the suzerainty of the Chinese throne, and to consolidate the Pax Sinica in Asia (Jesus, 2005). According to historian Paul Kennedy, "In 1420, the navy Ming was recorded as possessing 1,350 combat vessels, including 400 large floating fortresses and 250 ships designed for long-range cruising" (Kennedy, 1989: 4).

When the Admiral concluded his last voyage, he reported to the emperor that there was no outside place that was better and richer than China, and there was nothing China really needed from the outside world. The emperor then, in 1521, ordered the destruction of the ocean-going vessels and banned trade outside Chinese territorial waters. This imperial mandate was connected to the fact that emerging rich merchants with their wealth based on world-wide trade were

1

becoming a challenge to imperial power, which was based on tribute from the land (Brown, 1993: 16).

China's relations with the West, especially its early encounters with Europe, are often viewed through the prism of a great civilization and a regional hegemon, as well as a victim of century-long humiliation under Western imperialism. Not only do Chinese *technological inventions* (gunpowder, the compass, printing, paper-making) together with a number of other items such as medicines, plants and minerals that were first discovered and cultivated by the Chinese, provide a good starting point for discussing both the achievements of the Chinese civilization and China's influence on the West (Bodde, 2004a), but so do *Chinese ideas* and their impact on the historical development of the West, such as civil service, alchemy, chemistry, agricultural methods, some of the inspiration for the Age of the Enlightenment, Western literature, as well as Western political and economic theories (Bodde, 2004b). This questions the Eurocentric myth that Greece was the only source of all of its science and knowledge. The Chinese culture, philosophy and socio-political institution had an indispensable influence in the European Enlightenment, in which the leading figures of the Age of Reason, such as Leibniz, Voltaire, and Quesnay, among others, found great inspiration in many aspects of Chinese society and political organization (Billington, 1995). As a Chinese scholar summarizes the impact of Confucianism on the European modern civilization:

> The human-based ideas of Confucianism that people are the foundation of the country, the governing way of "Governance with virtue", the way of personnel placement that men of great virtue and talent are elected who will cultivate mutual trust and promote universal understanding, the nationwide education thought that there should be education for everyone without distinction and the imperial examination system under the idea that those who excellently learned should serve (in the government), have exerted beneficial influences on the European modern civilization. (Yu, 2009: 10)

For centuries the "Middle Kingdom" had no interest in dealing with outside "barbarians" and wanted nothing from the West. But the West wanted a great deal from China and its ambition was not only to urge the Chinese and their own government to open-up trade, but also to allow passage for other products.

The *Opium War*[1], in the middle of the 19th century, ended with China's total defeat. The *Treaty of Nanjing*[2] forced China to pay a huge indemnity to Britain for the cost of war and imposed a tariff on all goods imported into China. Ever since then, Chinese civilization has been greatly contested and challenged, while the well-equilibrated Chinese imperial system gradually collapsed. Unlike the downfall of previous dynasties, when China was ruled by its minority ethnic groups (including the last Qing Dynasty) which did not inflict any fatal damage to the main features of the Chinese way of life and the identity of Chinese culture, the decline of Qing Dynasty was unanticipated and had the whole face of civilization collapse. The Middle Kingdom experienced the unprecedented trauma of "century of humiliation."[3] Since then, a strong national sense of "victim mentality"[4] has been a major driving force behind the emergence of Chinese nationalism and behind China's persistent effort to reclaim its lost status as a global power.

The causes of China's decline were both multiple and complex. There were a number of internal factors and external forces that contributed to this state of affairs. The followings are some of the major conceptualizations and interpretations from a variety of perspectives:

Internal cultural, political and social constraints

The decline of Chinese civilization and its underdevelopment has been a subject of interest in social science and especially in the field of development studies. Both Western and Chinese scholars and researchers have attempted to find answers to questions such as, "Why did capitalism evolve in medieval Europe and not in China, India or anywhere else?" A number of theoretical explanations, embracing both internal and external factors, have been advanced to explain the rise of capitalism in Europe (Li Xing and Hersh, 2004) and the causes of non-European countries (including China's) inability to overcome the static limitations of its feudalism and move to capitalism.

One of the Eurocentric frameworks for understanding and interpreting the causal correlations lie in the discussion of how cultural values and social processes interact to shape and reshape socio-economic development in the evolution of market capitalism. Among the interpretations by central Eurocentric thinkers, Hegel, in his *The Philosophy of History* (1837), states that universal or world-history travels from east to west. Asia is the beginning, while Europe is the end of history. The "beginning", on one hand, stands for the source of human civilization, but, on the other hand, represents a primitive cultural tradition – a "childhood of history":

> The first phase - that with which we have to begin - is the East. Unreflected consciousness - substantial, objective, spiritual existence - forms the basis; to which the subjective will first sustain a relation in the form of faith, confidence, obedience. In the political life of the East we find realised national freedom, developing itself without advancing to subjective freedom. It is the *childhood of history*. In the gorgeous edifices of

3

the Oriental empires we find all national ordinances and arrangements, but in such a way that individuals remain as mere accidents. These revolve round a centre, round the sovereign, who as patriarch stands (not as despot, in the sense of the Roman imperial constitution) at the head. For he has to enforce the moral and substantial; he has to uphold those essential ordinances which are already established; so that what among us belongs entirely to subjective freedom, here proceeds from the entire and general body of the state. (Hegel, ibid. *italic* added)

In the eyes of Hegel, societal development history can be described as the evolutionary development process of a human being. The application of the "childhood" metaphor intends to describe the contrast between European modernity and Asian/African regression. Asia and Africa were seen as being "static, despotic, and irrelevant to world history" (Said, 1993: 168). Hegel's view of history was highly influential and had a great impact on Marxist, culturalist and humanist historiography. Hegel opened the window for a strong Eurocentric understanding and interpretation of world history.

Karl Marx, whose theories and insight inspired the Chinese Communist Revolution, described China a society "vegetating in the teeth of time….. the representative of the antiquated world" in contrast to Europe, a "representative of overwhelming modern society". Marx discovered in the Great Wall of China a metaphor for the universal resistance of non-European societies to change (Marx as quoted in Dirlik and Meisner, 1989: 17). Despite his strong critique of and opposition to the systematic problems of capitalism, Marx was, nevertheless, impressed by the dynamism of European capitalism, while dismayed by the backwardness and stagnancy of China and India.

What is most influential to contemporary sociology and development studies, is Max Weber's Eurocentric culturalist interpretation on the relationship between cultural values/orientations and economic rationality. His theory on the *Protestant ethic* – the spirit of capitalism – has had a strong influence on 20th century history, sociology, and political science. Many scholars, including Weber himself, used this theory to justify their claim about the reason why occidental modern societies were able to realize industrialization, whereas, despite favourable conditions for rationalization in traditional China, the Confucian ethos of humanism, as opposed to the ethics of ascetic Protestantism, was inimical to the development of the spirit of capitalism. In his own words, Weber made the following comparison:

The relentlessly and religiously systematized utilitarianism peculiar to rational asceticism (Puritanism), to live "in" the world and yet not be part of it, has helped to produce superior rational aptitudes and therewith the spirit of the vocational man which, in the last analysis was denied to Confucianism. That is to say, the Confucian way of life was rational but was determined unlike Puritanism, from without rather than from within. The contrast can teach us that mere sobriety and thriftiness combined with acquisitiveness and regard for wealth were far from releasing the "capitalist spirit." (Weber, 1951: 248)

Following Weber's interpretation, the worldviews of Chinese Confucianism and Taoism embody the religious ethic of the privileged or vested interests, where the educated and the patrimonial state maintained the dominance of tradition (Weber, 1951). Confucianism sees tradition as being sacred and believes in ancestral spirits. Tradition is maintained through education, and education also aims to fulfill a form of personal cultivation, rather than simply being a source of expertise and functional technology (Weber, 1951). Weber's central conclusion was that Chinese traditional culture, like other major non-Western cultures of the world, was not able to generate cultural forces strong enough to break the constraints of religious and traditional values in terms of accepting and engaging profitable economic activities.

But the challenge to the Weberian interpretation is how his hypothesis would explain the astonishing stagnation of Europe from 300 to 1100 CE (the Dark Ages), vis-a-vis the great advance of China during this period. Professor Joseph Needham, a renowned scientist and historian of science, was one of the Europeans who endeavored to study the impact of cultural, social and institutional durable permanency on the development of technology, science and civilization in ancient China. With the assistance of an international team of collaborators, Needham's research project produced a series of volumes, entitled *Science and Civilization in China* (Needham et al., 1954). Needham spent the latter half of his productive life on the study and publication of Chinese science and civilization. His research outcomes prompted a number of serious questions which probed the perceived Eurocentric myth, i.e. that Greece was the only source of science and knowledge for Europe. Owing to his great efforts, Chinese contributions to the world's history of science and technology are well documented today. But Needham also posed an interesting grand question, known as "The Needham Question", which is: despite the rich history of science and technology in China and India, why did the modern scientific and industrial revolution first take place in Europe and not in China, and why was China overtaken by the West in science and technology, despite the fact that it was ahead of Europe for fifteen previous centuries?

The "Needham question" leads us to ponder a number of related questions: what happened, culturally and socially, in the history of China that made development, investing in and commercializing science and technology less important? What are the cultural, religious, economic and political factors that caused China to be static? In particular, what are the sources of the stability and longevity of the Chinese centralized bureaucracy which had survived for more than two thousand years, and continues to be a major complication to the development of a market economy and a modern society (Elvin, 1973)?

Inspired by Needham's research and, perhaps as an attempt to partially answer his puzzling questions, some scholars attempt to theorize about the socioeconomic causes that blocked China's breakthrough from feudalism to capitalism. The theory *traditional equilibrium*, developed by Eckstein, Fairbanks and Yang (1960), offers us an explanatory model. It argues that China, in the early 19th century, was in a state of traditional equilibrium in which "minor growth, innovation and technological change may occur but...[are] not sufficient to break the rigid and inhibiting bonds of the traditional framework of social and economic institutions" (Eckstein, Yang, and Fairbank, 1960: 1). Western overseas expansion and colonial occupation, combined with population pressure and administrative decay, left China in "a century-long process of disintegration, transformation and slow gestation within the traditional Chinese order" and "an acute degree of tension, in the minds of proud conservatives and later in the minds of modern patriotic Chinese ... gradually built up to explosive proportions until the shackles of the old order were violently broken and the Chinese economy erupted at long last into the industrial take-off under totalitarian control which we are witnessing today" (Eckstein as quoted in Lippit, 1980: 19).

According to the logic of this theory, the social and economic institutions of China's traditional order blocked development until the advent of Western expansion, which, after a long period of gestation and psychological anguish, unleashed the forces of modernization. It is an attempt by Chinese scholars to explain underdevelopment in China specifically, from the perspectives of its internal factors in relation to a number of features of Chinese political and social structure. It stresses the social structure symbolized by the Chinese family-system, a conservative bureaucracy and ruling ideology, a parasitic elite, and fatalistic attitudes, etc., as obstacles to modernization. Seen from a comparative perspective, Chinese bureaucratic feudalism was culturally and socially much more durable than the European aristocratic feudalism which was defeated by the rising industrial capitalist class.

The shortcomings of China's traditional social and economic structure are perceived to be the cause of economic stagnation in the traditional Chinese rural economy, leading to obstacles to technological innovation. Elvin proposes an explanation for the persistence of technical stagnation in the late traditional economy, in terms of his notion of the Chinese economy being caught in what may be called a *high-level equilibrium trap*: "a situation to which most of the usual criteria of 'backwardness' do not apply, yet characterized by a technological immobility that makes any sustained qualitative economic progress impossible" (Elvin, 1972: 170). The trap, according to Elvin's interpretation, is that China had developed substantial technology, such as in agriculture and water transport, without a discontinuous jump involving the application of modern scientific inputs (Elvin, 1973: 305, 306, 312).

The arguments of this theory suggest that the requirements of modernization were incompatible with the requirements of Confucian stability and the hierarchy system. Its analytical framework is somehow influenced by the Weberian approach to capitalism and rationality. The question addressed, is why Japan was able to mobilize internal resources to resist Western penetration and colonialization, despite the fact that only one hundred years ago it did not seem to have favourable internal and external preconditions for a national take-off. The conclusion in line with this theoretical explanation is that the external impact on China and Japan was basically similar; and the reason why Japan was not hampered and disrupted was that Japanese society "was receptive to innovations based on western ideas and institutions" (White, 1982: 115).

The mode of production

In the same line as that of the Needham questions, Pomeranz (2000) raises the classical puzzle of, "Why Europe conquered China, not China conquered Europe?" At the time when Europe entered the stage of industrialization, leading the world from the age of World Empire into the age of world economy, there were multiple core regions in the world. So, why did sustained industrial growth begin in Northwest Europe, despite surprising similarities between the advanced areas of Europe and China?

Pomeranz (2000) shows that the core regions in the Chinese Empire in the mid 18th century, such as the Lower Yangtze Delta area, were at the same level of economic development as England in terms of life-expectancy, consumption, product and factor markets, and the strategies of households. Pomeranz even demonstrates that the core regions of the Chinese and Japanese Empires were no worse off ecologically than Western Europe, with both facing comparable local shortages of land-intensive products. According to his analyses, two developments contributed to further rise of Europe: 1) the use of coal as the replacement of timber, and 2) the expansion of trade. The transition from using coal to replace timber was one of the most fortunate developments in Europe, reducing the pressure on the intensive use of land, while promoting growth towards energy-intensive industries. The discovery of new territories opened more trade routes and America became a greater source of necessary primary products for European industrialization. Marx and Engels emphasized the great contribution to Europe's industrialization by the geographical expansion of economic relations to America:

> The discovery of America, the rounding of the Cape, opened up fresh ground for the rising bourgeoisie. The East-Indian and Chinese markets, the colonization of America, trade with the colonies, the increase in the means of exchange and in commodities generally, gave to commerce, to navigation, to industry, an impulse never before known, and thereby to the revolutionary element in the tottering feudal society, a rapid development. … Modern industry has established the world-market, for which the discovery of America paved the way. (Marx and Engels, 1958: 35)

The expansion of import from the trade with America helped Northwest Europe to further grow their specialization in manufacturing, which was assisted by free labor from the land.

Pomeranz' explanations on the rise of European industrialization and the failure of China's industrial take-off, echo some aspects of the Marxist theory *Asiatic mode of production*. By "mode of production", Marx refers to the relationship between the forces of production (land and natural resources, necessary for the production of material goods) and the relations of production (people's socio-economic relationships to production). The theoretical departure of the Asiatic mode of production was based on several conceptualizations: geographically, the landscape of China and other Asian communities was dependent on irrigation-systems which required a centralized authority and collectivity to co-ordinate and develop large-scale hydraulic works; politically, the primitive form of Asian states with self-sufficient agricultural communities, created stagnant societies dominated by a despotic state class and centralized governance; and socioeconomically, the Asian economic bases consisted of economically self-sufficient village communities combining agriculture and handicrafts. The central argument of the theory suggests that "Asiatic societies were held in thrall by a despotic ruling clique, residing in central cities and directly expropriating surplus from largely autarkic and generally undifferentiated village communities" (Lewis, Martin and Wigen, Kären, 1997: 94).

The debate about the Asiatic mode of production has raised questions in relation to the relevance of Marxist concepts outside the European context, as well as the character of materialist explanations of class society, revolutionary change and world history (Bottomore 1983: 32). The concept of the Asiatic mode of production was used by Marxists to endorse "the privileged position of occidental over oriental history: the dynamic and progressive character of the West versus the stationary and regressive features of the East" (ibid.: 33). The oriental pre-capitalist economic formations, together with their "primitive" societal forms and class structures, were unfavourable for the emergence of the "capitalist mode of production", whereas the existence of occidental feudalism in politically independent cities was crucial for the growth of the production of exchange values, and for the rise of a bourgeois class and industrial capitalism.

Even among Marxists, opinions are divided regarding whether the birth of capitalism in Europe is attributable to the conflicts among the classes in feudal society, or whether the emergence of an external market sector served to weaken feudalism and to stimulate new forms of production (Lachmann, 1989).

External factors by Western imperialism

The colonialism and imperialism thesis can ben seen as a radical approach, viewing underdevelopment essentially as an outcome of a historical process caused by Western colonial-imperialist expansion. China's external relations, such as in trade and contact with Western imperialist powers and Japan, tended to promote underdevelopment. In the view of this theory, underdevelopment is not inherent to preindustrial societies, but is a consequence of a specific historical process. It argues that, even though imperialist penetration did bring elements of modern economy to China, the impact was both geographically confined and sectorally skewed to serve foreign interests, producing a form of "false modernization" (Esherick quoted in White, 1982: 114).

Although China was not historically "colonized" by any European power, and in line with the explanations from this progressive Marxist perspective combining internal and external factors, the development of China's peripherization was the result of Western imperialist penetration, and such a result was made possible due to China's internal weakness in term of its domestic class structure. The imperial structure of the gentry-dominated social formation failed to provide a basis for China to make a smooth transition to a new modern state. The imperial society, ruled by the gentry, despite its sophistication and power was, on its own, unable to make the economic and political breakthroughs that were achieved in Europe in the last several centuries (Blecher, 1997: 12). The impact of Western imperialism on China had the effect of creating political and economic challenges, and heightening internal social contradictions. Thus, the gentry forces that prevented China from making a timely economic transformation were unable to survive the challenge posed by Europe and Japan in the middle of the 19th century (ibid: 12). However, this approach can be applied to all third world countries which have suffered the adverse effects of Western penetration and colonialism, and it still implies the hypothesis that, if those countries were internally strong enough, they would have escaped

9

underdevelopment (Riskin, 1980: 109). The logic goes: if they were like Japan, they would have escaped it.

Marxism-Leninism opened the horizons to Chinese progressive revolutionary intellectuals, and made them more open-minded and internationally oriented. It offered them a great source of inspiration to take positions from, and to analyze the world from different perspectives. China, as they saw it, was no longer an isolated centre of the globe surrounded by barbarians, but a part of the world full of different forces and ideas. China was identified as a "proletarian nation", although it lacked the strong social force of a proletarian working class. The Chinese proletarian revolution was associated with the worldwide proletarian movement against international capitalism. Henceforth, the Chinese view on its role in international affairs changed, from regarding itself as the centre of the world and the universal authority, to seeing China's problem as being part of the World's problems, and the Chinese revolution as being relevant to the outside world.

The Embedded Sinicization:
From a "Civilization-state" to a Nation-state

The introduction of the above various theoretical explanations concerning the development of China's underdevelopment is not aimed to stimulate a new round of academic debate. Rather, it intends to highlight the central thesis of this introduction, namely that China's modern history since its defeat in the Opium War is one that links its decline with its forced integration with the outside world, especially with the West-based capitalist world system. It is also a history of clashes between the cultural and political imperatives of the Chinese civilization state, and the cultural and economic logic of the capitalist nation-state order. One of the great legacies of Eurocentric historicity since the era of European colonization and domination is the universal acceptance of the nation-state[5] as the basic conceptual unit and actor in international relations and international political economy. Since it encountered China in the 19th century, the West has been struggling to learn how to describe and conceptualize China from the logical frameworks of a nation-state; however, in essence, China has always remained a civilization state, and it is still seen as such by some scholars (Pye, 1990)

The underlying assumptions of contemporary development and international relations theories all perceive a causal and lineal process of the Eurocentric modernization path, driven by market, competition and technology. The perception was even claimed to represent the "end of history" (Fukuyama, 1989), i.e. that humanity has entered the ultimate phase of its evolution, where West-based market capitalism and liberal order is the most fundamentally satisfying form of government and economic organization. In contrast to Fukuyama's worldview, Huntington saw the post-Cold War history as the battle ground of the "beginning of a new history", in which the fundamental conflicts in the future international order would not be between nation-states, but rather between civilizations. In the context of interpreting the rise of China and the challenges it is posing to the liberal order, Huntington is perhaps right in some aspects. This is because what needs to be remembered is that modernization is also unavoidably shaped by history and culture. One of fundamental reasons for the constant failure of the West in predicting China's evolution and transformation is its failure to understand and interpret its past and present.

"A civilization pretending to be a nation-state"

Like all countries in the world, China has, since the 1911 Revolution[6], described itself as a nation-state. However, for many scholars, especially sinologists and cultural-historians, China was, and still retains the essential features of a civilization-state. It is the longest unbroken existing polity in the world, dating back to the first unified Chinese Empire - Qin in 221BC. Unlike Western nation-states, China's sense of identity comes from its long history as a civilization-state. That is to say, to apply the unit of analysis of "nation state" (a term that has its historical root in the formation of the modern nation-state system in Europe) to China is paradoxical. The notion that China is a "civilization state" rather than a "nation state" was first raised by Lucian Pye in a very explicit tone:

> The starting point for understanding the problem is to recognize that China is not just another nation-state in the family of nations. China is a civilization pretending to be a state. The story of modern China could be described as the effort by both Chinese and foreigners to squeeze a civilization into the arbitrary, constraining framework of the modern state, an institutional invention that came out of the fragmentation of the West's own civilization. (Pye, 1990: 58)

Pye points out the paradoxes when applying some Western concepts to the Chinese context, such as the notion of "nationalism":

> [In] spite of the greatness of Chinese history, in spite of the manifest durability of everyday Chinese culture…the historical pattern of China's modernization has left China with a relatively inchoate and incoherent form of nationalism…. although China produced one of the world's greatest civilizations and still has a powerful and tenacious culture, it now has in modern times a relatively contentless form of nationalism. … the Chinese political class, in spite of such a formless nationalism, has been able to exploit

the mystique of patriotism to neutralize politically the very Chinese who
have been the most successful in modernizing. (Pye, 1993: 107-108)

The central features of *China as a civilization state* can be characterized by the
fundamental social and political culture defined under the "man-rule" order.
This order predetermines the narrow acceptance of a mono-moral and socio-
political arrangement, in which Confucianism had been the ruling ideology for
Chinese empires for centuries. Under this order the Imperial State not only enjoys natural authority, but also is taken for granted as the guardian of people and
society. The power of the State permits no challenge, and its power is absolute,
not relative. The State enjoys natural authority, legitimacy and respect. It is seen by
the Chinese as the guardian, custodian and embodiment of their civilization. The
duty of the State is to protect China's unity and integrity - unity is its first priority,
while plurality is the condition of its existence.[7] The legitimacy of the State, therefore, lies deep in Chinese civilizational history. The Chinese concept is quite different from how the State is perceived in Western societies.

Therefore, after China's defeat in the Opium War, and especially when the imperial system broke down in the early 20th century after the 1911 Revolution - releasing a great deal of cultural iconoclasm among Chinese intellectuals toward Confucian political and moral order - it was still commonly accepted that the State granted
rights and determined their limits (Peter, 1991). Likewise, during the periods of
revolutionary socialism after the victory of the Chinese communist revolution, the
role of the Chinese State was radicalized with the injection of the dictatorship of
a party state[8], in which orthodox Marxism and Maoism became the single para-
digmatic and political moral order[9], where Confucian stability and harmony was
replaced by class struggle, and political mobilization was radicalized for economic
development and socialist construction. Economic reform in the past three decades has gradually separated the political role of the Communist Party and the
administrative role of the State (government management).

The inherent sinicization in the process of China's transformation

Understanding the characteristics of China as a "civilization state" provides a
framework of understanding the Chinese developmental state and its unique
state-market relations reflected in the so-called "Chinese model". The post-Mao
transitional market economy, along with fundamental institutional transformations, characterizes a distinctive style of capitalism in which the marketization
of the former command economy, the active role of the Chinese party-state and
local government, the variety of forms of property and business ownership, the
traditional culture of clientele-based social relations, the institutional legacies of

socialism, and the emergence of market-based institutions, all provide a rich empirical context to conceptualize and theorize the "embeddedness" characteristics and the new socio-institutional hegemony in post-reform China.

Historically, China has been able to display the capacity of absorbing foreign ideas and influences, as well as sinicizing and transforming them into an integral part of native value-systems, such as the sinicization of Buddhism and Marxism-Leninism. Today, in order to understand the success of Chinese capitalism and its integration with the capitalist world system, it is imperative, likewise, to examine how China has been able to ideologically transform and sinicize a free market capitalism into a state capitalism with Chinese characteristics (Li Xing, 2004), such as "socialist market economy" or "market economy with Chinese characteristics", and "Confucian businessman", which are econo-politically and culturally contradictory.

Sinicization provides an analytical account of the success of the Chinese development model, in which the Chinese socialist state has moved from a planned economy with public ownership towards a hybrid regulated market economy with the existence of a larger proportion of private economy that still remains much embedded in the state system that spawned it. Sinicization also provides us the framework to enable us to understand the features of embeddedness in the processes of China's socio-cultural and sociopolitical adaptation, through marketizing decision-making powers and commodifying state institutions. The Chinese "socialist market economy" is a distinct form of capitalism characterized by active state intervention and close state-business relations. The emergence of new institutional entrepreneurs and their role in institutional innovations, play a positive role in encouraging marketization and decentralisation of state capacities and public resources, without falling into economic and social disembeddedment.

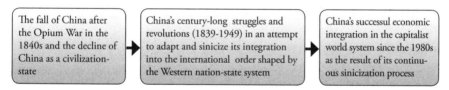

| The fall of China after the Opium War in the 1840s and the decline of China as a civilization-state | China's century-long struggles and revolutions (1839-1949) in an attempt to adapt and sinicize its integration into the international order shaped by the Western nation-state system | China's successul economic integration in the capitalist world system since the 1980s as the result of its continuous sinicization process |

Figure 1. China's persistent sinicization in its historical transformation and integration into the international order

Chinese State Capitalism and the International Liberal Order

The rise of China as a key political and economic actor since the beginning of economic liberalization in the late 1970s may well turn out to be one of the most important developments in the international system in modern world history. China's economic impact is already felt worldwide, cemented by its recent status as the world's second largest economy with the highest saving rate, after China overtook Germany in 2009, followed by Japan in 2010. The question is now how China's increasing economic and political power will impact on the existing capitalist world system and the established institutional order (Li Xing, 2010), and, more importantly, on Western principles and liberal values that are not shared by China (Flockhart and Li Xing, 2011). As an American scholar has asked, a central question which is in the minds of most Western political elites is whether China will overthrow the existing international liberal order or become part of it (Ikenberry, 2008, 2011).

To understand China and its requirements and expectations of the capitalist world system, it is important not only to appreciate how radically China has already changed in the short space of the 20th century, but also to understand that radical change is alien to Chinese culture and the philosophy in which balance, stability and harmony are highly prioritized. Yet, despite a deep culturally-determined desire for harmony politically, China has transformed from an imperial monarchy to a short-lived republic and from a weak warlord state to a centralized revolutionary socialist state. Economically, China has gone through state-led industrialization based on a planned economy and socialist egalitarianism, to reliance on market mechanisms, leading from repeated shifts from crisis to failure, to rapid growth and modernization. From a cultural and ideological perspective, the Chinese value system has been radically transformed from feudalism to socialism, from collectivism to individualism, and from fundamental egalitarianism to huge inequalities. Yet, throughout the fundamental changes of the 20th century, China's deeply-felt desire has been to restore the "heavenly order" and "harmony and stability", and to regain the status of what is regarded as the "loss of historical and civilizational supremacy" and the return to the Middle Kingdom.

From "riding the tiger"[10] to "sinicizing the tiger"

The post-Mao economic reform initiated in the late 1970s, which prioritized economics and trade over politics and ideology, implied that Chinese leadership effectively "hitched a ride on a tiger". China has been "riding the tiger" for the past three decades, turning itself into a key global political and economic actor, thus fundamentally changing relations with the principal states of the liberal world order. However, China is also caught in a "riding-tiger-dilemma" and is still struggling to figure out how to dismount the tiger safely or simply how to keep riding without falling off. Consequently, the country is now driven by capitalist market forces and no longer has any other choice than to accept and follow the basic logic of the market. Yet, the essential logic of the market is shaped by Western cultural and religious norms and values that, in return, promote particular forms of human interactions and social relations (Li, Xing and Hersh, 2004) that are very different from – and in many ways opposite to – Chinese cultural and social tradition. Many of China's concerns about the liberal world order are generated and driven by the contradictions between internal market forces versus deep-rooted Chinese nationalism and cultural norms, as well as past memories. China is, therefore, now faced with two conflicting priorities: benefiting from the capitalist world market, while preserving its political and national identity.

> Will the rise of China lead to the sinicization of the international regime and the liberal order through the process of its historical transformation from being in a semi-periphery position, to becoming part of the core? Will China be a cooperative actor or a disruptive one? A force for continuity or a force for change?

There is no doubt that China, as a rising power with sustained economic growth and rising military strength, has great power interests that cannot always be reconciled with the interests of other core states in the liberal order. However, on some issues where the West sees Chinese intransigence, the actual state of affairs may be a China that is itself severely restricted in its actions vis-à-vis domestic considerations, and a perceived need to sinicize China's internal political and economic structures. The current mixture of "neo-liberalism" and "nationalism" has caused ambiguity in China's ideological consistency and policy planning, especially in regards to inequality, property rights, energy security and environmental concerns, all of which conflict with a priority for order and party rule.

As a result, the "ride on the tiger" has created unintended consequences, ambiguities and dilemmas that China's leaders are constantly struggling to reconcile in its dual interaction with its domestic society and the liberal world order. China wants the US-led capitalist world system to acknowledge its "Chinese characteristics" in the process of becoming the order's new member. In this process, Chinese leadership discovers a method to pacify domestic dissatisfaction and build new bases of legitimization by using "national uniqueness" in opposition to the external other of the West. However, although resistance, suspicion and antagonism toward the liberal world order certainly exist among Chinese politicians, intellectuals and students, Chinese leadership is still not very clear as to what is to be expected from its complete integration into the liberal world order. During the Mao period, the goal was to mobilize people to build China as a self-reliant country *independent* from the capitalist world order. Today, the aim seems more likely to be to turn China into a "normal" great power in the liberal world order. However, an *interdependent* relationship, shaped by the rules of the game of international regimes (Keohane, 1989), is further keeping China in a tiger-riding-dilemma, because it is continuously constrained by the complex relationship of interdependence with the capitalist liberal order (Keohane and Nye, 1989).

China's economic marketization and its deep integration in the global economic system present new economic opportunities and impetus to liberal cores states. However, as Chris Patten points out, China is "the first example of a country which has done astonishingly well in this international system, but challenges its basic foundations" (as quoted in *BBC News* 2008), implying that China's success not only contradicts but also challenges some basic beliefs held in the West about a set of mutually-dependent relationships. These sets of relationships point to the hardcore belief system of the West about what makes a country grow, such as the relationships between property rights and economic growth, between the rule of law and market economy, between free currency flow and economic order, between political system and popular sentiment, and between democracy and development. The economic development model of China, labeled as the "Beijing Consensus" (Ramo, 2004) is now particularly attractive to many developing countries in terms of how to manage state-market-society relations and political economy in international relations.

For the time being, the US-based capitalist liberal order has great difficulty in viewing China as a "responsible stakeholder" in the international political system (Kaplan, 2010). The US mainstream media has described China as a "free-rider" (Lee, 2010), and some representative opinion-makers have claimed that the liberal order is facing a threat because "China is transforming the world as it transforms itself. Never mind notions of a responsible stakeholder; China has become a revolutionary power" (Economy, 2010: 142). However, the international debate on China's rise is controversial, and there is no consensus on whether China's behavior and foreign policy are actually more Westphalian[11] than the West (Etzioni and Ikenberry, 2011), or whether the rise of China represents a global economic and political "paradigm shift"[12].

Nevertheless, it is expected that, within the near future, various schools of "Chinese social science theories" will gradually emerge to challenge the existing ones which are rooted in the Eurocentric tradition, and which have been defined, constructed and dominated by the West for centuries. As a Chinese scholar explicitly indicates the trend, China's economic and political rise, together with its social achievement, will eventually lead to the emergence of Chinese schools of "international relations theories" (Qin, 2007).

What kind of nation will China be? What will China's relationship to the existing international order be? Will China be destructive or constructive? A cooperative actor or a disruptive one? A force for continuity or a force for change? These questions still remain, and will continue to remain in the minds of Western elites. For the time being, it is important for the core not only to recognize that China's inner transformation contributed – and will continue to contribute – to shaping and reshaping the capitalist world order and that now liberal core states have to adjust themselves to the opportunities and constraints brought about by China's rise, but also to understand that, once China started its "ride on the tiger", it was doomed to either 'hold on and stay the course – or to fall off'!

The Book's Objective:
The Impact of China's Rise on Semi-periphery and Periphery Countries

In recent years, the tone of the rhetoric concerning China's activities in Africa and Latin America in Western mainstream media and literature cannot be said to be positive. Instead, the collective Western opinion has been mostly negative and even to the extent of being conspiratorial in character, with insinuations that China's involvement in the two continents is driven primarily by resource exploitation, and labelling China's approach to trade and investment in the two regions as repeating the neo-colonial pattern of relationships.

More importantly, China's competitive advantages in the course of its full integration with the world capitalist system are weakening the relative monopoly of the existing semi-peripheral states in certain commodity chains, and are exerting pressures on their production costs and wage levels --- the danger of *peripheralization of the semiperiphery* in the current capitalist world system (Li, Minqi, 2005, 2008). More radical views see China as using capitalist globalization to create the last great modern empire through the invention of a new form of economic imperialism (contra the US as military imperialism), i.e., a new "workshop of the world" (*Political Geography*, 2011).

Since the end of the 1990s, the debate on the relationship between China and various African countries has been ongoing, within an extensive context. More recently, the debate also extended to the relationships between China and some Latin American countries. The transformation of the nature of South-South relations from an alliance-based political relationship during the Cold War, to a market-based economic relationship in the current era of globalization, imbues this debate with special importance for intellectual scrutiny. However, in the current political and intellectual world, there are far too many more opinions and assumptions than there are substantial concrete research outcomes that are able to support these opinions and assumptions.

Therefore, methodologically, this book aims to provide a framework of understanding China's re-emergence in the nexus of the historical, economic, political and world system perspectives. By doing so it will help readers to understand the triple impact of China's rise to the core, semi-periphery and periphery countries with a focus on the latter two groups of countries. Is China's rise and its economic impact ushering in a new world order for semi-periphery and periphery countries, or bringing them neo-colonialism in the 21st century? Will the imperative logic behind the rise of Chinese capitalism (its thirst for market and resources) eventually bring about neo-colonialism in the developing world?

The idea of the semi-periphery was first applied to the modern world-system by Immanuel Wallerstein (1974a, b), and it has been developed and further explored by other scholars (Arrighi, 1985; Chase-Dunn and Grimes, 1995). Compared to other regions in the world, Africa and Latin America are seen as having relatively stable market niches as energy suppliers. China's central policy objectives in Africa and in Latin America are stated clearly in its policy papers - *China's African Policy Paper* (2006), and *Latin American policy paper* (2008). The policy objectives are aimed at strengthening diplomatic and political ties with these two resource-rich regions, while, at the same time, securing and diversifying energy supplies and other raw material resources, including the opening of these regions' commodity markets. China has had a positive economic spill-over effect on the rest of the world, especially in developing regions: Latin America, Southeast Asia, Africa. Currently, China is one of the key investors in Africa and its trade and investment relations in Latin America are going to accelerate in the coming years. China's increasingly dynamic economic relations with these regions are seen, by some Western critics, as challenging the traditional ties between these regions and their historical colonial relationships with Western powers.

Seen from the world-system perspective, in the past three decades China is progressively and slowly moving from the periphery to the semi-periphery, and now China is seen as heading towards the core. Historically, the cyclical rhythms of the rise and fall of new powers result in regular slow-moving – but significant – geographical shifts in capital accumulation and power, without changing the fundamental relations of inequality within the system, i.e. the basic structure of the core, periphery and semi-periphery remain in place (Wallerstein, 1997). Moreover, this hierarchy of positions is a potential source of conflict, as peripheral countries attempt to move up the system, while semi-peripheral countries both struggle to join the core and avoid becoming peripherized. At the same time, the core countries strive to maintain their dominant position in the system as a whole, through trade relations and international institutions on the basis of the established rules of the game.

As indicated before, intensification in China-African and China-Latin American economic relations also accelerates the "neo-colonialist" or "neo-imperialist" argument claiming that China is imposing on the regions a renewed version of the "dependent" relationship which was historically formed by European colonial powers. However, despite the criticism of China's realism-oriented policy in its economic and political relations with the two regions, the Chinese style of approach and engagement – especially its aid policy and practice – will indeed have far-reaching implications for the long-term and permanent realignment of power relations in the conventional international aid system, and has already changed the system in many ways (Opoku-Mensah, 2010)

> Is China presenting an alternative development model to the developing world? Does it represent a new "beginning of history" rather than the "end of history?" Will the rise of China lead to the peripherization of existing semi-periphery countries, and to the altering of the traditional pattern of relationships between the West and the developing world?

Seen in this light, China's economic rise and its active engagement, especially in the semi-periphery zones, are predicted to pose severe challenges and constraints to the established capitalist world system:

> China's competition will completely undermine the relative monopoly of the existing semiperipheral states in certain commodity chains. The value added will be squeezed, forcing the traditional semi-peripheral states to accept lower wage rates close to the Chinese rates. … Should the Chinese workers generally receive the semi-peripheral levels of wages, given the size of the Chinese population, the total surplus distributed to the working classes in the entire semi-periphery would have to more than double. This will greatly reduce the share of the surplus available for the rest of the world. (Li, Minqi, 2008: 436, 437)

Within the capitalist world system, a layer of the semi-periphery – the "middle stratum" – represents the stability of the world order as well as the hopeful modeling of the Western "modernization" and "development" path – a driving force for upward mobility. The larger such a layer becomes, the more stable the system will be. Otherwise, should this layer be reduced and move to further peripherization, the world system would likely become highly unstable (Li, Minqi, 2005: 436-437).

China's policy on periphery countries, particularly its development aid policy in African countries, is argued by some Western elites to be threatening to dislodge a carefully-crafted governance and transparency agenda that the West has been investing in in Africa for decades. Many questions are being raised regarding China's role in Africa, such as "Is China's policy and practice in Africa and other parts of world's periphery fundamentally redefining the nature of the international aid system?"; "Does China aim at effectively pricing out other aid players?"; and "Is China challenging the normative principles underlying the international aid system?" To reach a consensus is not easy, but many share the following conclusion on the assessment of China's development aid in Africa:

> The entry of China into the aid system is changing this power of the traditional aid system to shape the development route, as it offers a new set of ideas and practices that, first, is breaking the monopoly of Western aid to define, and second, is also proving attractive to aid recipient countries, particularly in Africa….. [Chinese aid] itself does not indicate a permanent restructuring of power relations in aid. But it does indicate that change is certainly in the making in the international aid system of power relations. (Opoku-Mensah, 2010: 81, 82)

Despite the fact that China represents an enormous opportunity to other semi-periphery and periphery countries, both in terms of China's growing appetite for imports and in terms of Chinese outward FDI – and, in some cases, also as a source of foreign aid – it also represents a challenge. China has now become the world's biggest exporter and it is a powerful competitor, particularly in manufacturing exports where its market share has been rising markedly and it is now by far the biggest manufacturing exporter (Gallagher, 2010: 5). This is particularly a challenge to the competitiveness of semi-peripheral countries that often see themselves outcompeted in the home market and in traditional export markets by Chinese producers. For peripheral countries China's emergence as a manufacturing powerhouse may increase their difficulties in diversifying their economies into manufacturing activities, thereby keeping back their modernization. A further problem area, which both peripheral and semi-peripheral countries with growing commodity exports to China may face in the future, is a growing dependency on the Chinese market, which potentially makes them vulnerable to policy decisions made by China.

The challenge facing the semi-periphery and periphery countries concerned is how they will manage their relationship with China; that is, how they will smartly play to their own strengths and explore areas of synergy and opportunity, while minimizing their weaknesses, disadvantages and vulnerabilities.

The Chapter Contributions

Chapter 1 by Li Xing and Steen F. Christensen takes the theoretical assumptions by Li Minqi as its point of departure, in which the rise of China is seen as moving the capitalist world system towards a dead-end in terms of the limits of global resources and the environment. The paper's focus here is primarily directed at one of his central arguments, that is that the rise of China-led global competition is exerting heavy pressures on the existing semi-periphery countries, thus making the capitalist world system unstable.

This chapter intends to, on the basis of the same theoretical framework of world-system theory, construct a different interpretation in which the economic rise of China is seen as potentially 1) representing some positive features of an emerging hegemonic power; 2) playing a stabilizing role in the current global crisis; 3) becoming the engine of economic growth for many development regions and countries; and 4) becoming an attractive development model to learn from. The paper uses Brazil as the pivotal example to support this position from a variety of economic data. It is shown that, although China presents Brazil with significant challenges, particularly in terms of its competitiveness in the manufacturing sector in the home market and in traditional export markets, China's influence has mainly been benign in the first decade of the 21st century. It is shown that Brazil has gone through very positive socio-economic development in this period, not only due to China's impact on Brazilian development, but also due to domestic political decisions. Furthermore, bilateral relations between the two countries are seen as a potential avenue for minimizing the risks associated with the impact of China's 'rise' for Brazil.

Chapter 2 by Raúl Bernal-Meza mainly focuses on the largest countries of MERCOSUR: Brazil and Argentina, including Chile, countries that established diplomatic relations with China between the early and mid 1970s. These three countries have opted for a pragmatic view on policy toward Beijing, which is expressed in their non-questioning the issue of human rights, in their support for the status of Taiwan as part of China, and in granting China the status of "market economy." The main explanation lies in the role of the Chinese market in the structure of commodities exports from Brazil, Argentina and Chile, although the main South American country, Brazil, shares with China in international policy an interest in the creation of counter-powers, allowing the neutralization of the unipolarity that the superpower United States has pursued since the end of the Cold War.

China has given different statuses to their relations with these countries. While Brazil and Argentina have been designated "strategic partners", Chile has been designated as a "cooperative partner". However, Chinese and Latin American interests, as well as those negotiated bilaterally with each of the MERCOSUR countries, will not necessarily be the same in the medium and long term. Although both sides are united by the concern for development, there is no doubt that China aspires to become a world power, a purpose and overall status that, in Latin America, only Brazil aspires to. China's relationship with the countries of MERCOSUR is in doubt. Chile, which is the country with the least significant status of "cooperative partner", while Argentina and Brazil are "strategic partners", appears more satisfied with the progress made in their relationship. In contrast, perceptions of Brazil and Argentina, which are its "strategic partners" and for different reasons, seem to agree that China is pursuing a *realpolitik* with them, away from the speeches of Chinese South-South relations, and from the spirit of a closer society of friendship.

Chapter 3 by Eduardo Daniel Oviedo looks into the stratification of the world economy, and shows both the success of Asian political classes and the failure of Latin American leaders to reach the objective of economic modernization. In particular reference, China, with a "stabilized one-party totalitarian regime", has reached a position in the Directory of great economic powers. Therefore, it is important to consider two aspects: a) the patterns of political behavior that the Chinese government adopted should be taken into account when discussing modernization in Latin American countries; and b) how the struggle to achieve modernization affects Chinese-Latin American interests. In this sense, the link between the objective of modernization and the political will of governments provide two kinds of external orientation in Latin America. On one side, there are nations that accept the "primarization" of their economies and the new international division of labor. On the other, there are other political units that accept the economic reality based on the North-South framework, but seek to overcome this situation with the "de-primarization" of their economies. In the first case, cooperation exceeds the tension; in the second, the tension tends to surpass the cooperation in the rhythm of modernization process progress. However, because of the emerging stage of industrialization in Latin America, harmony and tension of interests will coexist in the short and medium terms.

Chapter 4 by Ignacio Frechero analyzes China's global rise from a Latin American perspective. Beijing's own-made reforms are sometimes publicized in developing countries as a miraculous alternative to the Washington Consensus, so the first objective is to provide a brief account of the inner transformation the country has been through since the death of Mao Zedong, its performance, achievements and unresolved issues. Secondly, to understand China's new international protagonism in both structural - its power position in comparison with the other great powers and the United States - and dynamic terms - its increasing participation in international organizations and its diplomatic efforts to reach all regions and nations. And finally, to explore the implications of China's growing involvement in Latin America, highlighting opportunities and challenges to the countries in the region. The main argument is that China, though its importance as a source for exports' revenues and investments in Latin America, poses the following threats: the re-establishment of a *North-South* trade pattern and of an extractive investment trend, a socio-environmental degradation and the overexploitation of natural resources, and a potential collision of interests with Washington over the Western Hemisphere.

Chapter 5 by Jørgen Dige Pedersen presents the challenges of China's rise to another important semi-periphery country which is also China's neighbor – India. The rise of China has been a cause of anxiety for its big neighbour India, but it has also created opportunities and a tremendous increase in mutually-advantageous economic relations. In addition, India has, on a large variety of international political issues, seen rising China as a potential ally rather than an adversary and potential competitor. China's close friendship with Pakistan and outstanding border conflicts with India still continue to define the relationship between the two great Asian nations, but, at the same time, and despite the historically-rooted animosity, the two nations have expanded their mutual collaboration. This chapter traces the evolution of these partly contradictory trends in the relationship between China and India, and provides an assessment of the direction of future developments.

Chapter 6 by Johanna Jansson explores the Chinese emerging relationship with the Democratic Republic of Congo. The chapter argues that, whilst the Democratic Republic of Congo (DRC) may be a periphery economy in the traditional sense of the term, the mineral-rich country is anything but peripheral to the global economy of resource extraction. As a result, the rise of China in Africa and other concurrent developments in the global political economy have generated a multitude of responses in the DRC. Based on comprehensive field work in the DRC from 2008 to 2011, the chapter disentangles these dynamics, analysing Chinese aid, trade and investment in the country. It argues that each of these vectors should be understood as phenomena which indeed originate from the changes in China, but which have different specific drivers and aims, and whose local implications are conditioned by a range of different global and local factors. The chapter presents a multilayered argument as to why the Chinese presence produces impulses both for continuity and change in the DRC.

Chapter 7 by Elijah Nyaga Munyi examines what is meant by "China-Africa" relations and cautions on the simplification and collectivization of African economies' interests and responses to Chinese economic encroachment. Since there has not been much in the development of a collective African policy framework for economic engagement with China, this chapter seeks to shift the focus from the debate on the pros and cons of China-Africa relations, to arguing that the time is auspicious for Africa to develop common policy measures to manage the dramatic rise of China's presence, and for making provisional policy proposals on how to engage China from a regional perspective. The chapter's central arguments are twofold; first, an incipient African disenchantment over China (as outlined in the post-FOCAC 2009 African Union report) provides a prod to coalesce an African "Chinese policy" to manage China-Africa relations. Secondly, if widely adopted, an African "Chinese policy" would not only refine a coordinated continental response to China, but would also enhance the consolidation of regional convergence in key policy areas in Africa. The chapter proposes pragmatic policies for embracing China, beyond the opinion-based dichotomy of praise versus criticism.

Notes

1 The Opium Wars (1839-43, 1856-60) were fought between Great Britain and China. They began when the Chinese government tried to stop the illegal import of opium into China by British merchants. China was defeated in both the wars. As a result, European powers, especially the British, gained significant commercial privileges and territorial concessions, such as Hong Kong.

2 The Treaty of Nanjing was signed on August 29, 1842. It was the first unequal treaty in the history of China's foreign relations following its defeat in the first Opium War (see note 1). The Treaty forced China to pay a huge indemnity to Britain for the cost of war and imposed China a tariff on all imported goods. It allowed Hong Kong to be given to the British on a 99-year lease. The treaty also stated that the coastal ports of Xiamen, Guangzhou, Fuzhou, Ningbo, and Shanghai should be opened to foreign trade. What was most damaging to China was the loss of its sovereignty: the fixed tariff, extraterritoriality, and the most favored nation provisions.

3 The notion of "century of humiliation" refers to the period between the first Sino-British Opium War (1839) and the end of the Chinese Civil War (1949), during which the political incursion, economic exploitation, and military aggression by foreign imperialist countries are regarded as the key factor that undermined the historical glory of the Chinese civilization and humiliated the Chinese nation.

4 The notion of "victim mentality" is connected with China's painful experience of the

"century of humiliation" (see the above note 2), and it has dominated the Chinese consciousness of its relations with the Western world. It is one of the central factors that instigated Chinese revolutions in the 20th century, including the communist revolution, and has shaped China's foreign policy and international relations since the founding the People's Republic in 1949.

5 The emergence of the "nation-state" as a concept and a "unit" of international relations is a relatively contemporary phenomenon, and was formally derived from the Westphalia Treaty. The political and cultural legitimacy of a nation-state is based on sovereignty and ethnic identity within a defined territorial unit. Historically and culturally, as a civilizational state, China was not familiar with, and was not shaped by the nation-state framework of understanding.

6 The Republican Revolution of 1911 overthrew the last dynasty - Qing Dynasty (1644–1911) and turned China into a republic. It is also called *Xinhai Revolution* in Chinese because the year 1911 was a Xinhai Year in the sexagenary cycle of the Chinese calendar.

7 Despite the historical rise and fall of different dynasties, "national unity" has always been the priority for Chinese rulers. This can be offered as an explanation for why China could offer Hong Kong and Macau "one country two systems", a formula alien to the Western nation-state framework of understanding. This can also be seen as indicative of why "the separation of Taiwan from the Mainland" has always been an issue of great controversy, embedded with political risks, regardless of the gap between the two sides of the strait.

8 China is a single-party state, in which the Chinese Communist Party (CCP), as the ruling party, forms the government, and no other parties are permitted to run candidates to replace the CCP. Even though China has other political parties, they, more or less, function as allied parties to exist as symbol of national unity, democratic politics and political participation.

9 Even the neo-Marxist theories, such as Kauskysm and Gramscianism, were not recognized to be "politically correct" in connection with orthodox Marxism and Maoism.

10 "Riding a tiger" is a Chinese idiom implying the dilemma of riding on the back of a tiger and finding it hard to get off. Today, China is seen as being caught in a "riding the market economy" and "riding the capitalist liberal order", i.e. any slow-down in economic growth would put the country in a risky situation, leading to social unrest and political illegitimacy, while, at the same time, China is constrained by the rules of the game of international regimes.

11 See note 5.

12 The connotation of "paradigm shift" here implies a controversial and debatable fact that in many ways China's economic success cannot be explained by Western mainstream economic and political theories. The question behind it is whether the Chinese development experience can be seen as an alternative development model.

References

Billington, Michael O. (1995) "The European 'Enlightemnet' & The Middle Kingdom", *Fidelio*, IV(2). Available at http://www.schillerinstitute.org/fid_91-96/952_middle_kingdom.html

Blecher, Marc (1997) *China against the Tides.* London: Pinter Publisher.

Bodde, Derk (2004a) *China's Gifts to the West.* Prepared for the Committee on Asiatic Studies in American Education. Reprinted with permission in *China: A Teaching Workbook*, Asia for Educators, Columbia University. Available at http://afe.easia.columbia.edu/chinawh/web/s10/gifts.pdf

Bodde, Derk (2004b) *Chinese Ideas in the West.* Prepared for the Committee on Asiatic Studies in American Education. Reprinted with permission in *China: A Teaching Workbook*, Asia for Educators, Columbia University. Available at http://afe.easia.columbia.edu/chinawh/web/s10/ideas.pdf

Bottomore, Tom et al. (1983) *A Dictionary of Marxist Thought.* Massachusetts: Blackwell Publisher.

Brown, Michael Barratt (1993) *Fair Trade: Reform and Realities in the International Trading System.* London: ZED Books Ltd.

Chinese government (2006) *China's African Policy.* Available at http://www.gov.cn/misc/2006-01/12/content_156490.htm

Chinese government (2008) *China's Policy Paper on Latin America and the Caribbean.* Available at http://www.chinadaily.com.cn/china/2008-11/06/content_7179488.htm

Dirlik, Arif and Maurice Meisner (eds.) (1989) *Marxism and the Chinese Experience.* New York: M E Sharpe.

Eckstein, Alexander, John K. Fairbank, and L. S. Yang (1960) "Economic Change in Early Modern China: An Analytical Framework", *Economic Development and Cultural Change*, 9(1): 1-29.

Economy, Elizabeth C. (2010) "The game changer: coping with China's foreign policy revolution", *Foreign Affairs,* 89(9): 142-153.

Elvin, Mark (1972) "The High Level Equilibrium Trap: The Causes of the Decline in Invention in the Traditional Chinese Textile Industries," in William E. Wilmott, (ed.) (1972) *Economic Organization in Chinese Society.* Palo Alto: Stanford University Press.

Elvin, Mark (1973) *The Patterns of Chinese Past.* Palo Alto: Stanford University Press.

Etzioni, Amitai and Ikenberry, G John (2011) "Changing the Rules: Is China More Westphalian Than the West?" *Foreign Affairs*, 90(6): 173-176.

Ferdinand, Peter (1991) "Socialism and Democracy in China", in David McLellan and Sean Sayer (eds.) *Socialism and Democracy* ed. London: Macmillan Academic and Profession LTD.

Flockhart, Trine and Li, Xing (2010) "Riding the Tiger: China's Rise and the Liberal World Order", *DIIS Policy Brief* – December, Danish Institute for International Studies, Copenhagen, Denmark.

Fukuyama, Francis (1989) "The End of History?" *The National Interest* (summer): 3-18.

Gallagher, Kevin P. (2010) "China and the Future of Latin American Industrialization", in *The Frederick S. Pardee Center for the Study of the Longer-Range Future*, Issues in Brief 18, Boston University.

Helge, Georg W. F. (1837) The Ph*ilosophy of History*, edited by Glyn Hughes 2009. Available from http://www.btinternet.com/~glynhughes/squashed/hegelhistory.htm

Ikenberry, John G. (2008) "The Rise of China and the Future of the West", *Foreign Affairs,* 87(1): 23-37.

Ikenberry, G. John (2011) "The Future of the Liberal World Order: Internationalism After America", *Foreign Affairs*, 90(3): 56-69.

Jesus, Attilio (2005) "China's empire of exploration", *Le Monde Diplomatique,* September. Availabe at http://mondediplo.com/2005/09/18zhenghe.

Kaplan, Robert (2010) "Don't Panic About China", *The Atlantic*, 28 Jan. Available at http://www.theatlantic.com/magazine/archive/2010/01/don-apos-t-panic-about-china/7926/.

Kennedy, Paul (1989) *The Rise and Fall of the Great Powers: Economic Change and Military Conflict from 1500 to 2000.* New York: Vintage Books.

Keohane, Robert O. (ed.) (1989) *International Institutions and State Power: Essays in International Relations Theory. Boulder: Westview Press.*

Keohane, Robert O. and Nye, Joseph S. (1989) *Power and Interdependence.* Harper Collins Publishers.

Lachmann, Richard (1989) "Origins of Capitalism in Western Europe: Economic and Political Aspects", *Annual Review of Sociology*, 15: 47-72

Lee, John (2010) "China won't be a responsible stakeholder", *Wall Street Journal*, February 1. Available at http://online.wsj.com/article/SB10001424052 7487047223045750379931817880328.html?mod=WSJ_topics_obama

Lewis, Martin and Wigen, Kären (1997) *The Myth of Continents: A Critique of Metageography.* Berkeley: University of California Press.

Li, Minqi (2005) "The Rise of China and the Demise of the Capitalist World Economy: Exploring Historical Possibilities in the 21st Century", *Science & Society*, 69(3): 420-448.

Li, Minqi (2008) *The Rise of China and the Demise of the Capitalist World Economy.* London: Pluto Press.

Li, Xing and Hersh, Jacques (2004) "The Genesis of Capitalism: The Nexus between 'Politics in Command' and Social Engineering", *American Review of Political Economy*, 2(2): 100-144.

Li, Xing (2004) "'From 'Politics in Command' to 'Economics in Command': A discourse analysis of China's transformation", *Copenhagen Journal of Asian Studies*, 18: 65-87.

Li, Xing (ed.) (2010) *The Rise of China and the Capitalist World Order*. Surrey, UK: Ashgate Publisher.

Lippit, Victor D. (1980) "Development of Underdevelopment in China", in Philip C C Huang (ed.), *Development of Underdevelopment in China*. M E Sharpe, New York.

Marx, Karl and Engels, Friedrich (1958) "Manifesto of the Communist Party", *Selected Works in Two Volumes, Volume I*. Moscow: Foreign Languages Publishing House.

Needham, Joseph et al. (eds.) (1954) *Science and Civilization in China*. Cambridge: Cambridge University Press.

Opoku-Mensah, Paul (2010) "China and International Aid System", in Li Xing (ed.) *The Rise of China and the Capitalist World Order*. Surrey. UK: Ashgate Publisher.

BBC News (2008) "China is a threat to democracy", November 23.

Political Geography (2011), Guest Editorial "Thesis on labour imperialism: How communist China used capitalist globalization to create the last great modern imperialism", *Political Geography*, 30: 175–177

Pomeranz, Kenneth (2000) *The Great Divergence: China, Europe, and the Making of the Modern World Economy*. Princeton: Princeton University Press.

Pye, Lucian (1990) "China: Erratic State, Frustrated Society", *Foreign Affairs*, 69(4): 56-74.

Pye, Lucian (1993) "How China's Nationalism Was Shanghaied", *The Australian Journal of Chinese Affairs*, 29: 107-133.

Qin, Yaqing (2007) "Why is there no Chinese international relations theory?" *International Relations of the Asia-Pacific*, 7(3): 313-340.

Ramo, Joshua C. (2004) The Beijing Consensus. London: the Foreign Policy Centre.

Riskin, Carl (1980) "Development of Underdevelopment in China", in Philip C C Huang (ed.), *Development of Underdevelopment in China*. New York: M E Sharpe

Said, Edward (1993) *Culture and Imperialism*. New York: Vintage Books.

Wallerstein, Immanuel (1974a) "The Rise and Future Demise of the World Capitalist System: Concepts for Comparative Analysis", *Comparative Studies in Society and History* 16: 387-415.

Wallerstein, Immanuel (1974b) *The Modern World-System I: Capitalist Agriculture and the Origins of European World-Economy in the Sixteenth Century.* New York: Academic Press.

Wallerstein, Immanuel (1997) "The Rise of East Asia, or The World-System in the Twenty-First Century." Available at http://fbc.binghamton.edu/iwrise.htm.

Weber, Max (1951) *The Religion of China: Confucianism and Taoism,* translated and edited by Gerth, H. H. New York: Free Press.

Weber, Max (1958) *Protestant Ethic and The Spirit of Capitalism* translated by Parsons, T., Charles Scribner's Sons.

White, Gardon (1982) "Why Did China Fail to Follow the Japanese Road?" in Manfred Bienefeld and Martin Godfrey (eds.) *The Struggle for Development, National Strategies in an International Context.* New York: John Wiley.

Yu, Jianfu (2009) "The influence and enlightenment of Confucian cultural education on modern European civilization", *Frontiers of Education in China,* 4(1): 10-26.

LI XING
STEEN FRYBA CHRISTENSEN

Chapter 1

The Rise of China and the Myth of a China-led Semi-periphery Destabilization
The Case of Brazil

The Placement of the Discussion
The Destabilization of Global Capitalism by a China-led Semi-periphery Rivalry

The central thesis on the rise of China leading to the demise of the capitalist world system by Li Minqi was first clarified in his article "The Rise of China and the Demise of the Capitalist World-Economy: Exploring Historical Possibilities in the 21st Century" (Li, Minqi, 2005). This article was later further extended and explored in a well-written book (Li, Minqi, 2008a), where, along with his other publications (2008b, c, and 2010), he questions the sustainability of the capitalist world system. Throughout these writings, Li Minqi employs two central notions from the world-system theorist Immanuel Wallerstein: the "dichotomy of capital and labor" and the "endless accumulation of capital" (Wallerstein, 2004). In the view of the world-system school, the capitalist accumulation process has historically spread outward from Western Europe over the past four centuries. Evolved from distinct historical conditions, the social system of capitalism now encompasses the entire globe, "not only in the sense that just about every economic actor in the world today is operating according to the logic of capitalism, and even those on the outermost periphery of the capitalist economy are, in one way or another, subject to that logic" (Wood, 1997: 1).

With the full integration of China and India, the two most populous nations on earth, in the world economy, Li Minqi argues that the capitalist mode of production has approached the end of the "strategic reserves" of land, labor and resources, i.e., the system's strain upon ecological sustainability in connection with industrial production and environmental degradation. The logic of capitalism, as its backers and detractors maintain, is based upon the notion of "expanding to continue." Accordingly, Li Minqi holds that the rapid growth of the Chinese economy has stabilized the capitalist world system that has been sinking into slow growth since the US-led post-World War II period of prosperity and stability ended in the early 1970s. However, the China-led economic growth in the past three decades only provides a short-term solution to the system.

In the view of Wallerstein, for capital to be shifted away from the declining sectors into the rising sectors, the declining sectors need to be relocated from the core to the semi-periphery (or to the periphery according to the labour condition and the technological level). Some countries in the latter two categories will benefit from such global production and capital relocation. Historically, it was in such pivotal moments that opportunities for upward mobility within the system were generated and regenerated (Wallerstein, 1979: 69-73). China's high economic growth in the past decades can be regarded as reflecting the positive spill-over effect of taking advantage of the system's upward mobility. In line with this understanding, Li Minqi documents that "China has been the primary beneficiary of the latest round of capital relocation. Since 1993, China has consistently been the largest receiver of foreign direct investment among the "developing countries" (Li, Minqi, 2005: 435).

Notwithstanding China's own benefit, Li Minqi forcefully argues (and this argument has raised global debates) that China's state-led development model based on a strategy of cheap labour and export-orientation has, seen from a variety of perspectives, caused a "downward" recession for other semi-periphery countries:

> China's competition will completely undermine the relative monopoly of the existing semi-peripheral states in certain commodity chains. The value added will be squeezed, forcing the traditional semi-peripheral states to accept lower wage rates close to the Chinese rates. (Li, Minqi, 2005: 436)

> Should the Chinese workers generally receive the semi-peripheral levels of wages, given the size of the Chinese population, the total surplus distributed to the working classes in the entire semi-periphery would have to more than double. This will greatly reduce the share of the surplus available for the rest of the world. (Ibid.: 437)

Furthermore, among his critiques of the capitalist system in connection with the global debates on the consequence and impact brought about by the economic rise of China, one central point Li Minqi raises is that China's rise heralds the "autumn" of the current global system, leading the system into a "winter." His analytical propositions can be summarized as: a) Global relocation of production and capital accumulation from the core to semi-periphery makes China the key beneficiary that is taking a larger share from the relocation and capital movement; b) China's rise is exerting great pressure on other semi-periphery states, leading to the peripherization of the existing semi-periphery countries; 3) Once the semi-periphery world has gotten into trouble and become unstable, the entire capitalist world system would be in crisis. Here, Li Minqi outlines the possible consequences of the destabilization of the capitalist world system caused by the China-led semi-periphery rivalry:

> The semi-periphery plays the indispensable role of the "middle stratum" in the world system representing the hope of "modernization," "development," and an upward mobility for the great majority living in the peripheral states. Should this layer disappear and be reduced to no more than a part of the periphery, the world system is likely to become politically highly unstable. (Ibid.: 436-437)

> Peripheralization of the semi-periphery will deprive the capitalist world economy of a major source of effective demand. Moreover, the peripheralized semiperipheral states will inevitably face highly explosive political situations at home…. However, the peripheralized semi-peripheral states will not be able to simultaneously offer the relatively high wages and survive the competition against other peripheral or peripheralized semi-peripheral states in the world market. The entire semi-periphery will be threatened with revolution and political turmoil. (Ibid.: 437)

Li Minqi's conclusion is that China's rise is intensifying global competition over markets, and placing downward pressures on industrial wages both in core and semi-periphery countries. At the same time, it also puts upward pressure on commodity prices and threatens to destabilize the traditional pattern of relationships between core, semi-peripheral, and peripheral nations in the capitalist world system.

Research Question, Propositions and Objective

Although the Marxist approach to the critical analysis of the development of capitalism, with its deep insight into the system's embedded contradictions that result in recurring crises, was vindicated by the evolution of capitalism in the 20th century, capitalism has so far been able to pull out of its periodic crises.

This is especially true seen from the perspective of the historical experiences of the developed West, where capitalism has survived severe economic crises. The contemporary global financial crisis since 2008 can be seen as a manifestation of capitalism's recurrent crises, hence, it is still too early and difficult to declare the doom's day of global capitalism.

The question that remains unanswered is why capitalism, if history shows that it does indeed perpetually and periodically generate socio-economic crises, has so far been able to retain its legitimacy as a viable and sustainable socio-economic system. What is missing from the structural analysis of Marx is an approach that explicitly takes into account questions of social and political power, or, to put it differently, an analysis that attempts to conceptualize the dialectics of historical change within the capitalist system and to understand market society as a complex and dynamic rather than static structure.

In retrospect, historical capitalism has experienced periods of discontinuous change, which have been more typical than the "brief moments of generalized expansion along a definite development path like the one that occurred in the 1950s and 1960s" (Arrighi, 1994: 1). In modern times, capitalism underwent constant reforms and transformations from a laissez-faire capitalism to a more regulated system based on controlled and rationalized production – such as Fordism, Keynesianism, New Deal, social welfare capitalism, and so forth – with the state playing a positive role in many economic and social aspects. These far-reaching modifications in economic and political realms showed the adaptability of the ruling classes of modern capitalism in the acceptance of necessary reforms in order to defuse emerging societal contradictions. These concessions intended to regenerate and promote general consensus or consent through which social control and the mode of production could be preserved. Politically, social consent is believed to have its root in the system of democratic institutions and liberal ideology through which the mechanism of exchange of dialogues and ideas between the population and the state aims at maintaining social and political stability. In this way, the social order, which the bourgeois ruling class has created and recreated in a web of institutions, social relations and ideas, represents a basis for consent (Bottomore, 1983: 201).

History tends to repeat the similarities between the past and the present. If we turn to the work of Polanyi, especially his notion of "double movement" (Polanyi, 1944), which describes the evolution of "variant" market capitalism in the 19th and the early 20th century, we can understand why he was actually convinced that "our age will be credited with having seen the end of the self-regulating market" (Ibid., 1944: 148). This is because the disastrous social effects of free market capitalism were so obvious in his time. Polanyi's analysis is equally, if not more, relevant to our understanding of the similarly disastrous form of liberalism governing the world today. Likewise, the theoretical framework of Gramsci (1971), notably his concepts of "hegemony" and "passive revolution", helps us comprehend, without rigidly looking through the lens of the development of productive forces, how the legitimacy of the capitalist system is sustained. Gramsci provides a comprehensive framework for understanding the more complex and deeper social dimensions of *class culture* as well as a wide horizon of analysis of *ideology* and politics that escapes any simple causal explanation.

Furthermore, the methodological combination of both Polanyian and Gramscian theoretical and analytical categories enables us to conceptualize the evolution of the capitalist world order in a historical perspective, especially the changes in relations brought about by the intensification of globalization since the 1990s. It also promotes our understanding of the way globalization has reshaped the terrain and parameters of social, economic and political relations both at the national and the global levels, and has exerted pressure on the resilient capacities of capitalism (Li and Hersh, 2006).

In the context of comprehending the dialectics of capitalism in relation to the topic of this chapter, it is important to conceptualize to what extent the rise of China is creating new opportunities and alternatives for the further development and expansion of capitalism, and to what extent it is bringing about and accelerating the contradictory nature of capitalism into a full crisis. In order to do this, it is equally important to develop a holistic understanding of globalization and transnational capitalism in connection with the various aspects of crises, opportunities and alternatives that have different impacts on different countries and regions (Li, Xing, 2009).

This chapter aims to problematize Li Minqi's theoretical assertions on the demise of the world capitalist system brought about by, among other factors, China's economic rise. The chapter devotes a special focus on his claim that the rise of China will accelerate the contractions within the capitalist world system by reducing the development spaces of other semi-periphery countries. The China-led competition within the semi-periphery world will destabilize the global capitalist system leading to its demise. Our analyses and propositions are constructed and supported by the following areas:

1. Capitalism as a world system has indeed historically displayed recurrent crises including the recent financial crisis since 2008. However, the current crisis has the quite unique feature that it is a crisis generated by financial capital (Wall Street speculation and distortion) with a spill-over effect to the productive sectors. Make no mistake: the crisis originated right in the center of global capitalism (the US, Europe). Since 2008 no Western industrialized nation has

been immune to the economic recession caused by this crisis. Desperately and ironically, some Western politicians and scholars expected China's assistance to resolve the world's recession by taking advantage of her huge foreign exchange reserves. Remember this: China is still not recognized by the US and major European countries as a "market economy"!

2. The world system theory posits that the cyclical rhythms of the capitalist system consist of the rise and fall of successive guarantors of global order, with each one having its particular pattern of interactions with the system. The cyclical rhythms result in regular, slow-moving, but significant geographical shifts in the accumulation of capital and power without changing the fundamental relations of inequality within the system. China, albeit not yet a hegemonic guarantor, has shown some characteristics of playing the guarantor's role in reducing the negative impact caused by the contemporary crises, such as the Asian financial crisis in 1997, as well as the current global financial crisis since 2008.

3. Although it is true that there are, to a certain degree, contradictions caused by the economic competition between semi-periphery countries, what the world has witnessed in recent years does not conform with what Li Minqi claims to be "the China-led semi-periphery rivalry leading to the destabilization of the world system". On the contrary, the political and economic cooperation between the largest semi-periphery countries (the BRIC) in dealing with emerging global problems has generated a positive spillover effect to the rest of the world.

4. Various concrete economic statistics do not one-sidedly support the thesis of "China destabilizing the semi-periphery". For many years, although having exported more manufactured goods and imported raw materials, China has had trade deficits with the regions of Latin America and Southeast Asia. Some recent developments indicate that China's beneficial economic position in the world economy is being challenged in a number of ways. First, the value of Chinese currency has been raised under global pressure with an annual rate of 10% in the past years, which will be making Chinese products more expensive in the coming years. More pressures on the Chinese state to raise the value of its currency are expected to come in the near future. Secondly, the Chinese wage has been substantially increased due to both internal and external pressures. It is reported that the rising production cost in China caused by wage increases is pushing international and domestic companies to outsource or relocate their production and investment to China's neighbors or competitors where the production cost is lower (Jacob, 2011).

5. Although a favorable external environment and condition is very important for the upward mobility of a country, one cannot afford to ignore the internal

factors; rather, they should be emphasized. There is a scholarly consensus on the explanation of the success of East Asian development that such a success must be understood as the interaction of many mutually-supported external and internal factors. Namely, that it is *the synergy of external factors*, such as the US security umbrella, the post-war favorable international development environment, and foreign assistance and direct investment, *in correlation with internal factors*, such as the market-friendly role of the "developmental state," cheap and skilled labor, export-led development policy, and cultural resiliency and the role of education and social stability, etc. Over-emphasizing the external factors would lead us to a biased understanding.

This chapter uses Brazil as a significant empirical case, partly to verify the impact of the rise of China being felt worldwide, including in Brazil, and partly to falsify Li Minqi's hypotheses of China's potential negative impacts upon the semi-periphery. Brazil is the second biggest semi-peripheral country in the world, occupying the position as the world's 6th largest economy. Brazil is exceptional in the Latin American context for its relative success in maintaining a substantial manufacturing sector capacity through the "lost decade" of Latin American development in the 1980s as well as through the neo-liberal 1990s (Castro, 2009). Otherwise only Mexico, Latin America's second biggest economy, has likewise had a reasonable degree of success in this regard. For these reasons the analysis of this chapter does not attempt to generalize Brazil's experience to the rest of Latin America, nor to the rest of the semi-periphery, although the arguments and conclusions drawn may be of relevance to other semi-peripheral countries.

The Rise of China and Brazil's Economic Development

Considering Brazil's economic development experience in the last decade, it can safely be argued that Li Minqi's negative expectations for the semi-periphery have not materialized in Brazil, at least not in the short term. This is in spite of the negative shock experienced by the Brazilian economy as a consequence of the international financial crisis in 2008-2009. The IMF's Executive Board summed Brazil's recent development experience neatly up in a recent public information notice after its 2011 Article IV consultation with Brazil:

> Brazil has made remarkable strides over the last decade, emerging as a
> leading actor on the global economic stage. A strong policy framework
> and sustained political commitment to reduce inflation and public debt
> levels has increased the resilience of the economy to external shocks.
> Moreover, the increased macroeconomic stability, combined with well-

> targeted social policies, has allowed the country to take advantage of favorable external conditions over the past decade to accelerate growth and reduce poverty and inequality to historic lows. (IMF, 2011)

Viewed against the backdrop of these positive social and economic developments, Brazil is far from experiencing the kind of peripheralization and domestic political unrest that Li Minqi saw as the likely outcome of the impact of China's rise (2005: 437). In a 2010 study on global attitudes, the Pew Research Center compares attitudes in 22 countries: Brazilians are the second most positive about the current conditions of the economy, and 76% consider that the government is handling economic development well (Pew, 2010: 8-9). This is without a doubt a major reason behind the strong support given to President Lula; 84% see him as having a positive influence on the way things are going for Brazil (Pew, 2010: 13). These positive views are reflected in the atmosphere of optimism and the absence of political polarization and social and political unrest in Brazil, and largely a consequence of the successful social and economic development trajectory implemented throughout Lula's presidency.

The short-term good results do not allow us to say that Li Minqi's hypothesis of the peripheralization of the semi-periphery following China's rise is neither likely to become an issue in the case of other countries nor in Brazil's future. Brazil's social and economic developments in the last decade, which coincides with China's first decade as a member of the World Trade Organization (since 2001), have been extraordinarily positive in spite of the international financial crisis that broke out in 2008!

In the analysis, we seek to explain Brazil's economic development experience between 1999 and 2011, and we discuss how China's economic rise has impacted Brazil's development. The analysis is divided into two sub-periods corresponding to the period before the onset of the international financial crisis (2008) and the years after. The year of 1999 serves as a starting point for the analysis due to Brazil's financial instability in the late 1990s that led Brazil to devalue its currency that year and to re-evaluate its development-oriented policies.

In the analysis, we emphasize the challenges and opportunities that China has presented Brazil as well as we look into Brazil's own development strategy. This approach has been taken because China's impact cannot be properly analyzed without taking Brazil's own policies into account. As Deepak Nayyar has argued in an analysis of the impact of Chinese and Indian manufacturing exports on developing countries' development, it seems plausible to argue that developing countries will feel a negative impact from these exports, but such an impact cannot be proven (Nayyar, 2008: 91). Similarly, although Nayyar is right about the plausibility of a negative impact from Chinese and Indian manufacturing exports on other developing countries, another methodological problem is that the results upon development experienced by other developing countries cannot simply be explained as an outcome of China and India's impact. On the contrary, development results are also due to the overall situation in which a given developing country finds itself, and this situation is largely a path-dependent outcome of the policy choices pursued by the country itself. Therefore, the analysis will pay strong attention to Brazil's overall situation and to its own policy decisions when seeking to explain Brazilian development outcomes.

Brazilian Development and China's Impact: 1999-2008

Brazil came out of the so-called "lost decade" of Latin American development to a period of hyper-inflation and stagnation in the early 1990s. In response to this situation, the Brazilian governments between 1993 and 1998 introduced a stabilization policy based on economic openness, privatization, and stabilization based on an exchange rate anchor. This policy produced short-term success in terms of renewed economic growth, poverty reduction and control over inflation. The success was built on a shaky foundation however. This became clear as Brazil faced a financial crisis in 1998 and 1999 simultaneously with and connected to the financial crisis that hit Asia in 1997. Russia and Latin American countries experienced similar problems. Brazil's financial crisis should not solely be seen as a consequence of "contagion" from these various crises though. The country did exhibit a number of weaknesses and external economic vulnerabilities that made it crisis-prone. A central point of vulnerability was located in the rising current account deficit between 1993 and 1998 and an increasingly overvalued exchange rate that hampered the overall international competitiveness of the Brazilian economy and thus provoked the crisis (Palma, 2000).

The situation of financial instability in the country provoked rising financing costs, the driving up of public sector debt (Ocampo, 1999: 97-99), and the weakening of the international competitiveness of the import-competing sectors. As a consequence Brazil experienced a falling output in the industrial sector in 1998 and 1999 (BCB, 2000: 16) and a growing debt within the public sector. Between 1996 and 1999, public sector indebtedness thus rose from 31.4% to 43.2% (BCB, 2000: 93).

Brazil responded to the financial difficulties with devaluation in early 1999 as well as with a re-thinking of the overall framework of development-oriented policies. As Antônio Barros de Castro rightly argues (2009), the devaluation in 1999 and the new law of fiscal responsibility, passed by the Brazilian Congress in 2000 (BCB, 2001: 92), created new and better conditions for Brazilian development although the country obviously was facing major difficulties as well.

Some key economic figures from 1999 illustrate these difficulties vividly. In spite of a primary fiscal surplus of 3.1% of GDP in 1999, interest costs associated with the public sector's debt stood at 13.1% of GDP leaving Brazil with a nominal fiscal deficit of 10.0% that year. Also, while GDP per capita fell slightly in 1998 and 1999 when measured in the local currency, GDP per capita in US dollars fell from US$5,022 in 1997 to US$3,401 in 1999 due to the devaluation (BCB, 2000: 13).

These problems were not a consequence of a Chinese impact to any significant extent but rather a consequence of Brazil's own problems and unsuccessful policy choices. This is not to say that China did not present Brazil with challenges at the time. Mauricio Mesquita Moreira (2006: 1) argues that China had indeed become a formidable competitor to Brazil, and Latin America in general, in the 1990s and early 2000s due to China's successful manufacturing exports. Factors such as endowments, productivity, scale, and the government's role were the main reasons for the challenge posed by China in the manufacturing area. But, according to Moreira, the trade data up to that point had suggested a modest impact (although the trend was worrisome). He pointed out, however, that a tendency towards "de-industrialization" shared by Latin America and Brazil should not be seen as destiny but more as a consequence of a poor and volatile macroeconomic environment, and, in Brazil's case, also of long periods with an overvalued exchange rate (2006: 6). The solution for Latin American countries, he suggested, was to improve their macroeconomic conditions as well as to search for successful policy formulas that would lead a country towards the success of its manufacturing sector (2006: 27-28).

Brazil responded to the financial crisis of 1998-99 with macroeconomic policies aimed at improving overall macroeconomic conditions in order to stabilize the economy and resume a path of economic growth. It did so with a macroeconomic policy combining primary fiscal surpluses, targeting inflation, and implementing a floating exchange rate (Meyer, 2011: 3), thus leaving behind the semi-fixed exchange rate policy used to control inflation between 1993 and early 1999. In this context, the law of fiscal responsibility sought to control public expenses and get public sector debt under control (BCB, 2001: 92).

This policy was relatively successful in bringing down the nominal budget deficit to 4.5% in 2000 (BCB, 2001: 104) and in assuring renewed economic growth. However, it was an arduous and very challenging task to stabilize the budget and public sector indebtedness in a context where Brazil's neighbor, Argentina, a significant export market for Brazil, had entered a downward spiral in its economic development that led to default and devaluation in early 2002, thus reducing Brazil's exports to Argentina substantially (Bernal-Meza, 2002). Continued difficulties in bolstering confidence in the Brazilian economy were further spurred by the presidential election process in 2002 in which the left-wing Workers' Party of Luiz Inácio 'Lula' da Silva criticized, in its electoral propaganda, the neoliberal policies of Lula's predecessor Fernando Henrique Cardoso.

This situation led to a large increase in Brazil's risk rating, and the reserves in the Central Bank came under pressure thereby provoking devaluations (BCB, 2003) and creating a need for IMF financing. The main candidates came under pressure to clarify their policy position (Coggiola, 2004) and Lula promised in a "Letter to the People", published June 22, 2002, that, if he became president, he would honor the Brazilian public sector debt (Lula, 2002). Due to this unstable environment, Brazil's public sector debt increased substantially in spite of the policy of primary surpluses. From a debt/GDP rate of 48.8% in 2000, the level rose gradually to 58.7% at the end of 2003 (BCB, 2004: 106). However, once the uncertainty provoked by the 2002 elections passed with the swearing in of the new president and his coalition government, things started improving.

The new government emphasized the need to stabilize the economy not only through strict macroeconomic policies but also, as Lula emphasized in his inauguration speech as president, through the pursuit of a national development strategy with an active state presence in the economy, thereby, according to the president himself (Lula, 2003), going against the neo-liberal approach pursued by the former government. The emphasis on reducing the external economic vulnerability through a more active industrial policy, a renewed export orientation, and a policy aimed at getting the state debt under control was supported by CNI and Fiesp, the main employer organizations in the industrial sector (Abu-El-Haj, 2007: 108-11, Fiesp, 2002, CNI, 2002). This emphasis on a national development strategy and active state policies was soon to be found in the new government's industrial policy document, PITCE, which presented industrial policy as consisting of interconnected actions. These included industrial policies of the vertical pick-the-winner type, horizontal policies aimed at improving the business climate, along with policies in the area of foreign trade and technological development. Reflecting the government's emphasis on short-term stabilization, the PITCE document distinguished between a short-term strategy that was to stabilize the economy and a long-term strategy that entailed emphasis on technological development and improved production capacity in the industrial sector (Christensen, 2010).

With the new coalition government in place, the uncertainty regarding the policy orientation of the new government that had been present prior to the 2002 elections gave way to an improved atmosphere for economic development. The international context also turned out to develop in a direction that was relatively benign for Brazilian economic development in a number of ways such as the relative dynamism of global economic growth. For Brazil one of the most significant positive contextual factors in the international realm, however, was that Brazil experienced a strong improvement in its terms of trade. This improvement was associated with rising prices for commodities and agricultural products spurred in great part by growing Chinese demand for these products. Saslavsky and Rozemberg note that Brazil's terms of trade with China improved by 52% between 2001 and 2007 as Brazilian exports to China soared (2009: 191). The rising export prices in basic products were clearly a great asset in terms of the government's short-term strategies and stabilization efforts. Brazil's exports rose from approximately US$60 billion in 2002 to US$197.9 billion in 2008. This helped to ensure rising over-all trade surpluses until 2007 when the figure reached US$40 billion. The export of basic products made a great contribution to these results as it rose from US$18 billion in 2002 to US$73 billion in 2008 (BCB, 2003 and 2009).

These developments helped stabilize the Brazilian economy and create economic growth and social advancement on increasingly solid foundations. External economic vulnerability was reduced alongside the debt level of the public sector. These two elements were essential in the Lula government's quest for greater autonomy, understood as policy space to pursue its policies independently from outside pressure. This objective was pursued in several other ways from the outset. Tullo Vigevani and Gabriel Cepaluni (2007: 1313) have argued convincingly that the Lula government aimed at strengthening national autonomy through a mixture of an active state role in the economy along with a diversification of exports and of Brazil's international partners. This implied greater emphasis on South-South relations both in terms of economic exchanges and diplomacy such as the formation of coalitions with other developing countries in international economic negotiations. Amado Luiz Cervo sees this as a strategy of counter-power against the hegemony of the Triad powers, the US, the EU and Japan, with the aim of increasing the influence of emerging countries and the developing world in the global order (Cervo, 2008: 11).

This emphasis on relations with other developing countries was in fact initially pursued by the Lula government's predecessor when the Cardoso government in its national development plan 2000-03 put a stronger weight on its economic relations with South America and the biggest emerging markets such as China (Lessa, Couto and Farias, 2009: 95-96). The Lula government continued this trend, but arguably put even stronger emphasis on South-South relations, and in particular on innovative coalitions between developing countries in international politics with the goal of strengthening the voice and influence of the developing world in international affairs. Lessa, Couto and Farias (2009) emphasize the Lula government's strong emphasis on relations with the other

BRIC countries including South Africa, which was recently invited in to become a member of the informal BRIC group.

This strategic orientation helps explain Brazil's decision, as the first Latin American country, to accept China as a market economy within the WTO in 2004 (Saslavsky and Rozemberg, 2009: 203). As Amado Luiz Cervo (2010: 30) argues, the joint communiqués of Lula and China's leader Hu Jintao from 2004, as well as from 2010, show that both governments see their relations as strategic, based on principles of mutual trust, bilateral trade and the coordination of positions in relation to multilateral economic negotiations.

In other words, Lula's Brazil has treated China largely as an opportunity in terms of the government's development agenda and its search for a more prominent position in the global power hierarchy. The relationship with China and the overall strategy of counter-hegemony, however, is also controversial in Brazil, where some favor closer relations to the established Western powers both in political and economic terms. One critic sees the bilateral relationship with China as bizarre and argues that China is actually the main beneficiary (Almeida, 2010). The relationship, however, is also not without frictions, particularly when it comes to trade relations. The issue of competitive pressure from China in the industrial sector in the Brazilian domestic market, as well as in third markets, has been the main element behind worries of a negative impact from China on Brazilian development. Although Brazil does treat China as an opportunity, Henrique Altemani de Oliveira (2010: 89) sees the bilateral trade relations between the two countries as more competitive than equally supplementary. In any case, it is clear that the Brazilian government treats the trade relationship with China both as an opportunity and as a challenge.

Saslavsky and Rozemberg (2009: 223) argue that, overall, there has been only a limited negative impact on Brazilian industrial jobs as a result of competition from China although some sectors have been challenged, not the least in third markets such as the United States and the EU. In a study from 2007, Uziel Nogueira argues that Brazil, during Lula's first presidency (2002-2006), had been "rapidly losing market share in products such as shoes, textiles, clothing, transport vehicles, machine tools, chemical products and steel that were highly competitive in the past" (Nogueira, 2007: 17), although he emphasizes that this consequence was largely due to an unfavorable macroeconomic policy framework and decaying infrastructure in Brazil itself. Renato Baumann (2009: 13-14), focusing on Brazilian losses in the third markets, points out that Brazil lost market share in three key markets, namely the US, Argentina and Mexico, between 2003 and 2008, during which time China gained market share. According to the calculations made by Kevin P. Gallagher and Roberto Porzecanski on the basis of the United Nations' Commodity Trade Statistics, Brazil's share of global manufacturing exports stayed flat at 0.7% between 2000 and 2008, while China increased its share from 5.0% to 11.5% (Gallagher, 2010: 5).

On the other hand, Brazil's social policies and its economic policies, as well as its stabilization policy have, as a whole, led to economic growth, growing domestic demand, job creation and a reduction in unemployment. Nevertheless, an increasingly strong currency and import liberalization contributed to a growing level of Brazilian manufacturing imports from China. Brazilian industrialists reacted to this development by putting pressure on the government to pursue trade investigations and trade sanctions against China (Saslavsky and Rozemberg, 2009: 201). The government and its specialized bureaucrats in this area responded to some of these demands. They have been quite active in pursuing anti-dumping investigations of Chinese exports to Brazil, particularly in a number of capital-intensive sectors. According to Saslavsky and Rozemberg (2009: 202), Brazilian authorities were particularly active in enacting anti-dumping measures against China in the years 1998, 2001 and 2007. Renato Bauman shows that 34.9% of Brazil's anti-dumping investigations between 1992 and 2008 were directed at China, namely 43 out of a total of 123, and that, in this last year (2008) alone, 10 new investigations directed at Chinese exports were initiated (Bauman, 2009, 14). Following the end of quotas in the textile and clothing sectors pursuant to the former Multifiber Arrangement[1], Brazil introduced new regulations to limit imports of Chinese produced textiles and clothes in late 2005, and in early 2006 China and Brazil signed a memorandum of understanding in the area of textiles. Similarly, China offered voluntary export restrictions in a number of areas of interest to Brazil (Saslavsky and Rozemberg, 2009: 204-207). These examples show the widespread use of trade protectionist measures by Brazil against Chinese competition in the manufacturing sector, but they also show that disagreements may at times be managed through bilateral economic diplomacy. This means that while there is often a conflict of interest between the two countries in the trade area, the two countries are nevertheless able to advance in bilateral economic cooperation of mutual interest while also presenting a common front in multilateral economic arenas when they share areas of common interest.

As we can see from these examples, development impacts are not only produced through market signals. Politics at the national and bilateral levels, as well as at the wider international level, all have a role to play. The examples here suggest that the Brazilian government has been open to private sector views and is seeking to protect Brazilian jobs and production.

If we focus on Brazil's development record up to the financial crisis in 2008, it shows a quite positive picture. In this respect, Brazil has arguably benefitted from trade with China. Brazil's hopes for a positive impact from Chinese FDI into the country, however, were not met in the period under discussion. Although Brazil enjoyed high and rising levels of incoming FDI between 1994 and 2007, only around 0.1% originated from China (Saslavsky and Rozemberg, 2009: 212, 215).

We argue that China's short-term impact on Brazilian development in the boom years of the global economy prior to the international financial crisis should be considered positive due to the stabilizing effect of China's growing imports from Brazil and its positive impact on Brazil's terms of trade. Brazil's positive export performance as a whole has created the conditions for its successful economic growth on a relatively firm macroeconomic basis between 2003 and 2008. Our attention now turns to the social and economic development results experienced by Brazil in this period.

Brazil's economic and social development between 2003 and 2008 was impressive. The country moved from a situation characterized by economic stagnation, a high level of external economic vulnerability, and a high public sector debt/GDP ratio at the beginning of the period to a situation of renewed economic growth and reduced macroeconomic imbalances. The successful export performance, economic growth, and primary budget surplus created a solid macroeconomic basis for continued growth and social improvements. As we have seen exports rose from around US$60 billion in 2002 to around US$198 billion in 2008. This ensured current account surpluses in the years 2003 to 2007, and, in spite of a current account deficit in 2008 (Tesouro, 2011: 10), Brazil became a creditor country in the international realm that year after a long history of being a debtor country. This result helped improve the credit rating of the country as did the primary fiscal surpluses of between 3% and 4% every year between 2002 and 2008 (Tesouro, 2011: 4) that led to a strongly reduced debt/GDP ratio of 38.5% in 2008 (Tesouro, 2011: 5) while monetary policies helped keep inflation in check inside the target (Tesouro, 2011: 8).

These macroeconomic results helped to create the conditions for economic growth and job creation. Economic growth averaged 4.2% and, in per capita terms, approximately 2.9 % between 2003 and 2008. However, when measured in US dollars, average per capita income increased from US$2,861 to US$8,628 between 2002 and 2008 (BCB, 2010, 16) as the exchange rate gradually strengthened in response to improved macroeconomic conditions.

Manufacturing exports maintained a relatively stable share of total exports between 2002 and 2006, falling marginally from 54.7% in 2002 to 54.4% in 2006. However, this share fell to 52.3% in 2007 and to 46.8% in 2008 (Arraes, 2010: 205). At the same time, Chinese manufacturing exports to Brazil rose from US$1.8 billion in 2003 to an impressive US$19.0 billion in 2008 (Fiesp, 2011).

These developments created concerns regarding Brazil's de-industrialization and re-primarization (Arraes, 2010). On the other hand, the industrial sector experienced an average yearly economic growth of approximately 4.7% in the years from 2004 to 2008 (BCB, 2007 and 2009). This economic dynamism helped produce jobs and create higher living standards. Between 1998 and 2006 the industrial sector created 1 million new jobs according to the statistical bureau IBGE (Saslavsky and Rozemberg, 2009: 196) and the expansion continued strongly in 2007 (BCB, 2008: 25). According to calculations made by Saslavsky and Rozemberg (2009: 196) China was responsible for a small job loss in Brazil, while growing domestic demand and growing trade helped increase employment. Marcelo Neri (2009: 225) points out that 10 million new jobs were generated in Brazil between 2004 and 2007 and that most of them were in the formal sector of the economy. Clearly, this job creation was only possible due to strong macroeconomic results in which China played a positive role via its imports from Brazil and its impact on Brazilian export prices in commodities and in the agricultural sector. As Antônio Barros de Castro argues (2009: 262-4), there was a clear consistency between the macroeconomic stabilization policy on the one hand and economic growth (along with a reduction in both poverty and economic inequality) on the other. In this regard job creation, higher minimum wages and economic transfers to the poor through programs such as *Bolsa Família*, a conditional cash transfer program, all played their part. This produced impressive socio-economic results. Some 30 million people entered the middle classes, out of a population of approximately 200 million, during Lula's eight years as president (Meyer, 2011: 4). The high level of economic inequality in Brazil was gradually reduced (Neri, 2009: 230) and poverty figures went down from 26.7% of the population in 2002 to 19.3% in 2006 (Neri, 2009: 236).

All these figures go against the fears and expectations of Li Minqi. Also, the analysis has shown that while China's impact on the manufacturing sector seems to be negative, the overall impact of China on Brazilian economic growth has been positive in the period between 1999 and 2008, particularly due to rising Chinese imports from Brazil and China's positive impact on Brazilian export prices.

The economic outcomes, however, are in large part a result of Brazil's own social and economic policies as well as its trade policy, its foreign policy and the overall panorama of the global economy that was propitious for the Brazilian economy for most of the first decade of the 21st century. By 2008 Brazil was in the midst of a period of solid economic expansion due to a number of factors. This was the case, even though the very success of economic growth and stabilization had led to a situation with renewed deficits on the country's current account balance and in which the competitiveness of the manufacturing sector was threatened by a series of factors that had been facing the Brazilian productive sector for a long time. These factors included a high tax rate, high interest rates, poor infrastructure (Nogueira, 2007: 17-8), and an increasingly strong exchange rate.

Brazilian Development and China's Impact: 2008-2011

The international financial crisis thus hit Brazil in the last part of 2008 during a situation of relative economic strength due to the improved macroeconomic situation, and with a more solid external and financial situation, but also in a situation of growing competitiveness problems on the part of the manufacturing sector. The main 'victims' of the crisis were the United States and the EU, and the troubles experienced by these markets, as well as those of Latin America, had negative effects for Brazilian export performance. Brazilian total exports fell from US$198 billion in 2008 to US$153 billion in 2009 with industrial exports being hit the hardest (BCB, 2010: 101). Overall output in the industrial sector was also hit hard in 2009, particularly in the manufacturing sector and hereunder the capital goods sector (BCB, 2010, 16, 18 and 22). In other words, the sectors contributing the greatest value-addition were the hardest hit – a worrisome trend.

In these situations, China became Brazil's largest export market in 2009, absorbing some 13.3% of total Brazilian exports. Similarly, Brazilian exports to China and some other minor Asian countries actually rose in comparison with 2008 in sharp contrast with exports to the United States, The EU and Latin America. This year also saw Asia become the main regional destination for Brazilian exports after having been only in the third position in 2008, far behind Latin America and the Caribbean, as well as the EU (BCB, 2010: 118). This underlines the growing importance of the Chinese and Asian export markets for Brazil, and was one reason for the continued fall in the share of manufacturing exports in overall exports, which fell to 44.0% in 2009 (Arraes, 2010: 205). While these developments provoked renewed worries about the Chinese threat to the Brazilian industrial sector, José Roberto Mendonça de Barros rightly argues that Brazil's export diversification and global trade outlook came in handy for the country in the crisis context (Barros, 2010: 4) as markets expanded in Asia, particularly China, while falling everywhere else in 2009. Whereas 50.5% of total Brazilian exports in 2002 had gone to the United States and the EU, this share had been reduced to 32.5% in 2009 (BCB, 2003 and 2010). Barros furthermore argues that the tendency towards re-primarization of Brazil's export model is not as pronounced as critics sometimes suggest since the dynamic areas of agribusiness and offshore oil have a large technological component that analysts sometimes forget to take into consideration.

However, Brazil was indeed hit by the crisis. Apart from its negative effects on Brazilian exports, economic growth was affected negatively with GDP falling 0.2% (or 1.2% in per capita terms) in 2009 (BCB, 2010: 13). Brazil's strong exports to China and Asia and the government's counter-cyclical policies explain why the economic downturn was relatively mild.

In order to minimize the impact of the external shock to the Brazilian economy, the Lula government undertook a number of actions aimed at stimulating activity in the economy. In the fiscal area a number of tax exemptions were given in order to stimulate demand. In the monetary and financial area, the government sought to stimulate the credit-giving of the banking sector by reducing banks' compulsory deposits in the Central Bank. Also, public banks as the Banco do Brasil (BB), Caixa Econômica Federal (CEF), and particularly the National Development Bank (BNDES) were used to maintain liquidity in the financial market and to stimulate private investments (CEPAL, 2010: 11-13) at a time where credit from privately owned banks was being reduced (Albrieu and Fanelli, 2010: 19). The government furthermore stimulated investment directly with its own investments as part of its program of accelerated economic growth, the PAC (Albrieu and Fanelli, 2010: 18). These various government stimulous policies assured continued growth in real incomes inside Brazil, which, together with anti-cyclical policies such as increased public sector wages and increased social security spending led to growth in retail sales and a dynamic domestic market outcome (Barros, 2010).

In the area of commercial policy, Brazil was quite active in anti-dumping measures, which were mostly directed at China between late 2008 and late 2009 (SELA, 2010: 30).

Through these policy actions, and with the help of continued dynamism in parts of Asia, particularly China, the outlook for Brazilian economic growth for 2010 was positive (BCB, 2010, 13), and the economy rebounded strongly in 2010 producing a 7.5% growth rate. While GDP per capita grew by 6.5%, the tendency towards a strengthened Real meant that income per capita measured in US dollars rose to US$10,814 in 2010, a rise of almost US$2,500 when compared to the 2009 level (BCB, 2011: 14). This was as much a result of the US monetary policies of quantitative easing that led to a weaker dollar as it was a result of China's exchange rate policy and Brazil's own inflation targeting regime. This development in foreign exchange markets put the Brazilian manufacturing sector at a further disadvantage regarding its international competitiveness.

However, renewed global economic dynamism and improved export prices led to a strong rebound in Brazilian exports, producing a new record of US$202 billion in 2010 (BCB, 2011, 91). While exports increased in all sectors, manufacturing exports did not reach the 2008 level, in contrast to basics that soared (BCB, 2011: 92, 96). Furthermore, China's share of Brazilian exports expanded to 15.3% as the value of Brazilian exports to China increased by nearly 50% leaving Asia as the biggest export destination for Brazil (BCB, 2011: 99, 113). This development further exacerbated the tendency towards an export model increasingly dominated by natural goods, or, in other words, a tendency towards de-industrialization and re-primarization. At the same time, China's exports to Brazil also soared, and, although Brazil ran a trade surplus of US$5.2 billion in its bilateral trade with China in 2010, China enjoyed a US$23.5 billion surplus in bilateral trade of manufacturing goods with Chinese exports to Brazil in this area at US$24.9 billion against Brazil's US$1.4 billion of manufacturing exports going to China. While Chinese manufacturing exports to Brazil had increased to US$15.3 billion in 2009, Brazil's manufacturing exports to China stayed flat at US$1.4 billion both years (Fiesp, 2011). An article from the central national industrial employer organization in Brazil, the CNI, from November 2010, speaks of a virtual "import tsunami" from China (CNI, 2010). Worries regarding bilateral manufacturing trade were thus mounting in the Brazilian industrial sector.

The strengthening of this peripherization tendency has led to worrying developments such as a relatively stagnant output in the Brazilian industrial sector in 2011, as the exchange rate has maintained an upward bias. The Brazilian government has reacted to this in various ways in order to protect the Brazilian manufacturing sector as we will discuss in the following.

The government has reacted on a number of fronts in order to guide economic development. In 2010 it introduced a "buy Brazilian" policy that required the public sector to pay up to 25% above market prices in order to source products from Brazilian producers (Fleischer, 2010, July 24-30). This policy was used, for instance, to strengthen the ship building industry, an industry that the Lula government had successfully sought to promote throughout his period (Verdin, 2010). In December of 2010, Brazil increased its import tariffs for Chinese-made goods in the toy sector (Kennedy, 2011). In a similar move towards a strengthened protectionist orientation aimed at promoting jobs and production in the Brazilian manufacturing sector, the new government that took over the reins in 2011 under the leadership of President Dilma Rousseff has authored a new industrial policy known as "Brasil Maior" (Bigger Brazil). In this document the state is depicted as having a central role in the economy as a planner of development that is in constant dialogue with business organizations. The plan aims at stimulating innovation in national production in order to increase industrial competitiveness in the domestic and external markets as a means to ensure economic growth, job creation, and continued social inclusion. Amongst other things, the plan aims at confronting the tendency towards substitution of national production with imports through defensive anti-dumping policies in order to foster growth in national production of products with high levels of value-adding. Similarly, the plan presents the active use of government procurement as a tool to create new business and technological competencies. Apart from this, the plan points towards "vertical" policies as it singles out the desirability of developing supply chains in the field of energy, a sector in which Brazil is globally competitive. Finally, the plan sees as a strategic goal the further export diversification and internationalization of Brazilian businesses with the aim of promoting exports with a high technology component, and it details that the use of technology and scientific knowledge should be increased in sectors that are intensive in the use of natural resources (MDIC, 2011: 7, 11-12). In short, the plan aims at a combination of protection from international competition and promotion of national production in advanced sectors as a way to protect and advance the Brazilian manufacturing sector.

Here we see a plan that points towards a very activist industrial policy and possibly the further entrenchment of anti-dumping policies in order to protect the Brazilian manufacturing sector from external competition, not the least from China. Recent remarks made by Guido Mantega, Brazil's finance minister, point in this direction as well. He argues that the United States and China both seek to keep their currencies weak in order to benefit their own competitiveness thereby hurting Brazil and other developing countries.

With this he suggests that it is legitimate for Brazil to pursue policies that seek to protect the country from disloyal foreign competition from countries that seek to enhance their competitiveness by weakening their currencies. As a consequence of strong recent inflows of capital to Brazil that threaten to overheat the economy and further strengthen the Real, the government has furthermore now started a policy aimed at reducing stimulus in the economy (BRIC Policy Center, 2011). It is using a number of tools including higher import tariffs, higher compulsory deposits by banks to the Central Bank, taxation of capital inflows, and public procurement policies that further strengthen the "buy Brazilian" policy. Guido Mantega has recently made the point that the Brazilian government needs to intervene in the economy in order to reduce destabilization of the external account and in order to maintain Brazilian jobs. He further argues that Brazil's economic growth is sustainable, even in the adverse global scenario of 2011, due to its solid public accounts and its large and dynamic domestic market. This creates a huge advantage for Brazil in comparison with many other countries, an advantage that Brazil must maintain through careful policies that keep the economy from overheating while maintaining job creation (Lima, Peduzzi and Aquino, July 27, 2011). In other words, Brazil's dynamic domestic market should benefit Brazilian producers and Brazilian job creation.

Thus, the Brazilian government is treating the current situation in 2011 as a situation characterized by currency conflict and trade war, and Brazil must protect itself in such a situation. Chinese imports from Brazil have in the meantime maintained their upward trend. Furthermore, in 2010 China started focusing on investing in Brazil. According to CEPAL figures (2011: 25), Chinese investments in Brazil rose to above US$9.5 billion in 2010, a huge increase when compared to the past. Other sources put Chinese FDI in Brazil at 17 billion dollars, most of which is directed at the oil sector (Scissors, 2011). What is clear, though, is that Chinese FDI to Brazil virtually exploded to new heights in 2010. Thus, China's economic importance for Brazil is on the rise both in terms of China's importance as an export market and as a source of FDI.

Conclusion

When one analyzes Brazil's development during the last decade, which corresponds to the period since China has been a member of the WTO, Li Minqi's thesis of the peripheralization tendency of the semi-periphery cannot be verified in practice by the experiences of Brazil. In line with the views of the world system theory, there are three paths of achieving upward mobility: 1) promotion by invitation; 2) strategy of independence and self-reliance; and 3) seizing the chance of new opportunities.

"Promotion by invitation" refers to the upward mobility path enjoyed by a semi-periphery or periphery country, whose geopolitical position is vital during the period of global power struggles. This upward mobility is stimulated by the favourable external environment created by the promotion and protection of one core nation, or a group of core nations, to serve its or their own geopolitical and geo-economic interests. Japan and the East Asian Newly Industrialized Economies are good examples of this type of upward mobility by external promotion.

A "strategy of independence and self-reliance" implies the mobilization of internal forces as well as the protection or isolation, willingly or unwillingly, from the capitalist world economy. The Chinese socialist period from 1949 to 1979 was driven by this internally-driven upward mobility. The result of Chinese socialism indicates a dual consequence of both great achievements and serious failures (Li Xing, 1999). Many failures are "policy failures" because, seen from a world system perspective, socialist states are still situated within the interactions of the capitalist world economy, and their activities are very much constrained by the international system of the capitalist world economy (So and Chiu, 1995:139-40).

"Seizing the chance" indicates the ability to take advantage of a new situation or condition (by virtue of timing) that is taking place in the international political economy and to adjust the domestic development mobility accordingly. This chapter shows that Brazil fits well into this category. Brazil has experienced extraordinary progress in terms of socio-economic development based on a much improved macroeconomic foundation. After facing financial instability, Brazil has been able to turn its situation around since 1999, but especially after the arrival of Lula as president in 2003. Brazil has gone through a period of successful economic stabilization with reduced public sector indebtedness in terms of the GDP/debt ratio and a substantial reduction in external economic vulnerability. These results have been produced in part by policy design, particularly through a successful strategy of export diversification and export growth along with a fiscal policy emphasizing primary surpluses as a tool to ensure a reduced public sector debt. The success of these policies, along with a much-needed devaluation in 1999 that helped lay the groundwork for the improved international competitiveness of the economy, has led to strong improvements in overall incomes and job creation. As a result poverty and economic inequality have been reduced, while many millions of Brazilians have enjoyed a period of upward social mobility. This has created an increasingly strong domestic market as well as high levels of socio-political stability as reflected in the widespread positive views among the population of the Lula government.

China's impact on Brazilian development can be seen as quite positive on balance, particularly in the period up until the international financial crisis in 2008. Chinese imports from Brazil grew strongly in this period and have retained this tendency after the outbreak of the crisis. In itself, the growing Chinese market has contributed to Brazil's economic stabilization and improved macroeconomic situation, which has been decisive in gaining the strong development results of Brazil in the period, but China's positive impact on Brazil's terms of trade has been particularly important for Brazil and promoted a strong growth in Brazilian exports of basic products such as minerals and agricultural goods. The dynamism of this sector has been particularly decisive in bolstering Brazilian trade surpluses. At the same time, China has also been a source of challenges for Brazil, particularly with regard to China's strong competitiveness in global markets in the manufacturing sector. Before the international financial crisis, Brazil met this challenge in different ways such as through anti-dumping policies but also through bilateral economic diplomacy with China in some areas.

Brazil's economic growth success and its improved macro-economic situation, which led Brazil to becoming an international creditor country (according to the Brazilian government), together with stronger international confidence in the Brazilian economy, helped increase the resilience of the Brazilian economy when confronted by the external shock that the international financial crisis in 2008 meant. After a short-lived contraction of the economy, in which particularly the industrial sector and exports suffered, Brazil entered a new phase of economic expansion. Again, Brazil's own policy choices as well as positive impacts from the world economy, including the continuous growth of exports to China, also in periods where exports to other regions fell, ensured that Brazil weathered the crisis as well as it did and got out of the crisis relatively fast. Government policies of stimulus to production, expansion of social policies, and public sector wages helped boost the dynamism of the domestic market, and, as export markets also improved, Brazil quickly closed the economic growth gap with a 7.5 % growth in 2010. Apart from China contributing positively to this result as an export market for Brazil, a virtual explosion in Chinese FDI to Brazil that started in 2010 also helped.

However, Brazil has experienced a strengthening of its exchange rate in the last expansive period. The strong exchange rate has created renewed challenges in terms of Brazil's international competitiveness in the manufacturing sector. This problem has been exacerbated by expansive monetary policies in the crisis-ridden developed countries, not the least in the United States, and by China's exchange rate policy that concentrates on maintaining a competitive currency. The problem has been further complicated by Brazil's inflation-targeting policies that have produced the world's highest real interest rates in years. These have thus attracted increasingly strong capital inflows to the country that further strengthen the currency and weaken the competitiveness of the Brazilian manufacturing sector, both in the domestic market and in third markets where China in particular has increasingly been gaining market share. So far Brazil has managed to maintain job growth, economic growth, and a relatively strong macro-economic framework, but the country is at risk of overheating and of renewed external economic vulnerability. In an attempt to avoid that these challenges might provoke serious economic dislocations, a wide range of policies, from capital controls to anti-dumping policies, and still others aimed at protecting domestic production, have been employed, and the government has sought to cut back on stimulus policies in order to avoid the risks of overheating. It is not clear where this will all lead at the moment.

In conclusion, what should be stressed is that Brazil's experience in this last decade goes against Li Minqi's expectations and that the good results have in large part been produced through good economic policies in Brazil; nevertheless, economic diplomacy, e.g. with China, has also contributed to the good results. At the same time, China has had a positive impact through market mechanisms as well, particularly due to growing Chinese imports from Brazil and China's positive impact on Brazil's terms of trade. China has been mostly a challenge for Brazil when it comes to the manufacturing sector though. However, the growing domestic market in Brazil in particular has meant that, all in all, the manufacturing sector in Brazil has not fared that badly. To sum up, the better than expected development results in Brazil, when considering Li Minqi's expectations and Brazil's bad situation in the late 1990s, have in large part been the product of politics and in part also of market developments.

Notes

1   Between 1974 and 1994 textile and clothing quotas were negotiated bilaterally as part of the GATT system. The Multifibre Arrangement (MFA) contained the rules that governed trading in textile and clothing.

Reference

Abu-el-Haj, Jawdat (2007) "From Interdependence to Neo-mercantilism: Brazilian capitalism in the Age of Globalization", *Latin American Perspectives*, 34(5): 92-114.

Albrieu, Ramiro and José María Fanelli (2010) "The Global Crisis and Implications for Latin America", *WP 40/2010*, Real Instituto Elcano.

Almeida, Paulo Roberto (2010) "Never Before Seen in Brazil: Luis Inácio Lula da Silva's Grand Diplomacy", *Revista Brasileira de Política Internacional*, 53(2): 160-177.

Arraes, Virgilio Caixeta (2010) "The Brazilian Business World: The difficult adaptation to globalization", *Revista Brasileira de Política Internacional*, 53(2): 198-216.

Arrighi, Giovanni (1994) *The Long Twentieth Century*. London: Verso.

Barros, José Roberto Mendonça (2010) "The Impact of the International Crisis on Brazil", *ARI 38/2010*, Real Instituto Elcano. Available at http://www.realinstitutoelcano.org/wps/portal/rielcano_eng/Content?WCM_GLOBA...

Barros de Castro, Antonio (2009) "The Impact of Public Policies in Brazil along the Path from Semi-Stagnation to Growth in a Sino-Centric Market", in Mario Simoli, Giovanni Dosi og Joseph E. Stiglitz (eds.) *Industrial Policy and Development: The Political Economy of Capabilities Accumulation*. London: Oxford University Press.

Bauman, Renato (2009) *Some Recent Features of Brazil-China Economic Relations (Preliminary version)*. ECLAC, Office in Brazil.

BCB (2000-2011) *Informe Anuario*. Brasília.

Bernal-Meza, Raúl (2002) "Política Exterior Argentina: de Menem a De la Rúa: ¿Hay una nueva política?" *São Paulo em Perspectiva*, 16(1): 74-93.

Bottomore, Tom, et al. (1983) *A Dictionary of Marxist Thought*. Massachusetts: Blackwell Publisher.

BRIC Policy Center (2011) "A recuperação da economía mundial e a Guerra Cambial: Brasil e China em foco", *Policy Brief 2*. Centro de Estudos e Pesquisa BRICS, Rio de Janeiro.

Castro, Antônio Barros de (2009) "The Impact of Public Policies in Brazil along the Path from Semi-Stagnation to Growth in a Sino-Centric Market", in Mario Simoli, Giovanni Dosi og Joseph E. Stiglitz (eds.) *Industrial Policy and Development: The Political Economy of Capabilities Accumulation*. London: Oxford University Press.

CEPAL (2010) *La reacción de los gobiernos de las Américas frente a la crisis internacional: una presentación sintética de las medidas de política anunciadas hasta el 31 de diciembre de 2009*. Santiago, Chile.

CEPAL (2011) *La República Popular China y América Latina y el Caribe: Hacia una nueva fase en el vínculo económico y comercial*. Cepal, Santiago.

Cervo, Amado Luiz (2008) "Conceitos em Relações Internacionais", *Revista Brasileira de Política Internacional*, 51(2): 8-25.

Cervo, Amado Luiz (2010) "Brazil's Rise on the International Scene: Brazil and the World", *Revista Brasileira de Política Internacional, Ano 53, Special edition, 2010*: 7-32.

Christensen, Steen Fryba (2010) "Brasilien: Den kalejdoskopiske, vestlige BRIK", in Steen Fryba Christensen et al. (eds) *FREMTIDENS STORMAGTER: BRIK'erne i det globale spil. Brasilien, Rusland, Indien og Kina*. Aarhus Universitetsforlag.

CNI (2002) *A Indústria e o Brasil: Uma Agenda para o Crescimiento*. CNI, Rio de Janeiro.

CNI (2010) "Por que a produção industrial não cresce?" *Revista da industria*. CNI, Rio de Janeiro.

Coggiola, Osvaldo (2004) *GOVERNO LULA: da esperança à realidade*. Xama, São Paulo.

Fiesp (2002) *O Brasil de Todos Nós. Proposta da FIESP/CIESP para Discussão com a Sociedade*. Fiesp, São Paulo.

Fiesp (2011) "Brasil registra déficit comercial com a China de US$ 23,5 bilhões em manufaturados", 18-01-2011. Available at http://www.fiesp.com.br/agencianoticias/2011/01/18/brasil_registra_deficit_comercia.

Fleischer, Daniel (2010) *Brazil Focus* (weekly report), July 24-30.

Gallagher, Kevin P. (2010) "China and the Future of Latin American Industrialization", *Issues in Brief*, October 18. The Frederick S. Pardee Center for the Study of the Longer Range Future.

Gramsci, Antonio (1971) *Selections from the Prison Notebooks*. Quintin Hoare and Geoffrey Nowell Smith (eds.). London: Lawrence & Wishart.

IMF (2011) *IMF Executive Board Concludes 2011 Article IV Consultation with Brazil*. Public Information Notice (PIN) No. 11/108, August 3, 2011. Available at http://www.imf.org/external/np/sec/pn/2011/pn11108.htm

Jacob, Rahul (2011) "China's rivals gain as factory wages soar", Financial Times, September 7.

Kennedy, Simon (2011) Brazil Hits China With Tariffs as Potholes Erode New Silk Road *Bloomberg Businessweek, August 2. Available at* http://www.businessweek.com/news/2011-08-02/brazil-hits-china-with-tariffs-as-potholes-erode-new-silk-road.html.

Lessa, Antônio Carlos (2010) "Brazil's strategic partnerships: an assessment of the Lula era (2003-2010) *Revista Brasileira de Política Internacional, Ano 53, Special edition, 2010*: 115-131.

Lessa, Antônio Carlos; Couto, Leandro Freitas; Farias, Rogério de Souza (2009) "Política externa planejada: os planos plurianuais e a ação internacional do Brasil, de Cardoso a Lula (1995-2008), *Revista Brasileira de Política Internacional,* 52(1): 89-109.

Lima, Daniel and Pedro Peduzzi and Yara Aquino (2011) *Crecimento brasileiro é sustentável com cenário adverso da economia mundial, diz ministro.* The Brazilian ministry of Foreign Affairs. Available at http://www.itamaraty.gov.br

Li, Minqi (2005) "The Rise of China and the Demise of the Capitalist World-Economy: Exploring Historical Possibilities in the 21st Century", *Science & Society,* 69(3): 420-448.

Li, Minqi (2008a) *The Rise of China and the Demise of the Capitalist World Economy.* New York: Monthly Review Press.

Li, Minqi (2008b) "The United States, China, Peak Oil, and the Demise of Neoliberalism", *Monthly Review*, 59(11): 20-34.

Li, Minqi (2008c) "Climate Change, Limits to Growth, and the Imperative for Socialism" *Monthly Review*, 60(3): 51–67.

Li, Minqi (2010) "Peak Energy and the Limits to Economic Growth: China and the World", in Li, Xing (ed.) *The Rise of China and the Capitalist World Order.* Surrey, UK: Ashgate Publisher.

Li, Xing (1999) "Socialist Foundations of Market Reforms: Assessing Chinese Past", *Economic and Political Weekly*, 34(49): 3457-3463.

Li, Xing and Hersh, Jacques (2006) "Understanding Global Capitalism: Passive Revolution and Double Movement in the Era of Globalization", *American Review of Political Economy,* 4(1/2): 36-55.

Li, Xing (ed.) (2009) *Globalization and Transnational Capitalism: Crises, Challenges and Alternatives*. Aalborg-Denmark: Aalborg University Press

Lula, Luíz Inácio da Silva (2002) *Carta ao povo brasileiro* (a public letter). Available at http://www.iisg.nl/collections/carta_ao_povo_brasileiro.pdf

Lula, Luíz Inácio da Silva (2003) *A New Course for Brazil*. Address to the Congress by the President of the Federative Republic of Brazil (January 1). Available at: www.mre.gov.br.

MDIC (2011): BRASIL MAIOR: Innovar para competir. Competir para crescer. Plano 2011/2014. Available at www.mdic.gov.br/brasilmaior on August 9 2011.

Meyer, Peter J. (2011) *Brasil-U.S. Relations*. Congressional Research Service. Available at www.crs.gov.

Moreira, Mauricio Mesquita (2006) *Fear of China: Is There a Future for Manufacturing in Latin America?* INTAL-ITD Occasional Paper 36. Inter-American Development Bank, Integraton and Regional Programs Department.

Nayyar, Deepak (2008) "The Rise of China and India: Implications for Developing Countries", in Philip Arestes and John Eatwell (eds.) *Issues in Economic Development and Globalization*. London: Palgrave Macmillan.

Neri, Marcelo (2009) "Income Policies, Income Distribution, and the Distribution of Opportunities in Brazil", in Lael Brainard and Leonardo Martínez-Díaz (eds.) *BRAZIL AS AN ECONOMIC SUPERPOWER? Understaning Brazil's Changing Role in the Global Economy*. Washington: Brookings Institution Press.

Nogueira, Uziel (2007) *China-Latin America Relations in the XXI Century: Partners or Rivals?* UNU-CRIS Working Papers, W-2007/7.

Ocampo, José Antonio (1999) *La reforma del sistema financiero internacional: Un debate en marcha*. Santiago: CEPAL

Palma, Gabriel (2000) *The Magical Realism of Brazilian Economics: How to Create a Financial Crisis by Trying to Avoid One*. CEPA Working Paper Series III, New School for Social Research, New York.

Pew Research Center (2010) *Brazilians Upbeat About Their Country, Despite Its Problems*. Washington: Pew Research Center.

Polanyi, Karl (1944) *The Great Transformation*. Boston: Beacon Press.

Saslavsky, Daniel and Rozemberg, Ricardo (2009) "The Brazilian Case", in Rhys Jenkins and Enrique Dussel Peters (eds.) *China and Latin America: Economic Relations in the twenty-first century*. German Development Institute, Bonn/Mexico City.

Scissors, Derek (2011) "China Global Investment Tracker: 2011", *The Heritage Foundation*. Available at http://www.heritage.org/Research/Reports/2011/01/China-Global-Investment-Tracker-20ll.

SELA (2010) *Evolución reciente de las relaciones económicas entre la República Popular China y América Latina y el Caribe. Mecanismos institucionales y de cooperación para su fortalecimiento.* Caracas, Venezuela.

So, Alvin Y. and Chiu, Stephen W. K. (1995) *East Asia and the World Economy.* California: SAGE Publications.

Tesouro Nacional (2011) *Brazilian Federal Public Debt.* National Treasury of Brazil. Posted on August 8. Available at http://www.tesouro.fazenda.gov.br/ english/public_debt/downloads/kit_divida_english.pdf

Verdin, Andrea (2010) "Brazil's shipbuilding industry: time for revitalization" *Latino Business-Review, May 10. 2010.* Available at http://www.latinobusi- nessreview.com/business-features/operations/brazil%E2%80%99s-ship- building-industry-time-revitalization.

Vigevani, Tullo and Cepaluni, Gabriel (2007) "Lula's Foreign Policy and the Quest for Autonomy through Diversification", *Third World Quarterly,* 28(7): 1309-1326.

Wallerstein, Immanuel (1979) *The Capitalist World-Economy.* New York: Cam- bridge University Press.

Wallerstein, Immanuel (2004) *World-Systems Analysis: An Introduction.* Dur- ham : Duke University Press.

Wood, Ellen (1997) "Back to Marx", *Monthly Review,* 49(2): 1-9.

Chapter 2

China – MERCOSUR and Chile Relations*

Introduction

The South American countries analyzed in this study, from the perspective of their relations with the People's Republic of China, are part of the group that many Asian countries identify as "Latin America and the Caribbean", a homogeneous view that several countries in the region itself, do not share.

This homogenous view of the region is an error on the part of China, as the region is profoundly diverse in terms of countries and sub-regions with varying degrees of capacities and linkages in the region and the world. The Southern Cone countries - Argentina, Brazil, Chile, Uruguay and Paraguay - share a set of doubts regarding the challenges, risks and opportunities that China presents to Third World countries as well as to many industrialized countries, as it has become one of the key players in the political and economical international system and the economic impact of its decisions is felt all over the world.

China's approach to Latin America and the Caribbean can be evaluated from different standpoints. Within the positive perspective, there are those that emphasize that the region's relations with China may reinforce a greater independence *vis-à-vis* the political influence and economic domination of the United States and the international organizations. In a similar way, China has become an export market of great potential for Latin American countries, although mainly in the area of primary sector exports. In relation to this, Chinese demand has substantially improved the price of several Latin American export commodities. Also, Chinese investments have improved the external conditions of the region's economies. However, China also presents Latin America with some potentially negative factors. One example is the concern that the region is exchanging one kind of dependency for another, and yet another is that Chinese long-term "geopolitical" ambitions could create conflicts with the United States. Also, China's competitive advantages are weakening the relative monopoly of semi-peripheral states in the commodity chains, as determined by production costs and salary levels, as well as displacing the region's traditional exports towards industrialized countries. More-over, Chinese manufactured goods, since they have increased China's presence in Latin American and Caribbean markets, have also displaced these countries' pro-duction from their historical export markets. As a result, these countries have lost markets. Thus, China may be creating the emergence of a new pattern of interna-tional commercial specialization in the region (Ellis, 2009; Li Xing, 2010). There-fore, the structural framework of China's relations with Latin America and, in particular, with the countries analyzed here is in process of transformation and change, an evolving relationship with multiple and complex dimensions.

This paper focuses on the two largest countries in MERCOSUR, Brazil and Argentina, as well as Chile, and will also briefly touch upon the smaller MERCO-SUR countries Paraguay and Uruguay. The three first-named countries established diplomatic relations with China between the early and mid-1970s, while Uruguay followed suit just a decade later and Paraguay remains as the only member that has no diplomatic relations with Beijing.

Paradoxically, the South American country that has less formal relations with China is Paraguay. At the same time, the most influential in China-MERCOSUR relations to the extent that its diplomatic recognition of Taiwan prevents MER-COSUR from having a block-level relationship with China. The lack of agree-ments at this level has meant that Brazil and Argentina have deepened their rela-tionships both individually and independently[1].

Although the relations of the Southern Cone nations with China are domi-nated by economic exchange, they differ considerably regarding the predominant products involved, the relative role of imports and exports, logistics and infra-structure, and in the dynamics of domestic politics, wherein the hopes and fears generated by China, the technological cooperation, and other non-economical aspects of each relationship, are part of the nature of these relations (Ellis, 2009). In addition, they also differ in the interests of their respective political agendas. For example, Brazil and Argentina see China as a major international player be-cause of its concern over the reform of the Security Council of the UN, an issue less or even barely relevant for Chile, Uruguay and Paraguay.

Brazil, Argentina and Chile have adopted a pragmatic political vision towards Beijing, which is shown in their non-questioning attitude towards the issue of human rights, their support for the status of Taiwan as part of China and their granting to China the status of "market economy". The main explanation lies in the place the Chinese market inhabits in the export structure of these three countries, although in international politics the main South American country, Brazil, shares with China the interest of creating counter-powers that can neutralize the unipolarity that the United States has exerted as the only superpower since the end of the Cold War.

From the Chinese perspective, there is a significant coordination with these three countries, which is extended to the entire Latin American region, in fora such as APEC, WTO, and the United Nations. According to Chinese sources (CICIR, 2004) there has been a 95% Sino-Latin American agreement in voting on UN resolutions (Pérez Le Fort, 2006:126). However, China has a undifferentiated policy towards Latin America and the Caribbean and does not break the region down into sub-regions and countries in spite of the profound differences among these countries in their international insertion and, derived from this, also great disparities in their level of relations with China. Similarly, although Beijing has been efficient in building bilateral relations with each country, incorporating each one into its international networks according to its advantages, respective political circumstances, and to what each country has to offer in terms of resources, markets and strategic relations, China has neither a disaggregated view of them and their respective sub-regional environments, nor of their relations with the United States (Ellis, 2009).

Despite the efforts of the past 20 years, China and Latin America still suffer from great mutual ignorance that affects the future development of bilateral relations. The bonds are mainly concentrated in the trade area, with the exception of Sino-Brazilian relations, which have, besides an important international political cooperation, a relevant cooperation in the fields of biotechnology, informatics, new materials, medicine and pharmacology. These areas are also part of the network between China and Argentina, but have not yet reached the same size, despite the potential they have.

When comparing the processes followed by South American countries in their relations with China, we can see that Chile was the pioneer. It was the first country to establish diplomatic relations with the People's Republic of China, the first to recognize its status as a "market economy" (a process that began in 1999 and ended in 2001), the first to allow the entry of China into the WTO, and the first to sign a Free Trade Agreement with the Asian country.

China's joining of the WTO did not make it adopt a policy similar to Japan's towards MERCOSUR, namely to wield the principle of equality in order to avoid negotiating with MERCOSUR. China's diplomatic efforts fought to be recognized by the block as a market economy, but the lack of unified action among the member States of MERCOSUR could be seen when Argentina and Brazil recognized that status separately during the visit of Hu Jin Tao in

61

November 2004. Uruguay only recently acknowledged this status during the visit of President Vazquez to Beijing in March 2009 (Oviedo, 2010a).

Currently, relations with China[2] are very important to these South American countries. The most important political opening to China from Latin America was manifested in the case of Brazil in the mid 1980s, when Itamaraty studies showed that China was the country with which Brazil had the largest number of coincidences in terms of voting in the UN General Assembly. In the international context of the 1980s, the Western world was imposing political constraints on Chile during its dictatorship in consideration of its systematic violation of human rights. This provided a context that could have potential impact on the changing model of Latin America's insertion into the global economy. Yet, the positive factors that deepened Brazil's insertion into the Pacific Rim from the mid 1970s onwards, a region that indeed relied on many countries similarly criticized for abusive authoritarian political systems, were not impeded by these issues when the latter was deciding its external relations. So, consequently, there would be a constant strengthening of bilateral Sino-Chilean relations.

From Argentina's side, although both countries have maintained diplomatic relations since 1972, and despite that during the presidency of Raul Alfonsin (December 1983 to July 1989), there were coincidences in the positions of China and Argentina in international fora, the key factor behind the strengthened emphasis on China has been the expansion of its exports of grains, particularly soybeans and soybean oil.

China has given different status to its relations with these countries. While Brazil and Argentina are in the category of "strategic partners,"[3] Chile has the minor category of "cooperative partner." It is necessary to point out that the strategic partnership is the main type of political and economic partnership for China.

However, Chinese and Latin American interests, as well as bilateral agreements with each of the MERCOSUR countries, may not necessarily coincide in the medium- and long-term. Although both parties converge on their concern for development, there is no doubt that China seeks to become a world power, a goal that Brazil, as the only country in Latin America, shares.

It is precisely in the context of this main goal of China in the world system, which it hopes to achieve by 2050, that bilateral relations with Latin America and the MERCOSUR countries in particular become relevant. This region and its major exporters provide China's resource demands (minerals, food, energy, etc.) and a market for its exports. In particular, countries like Brazil, Argentina and Chile share China's interest in building a multipolar world and they have assured support for some of the latter's concerns, including the Taiwan issue, support for the thesis of "one China", and admission to the WTO. However, the region is not a priority for China's foreign policy.

China's foreign policy has encouraged the use of peaceful negotiation and multilateral diplomacy, the abandonment of permanent strategic alliances and the rejection of isolationism. The skills and tools to this end are different from the previous decades, and framed in the context of a long-term vision in which the historical political realism, the state-centric conception, and the integration into the global economy remain characteristics (Oviedo, 2005: 38) that generally are also shared by these three South American countries with, however, some subtle differences (Bernal-Meza, 2003; 2004). For their part, the South American countries have different goals and nuances *vis-à-vis* China, differences that arise from their respective power resources and aims in the context of the global system.

There is a wide range of cooperation possibilities between these countries that has not been explored yet. Even though the scale and extent of problems and challenges that the countries of MERCOSUR and China face are very different in magnitude, the content is similar: how to create thousands (or millions) of jobs per year; how to develop policies to address the stresses that the ever-increasing urbanization creates upon infrastructure, transport and services; how to stop environmental deterioration and the loss of arable land; how to cope with energy shortages; and lastly, how to solve the growing social inequalities created by the increase in wealth due to the growth that, at different rates, characterizes all these countries in recent years.

Despite these great strides in China's relationship with the Latin and South American region and in the bilateral relations with the countries of the MERCOSUR, the current perceptions of the parties show worrying symptoms of discord. Chile, which is the country with the lowest status compared to Argentina and Brazil, is the one that appears most pleased with the progress made in the relationship. In contrast, the perceptions of Brazil and Argentina, which are for different reasons China's "strategic partners," seem to agree that China is applying upon them a *realpolitik* that is moving further away from the "South-South relations", further from the spirit of a close friendly partnership, and closer to a relationship influenced by Chinese political discourse.

The Post-Cold War Systemic Context

The last decades of the twentieth century showed a set of processes that were transforming the structural characteristics of the global system. Among those changes there were those related to the international economy, characterized by growing processes of globalization/internationalization and regionalism, and those related to global politics that led some countries to rise and others to fall in the global power pyramid. Among those that rose geopolitically, China's position as a regional power and its emergence as a world power became clearer on the basis of its remarkable economic growth, its increasing integration into the global economy, and the strengthening of its military-strategic power.

China is now one of the most important players in the global system. Its size and domestic market, its integration with the global economy, the amount of its international reserves, its demand for energy and commodities, as well as its policies on finance, currency, trade, security, environment, resource management, food safety and basic products prices, all increasingly affect the economies of millions of people outside China's borders. The Asian country has played an indispensable role in the triumph of global neoliberalism, and has, therefore, strengthened global capitalism in the current phase of globalization. China has shown a special ability to turn globalization's enormous forces to its advantage (Li Xing, 2010).

At the ideological level, influential sectors of the United States have placed China in the place formerly occupied by the USSR. Therefore, and in particular in those scenarios in which U.S. hegemony is exclusive, as is the case of Latin America, the strengthening of the relations with China is seen and presented as a threat.[4]

The emergence of China, on the one hand, will inevitably generate changes in world power and will reshape the international order, but, on the other hand, it will help the building of a new kind of balance of power in world politics based on multilateralism and institutionalism. China will demand a greater decision-making power in world affairs and there is no doubt that its sustained economic growth poses the greatest challenge to the existing world order since the end of the Cold War. Thanks to its participation in more than 1,000 global regimes and groups or organizations in which it participates, China will remain an increasingly important power in international affairs (Li Xing, 2010). In this context, the Latin American country that is most concerned with the problem of the possible consequences of these transformations is Brazil, being at the same time the most serious and the most interested candidate to become a regional player in global-scale politics (Bernal-Meza, 2010, 2010a). With regard to the perception of these shared interests, Brazil sought to develop a strategic relationship of global format, but failed in this attempt.

The end of the Cold War opened a unique opportunity for the development of international economic relations and, to a lesser extent, political relations. But the evolution beyond an East-West paradigm in the post-Cold War era coincided with China emerging as a major global power and, as the country developed its strategy of global integration, new theatres of engagement began to appear beyond the Korean Peninsula and the Yellow Sea in which the only remaining superpower would meet the emerging power. One of these theatres is precisely Latin America.

Within the framework of the WTO, the strengthening of the economic agenda over safety issues, due to the accelerated globalization of the capitalist economy, has given great impetus to the market economy and the negotiation of new agreements on trade liberalization (Bernal-Meza, 1994, 2000; Bayne & Woolcock, 2007).

The perception that China is a threat to U.S. security and that of its partners makes sense if the view is that China threatens the preservation of the *status quo* (Lewis, 2007), but there is no evidence that suggests that China seeks to change the relationship of Latin American countries *vis-à-vis* the United States, but rather to strengthen the South-South axis facing the unipolar tendencies of the superpower.

In line with this, China is an actor that may serve as an example for Latin American countries in the process of improving their economic performance and global integration. China's remarkable handling of the forces that constitute *globalization* to its own advantage, the internationalization of its companies, the capacities to attract investments and technology transfer, the efficiency in handling the relations between state, market and society and the practice of regionalism, are all some of the experiences that can be emulated to great advantage.

Chinese Foreign Policy

Since the years of Deng Xiaoping, China has begun to rationalize the communist ideology, adopting pragmatism as its guiding principle for international relations (Lewis, 2007). The reconfiguration of the global order and the impact of the events of September 11, 2001, increased the importance of Latin America to China at a time when the region was losing interest in the global policy of the United States.

Thus, China's leadership changed the tactics of its strategy, which has been to reach the rank of world power by the mid-21st century. From this systemic perspective, the Latin American country that agrees the most on the anti-unilateralist objectives is Brazil, a country with which China shares membership in the BRIC countries.

For China, "[t]he circumstances in which foreign policy has [been] reshaped after the Cold War and especially since September 11, 2001, have resulted in the increasing importance of Latin America not only as an important resource for the Chinese economic development, but also as political support in the framework of its global geo-strategic perspective" (Pérez Le-Fort, 2006: 123).

During the last decade, China's foreign policy became much more proactive, structured and pragmatic. One of the characteristics of this new policy has been the loss of the ideological burden. Contrary to traditional guidelines, the engine for external action has been the promotion of China's national interests and not ideological issues. China does not question the fundamental basis of the international order, nor does it promote an alternative model as it has done in the past. Instead, China is now seeking to join the existing order and maximize its position (Neves, 2006).

China has changed its foreign policy from its prior focus on North-South conflict to a foreign policy that treats South-South cooperation as a priority. This has led to strengthen relations with Latin America, to the extent that this approach would not be seen as a confrontational line *vis-à-vis* the United States. This position was reinforced by China's economic opening and the process of introducing market-oriented reforms.

Chinese strategic goals in Latin America have shifted towards bilateral strategic partnerships aimed at enhancing bilateral cooperation and coordination in international affairs as well as economic integration, following the model of the Sino-Russian strategic partnership. China promotes consensus with Latin America in international affairs by promoting multipolarity to confront U.S. unilateralism, and by reducing Taiwan's influence in the region (Pérez Le-Fort, 2006). However, this vision is not totally accepted, as it is also believed that "China is using bilateral diplomacy with market access as the main counterpart" (Oviedo, 2009b).

In some aspects, there are similarities in the views that Chinese and American academics have regarding Sino-Latin American relations. According to Jiang Shixue, there are five reasons for China's interests in Latin America: 1) as a developing country, China deems it politically necessary to share positions with the region in the fight for a fairer international economic order; 2) to reduce trade dependence on the U.S. and other developed countries, it is important for China to maintain economic relations with Latin America to increase its investments in the region; 3) to continue its internal development, China needs access to natural resources that are abundant in the region; 4) China can learn lessons from Latin American countries in the process of adapting to the *market economy*; and 5) since the end of the twentieth century, China has been interested in establishing diplomatic relations with some Latin American countries in exchange for the recognition of Taiwan as part of China (Jiang, 2002).

These interests and goals seem clear enough, but to achieve them implies a number of challenges. On the one hand, the great distance that separates the two regions, the difficult exchange of market information, and the precarious mutual understanding between China and Latin America due to differences in language, culture, and customs all imply challenges (Becard, 2008); on the other hand, Latin America's historical subordination to the hegemonic United States also implies a challenge. From this point of view, the main problem China must face in the process of expansion of these relations is the growing U.S. concern about the real (or perceived) Chinese objectives that could displace its interest in the region and how these might affect U.S. interests and political agenda in the region.

The Chinese political and academic discourse points out that these relations are part of the structure and prospects of South-South relations. However, this morphological claim hides a reality, namely the enormous difference in power between China and its Latin American partners, with the relative exception of Brazil.

From a hemispheric perspective, the mainstays of China's policy toward Latin America would be: 1) to promote bilateral relations in order to strengthen bilateral political cooperation, to complement mutual economic and trade needs, and to seek a cooperative strategic partnership with regional powers in Latin America; 2) to develop relations with Latin America in every way, not only in terms of economic and trade cooperation as well as at the government political level, but also in terms of regional organizations, parties, parliaments, NGOs, trade unions, etc.; 3) to develop regular mechanisms for dialogue and consultation, taking advantage of its accession to both regional organizations (the Rio Group, Latin American Integration Association, ALADI) and hemispheric ones (OAS, IDB), (CICIR, 2004:17-24).

The difference with the vision of Jiang Shixue is that, while the above hemispheric level of analysis emphasizes the importance of bilateral ties from a criterion of equilibrium and a common political interest, the vision of Jiang reflects a much more pragmatic and utilitarian perspective.

Nevertheless, to identify the characteristics of China's strategy toward Latin America and an explanation of the basis of this expansion, we can observe some coincidences between these views. In the view of Jiang the reasons are: 1) the existence of economic complementarities of both sides; 2) due to the processes of the economic reforms taking place for both parties, markets are increasingly open and regulations have been reduced; 3) Latin America cannot underestimate the great potential of the Chinese market; 4) in the process of diversifying their international economic strategies, Latin American countries need China and other East Asian countries; and 5) in the era of *globalization*, China and Latin America have common objectives, including issues such as South-South cooperation (Jiang, 2002). From the American view of the western hemisphere, its exclusive sphere of interest, the characteristics would be based on three aspects: 1) economic interest: as a growth area in foreign markets and procurement of energy, mineral, agricultural and wood resources; 2) political interest in promoting multipolarity and democratization of international relations; 3) diplomatic interest: to contain Taiwan's independence efforts (Pérez Le Fort, 2006).

Despite these interests and objectives, which would indicate some coincidences, the main problem China must face in the process of expansion of these relations is the growing concern of the United States. This challenge is particularly important in the case of Latin America and the Caribbean where the "yellow menace" is presented in both its political-military and economic-commercial aspects. Even though in this analysis, concerning the relationships of MERCOSUR countries with China, this is not the main topic of discussion, it cannot be denied that in each of the countries (Brazil, Argentina, Chile) there are actors who share this vision.

Identifying the relationships as "South-South" gives China the opportunity of denoting them as relations between similar actors, but this is not the reality from the perspective of countries like Argentina and Chile. To the countries of MERCOSUR, with the exception of Brazil, the relationship with China is a relationship to *a world power*. China is the only Third World country[5] that is part of the hierarchy of world power. Its military-strategic and economic capacity places it in the center of the global power system, with the influence to determine interests and global objectives resulting from that position, influence not shared by the Latin American countries.

The evidence of asymmetry in these relationships can be analyzed when studying the position that each partner has in the other's foreign trade. While Brazil, Chile and Argentina are the first, third and fourth trading partner of China in Latin America, in contrast, only Brazil might be able to become an important partner for China from the global perspective.

China is and will continue to be a major trade partner for Brazil, Argentina and Chile, but they can hardly become important partners for China's foreign trade. However, in the current international system, the relations between them do not *a priori* involve ties of subordination or domination, nor do these countries have a history of relationships exhibiting a pattern of imperialism.

The point of view of Argentina, Chile, Paraguay and Uruguay of China is very different from that of Brazil. While the former, especially Chile and Argentina, see China as an important trading partner as well as a partner in some scenarios (Asia-Pacific and PECC to Chile, UN agendas to Argentina), to Brazil the relationship currently means a political alliance of emerging powers that, in the context of BRIC countries, are seeking to reshape the global order through multilateralism, as well as an alliance of partners in a strategy of participation in global governance, but also has the potential to mean rivalry in the future reconfiguration process of world order.

The difference between Brazil and other South American countries looked at here is that none of these has the capabilities and resources of power of Brazil, a country that shares with China the vision that the ongoing transformations in the global system, along with the globalization process and end of the Cold War, have created new spaces of power that could help to improve their positions in the hierarchical structure of the global system.

China-Latin America Relations

China's view indicates that "[i]n discussing Sino-Latin American relations, we have to note three factors, namely, the Latin American factor in China's Development, the China factor in Latin American development, and the U.S. factor in Sino-Latin American relations" (Jiang, 2006:19). The "Latin American" factor in China's development is related to its economic growth: Beijing has become one of the largest importers of Latin American basic products and commodities; that demand has led to the sustained rise on its prices in the international market. This likewise has happened to some of the major export products of Chile (copper) and Argentina and Brazil (soy).

Since in the United Nations system each country represents one vote, politically, China needs Latin American support for many important issues. The Taiwan issue is not yet resolved, and 11 of the 25 countries that have diplomatic relations with Taiwan are Latin American or Caribbean.

In general, China is an important trading partner for Latin America and a source of investments.[6] Conversely, Latin America only represents 6% of China's foreign trade, but is a very important regional partner from the political point of view.

The *Latin American factor in China's Development* is related to the significant economic growth rates that have characterized China's development over the past 30 years. According to a Chinese scholar, who cites the data from the ECLAC, Beijing is one of the largest importers of basic products and commodities in Latin America:

> China is the world's top consumer of coal, tin, zinc, copper and cereals and is one of the leading consumers of fertilizers, iron and steel, bananas, oilseeds and oils, plastics, electronic equipment, optical, photographic and medical equipment, and nuclear reactors and machinery. China accounts for at least 20% of world consumption of 8 out of 16 selected products. In addition, it represents much of the net world demand for 8 of these products and is one of the three top world consumers of 15 of them. (Jiang, 2006: 35)

China represents a huge potential for the export trade in Latin America in addition to its potential as a partner in the international political and economic agendas. However, as noted, in recent years the idea of "China threat" has spread in Latin America, which tends to see China's approach to the region with fear:

> However, in recent years, the development of Sino-Latin American relations has come across an obstacle. In some Latin American countries there is a feeling that 'China is a threat' or there is 'fear of China'. Some Latin Americans tend to blame the rising unemployment rate on the expansion of Chinese exports. Starting with Mexico in the early 1990s, many Latin American countries have been using antidumping tariffs to limit Chinese exports. (Jiang, ibid.: 36)

But neither Brazil, Argentina nor Chile share that vision; indeed, Chile believes that the strong bond that unites it with the United States could become a hindrance to the strengthening of Sino-Chilean relations and make it less attractive to China than, for example, Brazil and Venezuela (Pérez Le Fort, 2006). However, there is no doubt that the Latin American countries, even in the case of emerging powers like Brazil, cannot avoid taking into account the North American opinion.

According to an academic specialist in the region, "though North-South relations are improving in certain parts of the world, developed countries still dominate the world order"; therefore, "developing countries need to raise their own bargaining power by getting more united" (Jiang, 2006: 20). However, this is not the prevailing view in the ruling classes and governments of most Latin American countries, and particularly of Chile and Argentina.

But Brazil and Argentina do apply antidumping measures against Chinese products. Moreover, the current difficulties between China and Argentina tend to expand the idea of the Chinese threat. Hence, it is important to enhance mutual understanding between China and the countries of MERCOSUR. In order to change negative perceptions there is a need for greater dialogue and exchange of ideas, for which academic cooperation is essential.

With respect to the U.S. factor in Sino-Latin American relations, and the "China threat" and "fear of China" that have been promoted by the international American press (Jiang, 2006; Lewis, 2007), the MERCOSUR countries do not see China as a threat to their relations with the United States. Despite that the presence of China in Latin America seems to be mutually beneficial, many observers in the United States are concerned about this political, military and economic interest in its "backyard" and to what extent it constitutes a danger to their own safety (Lewis, 2007: 28).

It is true that relations with China can strengthen the position of developing countries, in particular, in international negotiations. In November 2004, during his visit to Brazil, President Hu Jintao proposed several measures to boost relations between China and Latin America: "1) strengthen and enhance strategic common ground political mutual trust; 2) take practical and creative steps to tap potential for economic cooperation; and 3) attach importance to cultural exchanges to deepen mutual understanding" (Jiang, 2006).

On November 5, 2008, the Chinese government released its first paper on China's policy towards Latin America and the Caribbean.[7] The document consists of a prologue and five parts. In the prologue, the Chinese government expresses its general policy and defines that the document "is intended to express more clearly the objectives of the cooperation in various areas during a certain period of the future and promote the continuous healthy, stable and comprehensive development of Sino-Latin American and Sino-Caribbean relations". In the political arena, the paper discusses the trend to strengthen exchanges at the highest level, including legislative bodies, political parties and political organizations, as well as to establish and improve mechanisms for consultation, cooperation in international affairs, and the development of contacts between local governments. In economic terms, the document proposes to increase and balance trade, and to optimize its structure to promote common development while adequately resolving trade frictions through consultation and cooperation. In terms of investment, the document proposes to encourage and support Chinese enterprises that have a good reputation and are willing to invest in the region, and to welcome China's investments in Latin American companies. In the financial area, the document promotes exchange and cooperation between financial authorities, the establishment of branches of Chinese banks in the region, and banking supervision arrangements. It also supports cooperation in agricultural technology, staff training and the promotion of cooperation in animal and plant inspection in order to expand the trade in agricultural products and promote food safety. It also proposes areas of cooperation in industry, infrastructure construction, resources and energy, customs, quality and quarantine, tourism, debt reduction and relief, economic and technical assistance, and multilateral cooperation between chambers of commerce. In the cultural and social area, the paper argues for actively implementing cultural cooperation agreements, scientific and technological exchange such as aerospace technology, biofuel, technology, resources and environment and marine technology; in addition, promoting the dissemination and implementation of useful Chinese technologies in LAC in areas such as energy saving, digital medicine and mini hydro-electric. It also raises medical, health, and consular cooperation, and the exchange of journalists, popular links on environmental protection, climate change, human resources and social security, etc. In the so-called area for peace, security and justice, the document suggests military, judicial, and police exchange and cooperation, and non-traditional security, such as combating terrorism. The fifth part deals with the support of regional and sub-regional organizations. In order to gain influence on regional and international issues[8] China would carry on with the strengthening of exchange, consultation and cooperation in various fields (Oviedo, 2010b).

However, the document does not add anything new to the policy toward the region, at least not from the public level, but has the virtue of being a systematization of the different policies and positions that China has reiterated to each of the countries now presented in terms of the entire region. Its content emphasizes the region being considered as homogeneous, stating a general policy without understanding the peculiarities of each state (Oviedo, 2009b).

Two issues of importance to China highlight the mistake of considering Latin America as a homogeneous region: 1) the position of the countries as-regards their future policy with China; and 2) the position of the countries with respect to the status of Taiwan and with respect to diplomatic relations. Regarding these two points, Latin American countries differ in their policy positions.

The Sino-Latin American Economic Relations

Statistical data shows that the Latin American countries, in particular the countries studied here, were reorienting their economic relations with China, as it was becoming a major international buyer of raw materials and foodstuffs. The role that China began to occupy in the external sector of Latin American economies is expressed in the trade and investment flows. In 1998 China was the target of 2.7% of exports of MERCOSUR; in 2008 this rate reached 9.7% (Oviedo, 2010b). The importance of Sino-Latin American economic relations is explained by a Chinese scholar in the following way:

> [T]he outlook for increased trade appears promising. This is simply because: 1. Latin America has a wealth of natural resources, and China's rapid economic development will need more such input to sustain growth; 2. There is some economic complementarity between both sides; 3. As both China and Latin America undergo economic reforms, markets are opening and investment regulations are becoming more liberal; 4. Latin America cannot afford to neglect China's huge market potential, particularly after the latter entered the WTO. Moreover, as it diversifies its external economic strategy, Latin America will also need China and Other East

Asian countries; 5. In the age of globalization, China and Latin America have common interests involving such issues as South-South cooperation" (Jiang, 2006: 24-25).

China has entered the global investment market and this is also benefiting the Latin American countries. Chinese investments in Latin America are heavily concentrated in four countries (Brazil, Mexico, Chile and Argentina).

Apart from the impact of trade figures, the arrival of China, competing with traditional Western economic and financial powers, can be seen in the volume and diversity of investments. China has become one of the first investors in the region, particularly in countries like Brazil, Peru and Argentina. Among the main business concretized in 2010 the following should be highlighted: a contract between China's state-owned Wisco and the local LLX of approximately 3,300 million dollars to build a steel plant in the interior of Rio de Janeiro; the agreements with Brazilian Petrobrás (10 billion dollars); with Argentinean Bridas oil (3.1 billion for 50% of the oil), the purchase of the Brazilian oil field Peregrino (3 billion dollars, by Sinochem, purchased from the Norwegian Statoil); Toromocho copper mine (2.2 billion by Chinalco).

While there are interests and political concerns in the approach of some Latin American countries to China, the common element that identifies the interests of the countries of the region is external trade, specifically exports. When analyzing the more general data about the trade relations between Latin America and China, we can see that the bilateral trade structure reflects the creation of a specialization pattern.

The main countries of Latin America and the Caribbean which export to China are Brazil (37%), Chile (22.6%), Argentina (16.7%), Peru (9.7%) and Mexico (5.9%). But when analyzing the composition of exports, it becomes clear that they are highly concentrated in natural resources and natural resource-based manufactures, which account for 80%. Therefore, and given its endowment in natural resources, South America has become a major supplier of primary products to China, as it provides, for example, over 60% of soybean imports (mainly Brazil and Argentina), 80% fish meal (Peru and Chile), about 60% of sliced poultry offal (Argentina and Brazil) and 45% of wines and grapes from Chile (Roccaro, 2009: 12-13).

The economic bloc with the largest share of exports to China from Latin America and the Caribbean is MERCOSUR, which has come to represent 55% of the total. But the export basket, following the overall regional profile, concentrates on few products. For example, for Argentina three products (soybeans, soybean oil, and oil) explain over 86% of its total exports to China. A similar case is Chile, where three products (refined copper, copper concentrate and wood pulp) account for 85% of its total exports to China. For Brazil, six products (iron and concentrates, soybean, iron agglomerate, soybean oil, crude oil and wood pulp) explain 72% of its total exports to China (Ibid.).

The growth of the region's exports to China is due to China's growth rates and that the economies participating in the exchange are complementary. However, the growth of MERCOSUR's exports to China should not be seen as a result of an active policy of MERCOSUR to conquer that market. This can be seen from the fact that Chinese imports posted their biggest increase in the sectors in which Brazil and Argentina have the greatest comparative advantages. From this analysis it could be argued that bilateral trade between MERCOSUR and China is based on comparative advantages and there's virtually no intra-industry trade (Roccaro, 2009: 13).

China-MERCOSUR

The political focus of this relationship finds difficulties on both sides. On behalf of MERCOSUR, the fact that Paraguay has had diplomatic relations with Taiwan since 1957, prevents MERCOSUR from coordinating policies toward China because of the lack of unity of action of its members. On the side of China, this country has promoted its relations with Brazil, Argentina and Chile, countries that recognized its status of "market economy", while at the same time, did not engage in negotiating a free trade agreement with MERCOSUR (Oviedo, 2009). The bilateral trade growth is a central element of the interests in the relationship; while in 1998 MERCOSUR exported US$1,665 billion to China and imported US$2,358 million, in 2008 these figures had grown to US$23,663 million and US$29,138 million, respectively (Ibid.).

However, it is possible that one of the difficulties, the absence of diplomatic relations between Paraguay and China, could be solved shortly as the government of President Lugo has announced its interest in raising the level of relations that both countries maintain.

The foreign Policy of the Countries of MERCOSUR

Since the beginning of this decade, the differences in the foreign policies of the South American countries have deepened as a result of changes implemented by new alliances of government in order to deal with the crisis caused by the implementation of neoliberal policies during the 1990s. The differences are focused on four major topics: the vision of globalization, the degree of openness of the economy, relations with the United States and the type of regionalism or integration.

The wave of new governments with reactive political visions focused on strengthening the state and returning to economic nationalism, as well as the presence of models or types of non-convergent state, both in terms of policy development and international integration and foreign policy, led to the implementation of individual state policies, dismantled from a regional or subregional group as a whole. It also led to leadership disputes and the promotion of non-converging integration and cooperation projects.

a) Chile

Since the beginning of 1990 the "Concertación"[9] governments made the Chilean foreign policy a trade-state policy -that somehow came from the military regime- contained in a *pragmatic realism*, expressed in a rather conservative vision about what was possible in the new global context under the hegemony of the North American superpower. Chile returned to multilateralism, but put the United States as its main political partner. The main foreign policy paradigm was *open regionalism*.

This more open policy, "integration into the world", as expressed by open regionalism, was not only manifested in the economic sphere but also in political issues like human rights, disarmament, and the environment, under a concept borrowed from the cooperation mechanisms in the Asia-Pacific region and it was accompanied by a revival and implementation of new forms of cooperation in areas as diverse as infrastructure development, energy, technology development, physical integration and coordination of foreign policy (van Klaveren, 1997; 1997a). It is clear that the new Latin American regionalism became a paradigm of economic and political openness. *Open regionalism* was introduced as the new international economic integration strategy, the basis for the new features of integration agreements, which also nurtured political experiences in the formation of formal political forums for cooperation and international negotiations ("Contadora", "Rio Group", APEC), which were the result of the new presidential diplomacy and, in the economic arena, of the similarities between different countries in implementing programs of openness, economic liberalization and deregulation (Bernal-Meza, 2000: 349). For this reason, the concept became a basis for foreign policy.

Chile-China Relations

Chile was the first South American country to establish diplomatic relations with China, the first to support China's accession to the WTO and the first to sign a free trade agreement with Beijing. This history assures that Chile is a reference and an example for Sino-Latin American relations. The Free Trade Agreement between China and Chile can serve also as an example and model for a future agreement between China and MERCOSUR. According to President Hu Jin-tao, this treaty was an example to promote South-South cooperation.[10]

China and Chile share an experience of over thirty years of opening and economic reform. The two countries have cooperated in the UN Assembly. China supported the nomination of Chile as a non-permanent member of the Security Council for 2003-2004, and Chile supported the interests of China to enter as an "observer" of the OAS and the Latin American Parliament. Chile also granted recognition to China as a "market economy" and has supported some Chinese positions, including topics such as Taiwan and Tibet.

Both countries agree on the optimistic ideas about the global and regional environment they share. While China thinks that there will be 20 years of world peace and that this is required for further development (Zhang, 2006), Chile has been convinced for over 30 years that the Asia-Pacific region is the largest and most dynamic pole of the global world, that Chile is part of that environment and that the special relationship with China, given the geographical position of each, is essential to bring closer both shores of the Pacific. "The Chilean conviction to participate in the development of China and East Asia and the Pacific encourages the idea that Chile is the best choice for China in Latin America" (Zhang, 2006: 119).

Chile's strategy of expanding its commercial ties since the signing of free trade agreements diverges from the practice followed by member-states of MERCO-SUR, whose governments have been constrained to cease making bilateral agreements of this kind and subordinate their external trade policies to the decisions set by the block.

The Free Trade Agreement between China and Chile, proposed by China, deepened trade. In 2009, US$ 11,892 million was exported to the Chinese market, which translates into an increase of 18.9% of the total. But at the same time, imports from China reached US$5,117 million, representing a drop of 25%. Chile's trade balance surplus was thus US$6,775 million and trade reached US$17,009 million, representing an increase of 1.1% over the same period in 2008.[11] In 2009, the People's Republic of China ranked first among Chile's main partners and export destinations, attracting 23.8% of the total and 3.3% of the non-traditional shipments (Ibid.).

Chile's exports to China, sorted by productive sector, was dominated by the mining sector, which participated with 83.2%, followed by the non-food industry sector with 10.9%, food industry with 4.7%, and finally agriculture with 1.1% of the total exports during 2008.[12] Although the participation of non-traditional products remains low, the FTA has allowed the expansion of exports.

Chile has established itself as a trade nexus between Asia, Latin America and the United States. Although other nations in the region, including Peru, Ecuador and Costa Rica are trying to play that role, Chile is best poised to claim that position effectively by leveraging the combination of geographical location, good physical infrastructure, government and business infrastructure, and an interlaced network of FTAs. Furthermore, the Chilean customs administration has the reputation of reasonable efficiency and lack of corruption. This has led Chinese shipping companies to select Chile's ports from among the other alternatives in order to minimize delays and associated costs. In addition to its own public administration and infrastructure tools to support companies doing business in China, Chile has capacity within public and private sectors to support bilateral trade; its universities and other institutions offer Mandarin Chinese courses, and studies oriented towards doing business in China (Ellis, 2009).

Political relations have been strengthened by the incorporation of different sectors (economic, scientific, military, cultural) to the network of bilateral trade. Specialized studies indicate that the only major outstanding issue between the two countries is a controversy over allegations of Chinese overfishing in Chilean waters beyond 200 miles in the South Pacific, which has led the Chilean ministry in charge of fishing to limit Chinese fishing vessels' access to Chilean ports (Ellis, 2009: 47). However, on issues that are vital to China, the Chilean position has been of paramount importance: pragmatic as regards human rights and supportive on the recognition of "one China". Moreover, during the visit of Chilean President Michelle Bachelet to China in mid-April 2008, the two governments signed a declaration in which Chile recognized that Taiwan and Tibet belonged to China.

b) Argentina

The model of development and inclusion of "open economic nationalism" or "free market nationalism" that has characterized the Kirchner government as a paradigm of political economy has not had a correspondingly defined expression in terms of foreign policy (Bernal-Meza, 2009; Simonoff, 2009; 2010).

The break with the foreign policy of the neoliberal period (1989-2002) became clear in three issues:

1) It became clear in the vision or idea of globalization that is manifested in the type of relations commonly held with multilateral agencies like the IMF, the World Bank and WTO. In this case, the governments of the period 2003 - 2010 rejected agreement with the IMF regarding the supervision of economic policy and they refused to accept suggestions for amendments to Argentina's economic policy. With respect to the World Bank, Argentina joined the general critical view of the role of this organism, as one that functions to the detriment of developing countries and rather in favor of the interests of devel-

oped countries.[13] In relation to the WTO, Argentina rejected negotiations of the Doha Round unless a positive review of trade rules to the benefit for developing countries could be reached.

Argentina became part of the alliances opposed to the protectionist policies of major industrialized countries (USA, EU, Japan) that have integrated into the G-20, and then entered alliances with Brazil, China and India. After the change of Brazil's position, Argentina maintained its alliance with India and China.

b) It likewise became clear in the limited degree of economic openness, as evidenced by Argentina having followed a protectionist economic policy, even towards its MERCOSUR partners, accepting only protectionist regionalism projects.

c) Finally, it was shown in the type of relationship Argentina had with the United States and its hemispheric FTAA project, in that Argentina was part of the group against this American project (along with Venezuela and Brazil). Argentina has had a critical and confrontational stance towards Washington with regards to American hemispheric and global policies, as well as being against this superpower on hemispheric issues such as Honduras, the situation of military bases in Colombia, and adhering to the defense of countries challenged by the United States such as Bolivia, Venezuela and Cuba.

Taking into account its position on *regionalism* and the role of partnerships, Argentina has maintained its preferences for close bonds essentially within MERCOSUR and has privileged bilateral relations with Brazil (Bernal-Meza, 2009; Simonoff, 2009).

Argentina-China relations

According to an Argentinean specialist on these relationships, "China's rise widened the asymmetry of powers, changing the scheme of bilateral relations between China and Argentina from a traditional South-South model of cooperation to a North-South relation. Secondly, the trade between these two countries, indicated by Argentina's export of soybeans and soy by-products to China, is the staple for maintenance of productive political relations" (Oviedo, 2010).

Argentina and China signed a strategic partnership agreement in 2004. From then on contacts in various sectors were promoted and China became the 2nd destination of Argentinean exports. The exchange went from US$2,100 million in 2000 to over US$13,300 million in 2009, but since then China has become the third destination for exports, after Brazil and Chile. The trade balance between Argentina and China grew in 2010 and reached 13,822 million dollars, of which Argentina bought 6,132 million and sold 7,690 million.[14]

Although the two countries have a financial arrangement that allows Argentina to use its own money to pay for Chinese imports, this has been the subject of differences and difficulties that are affecting bilateral relations (although the problems are not only about trade).

While the commercial sector is important, Argentina is not only interested in trade but also in a strong technological and military cooperation. The deepening of trade occurred after the Argentinean recognition of China as a market economy, a decision that was linked to China's promise to invest US$20,000 million. However, the memorandum of understanding signed during the visit of Hu Jin Tao lacked the originally-promised investments (Oviedo, 2010a: 457).

Despite progress in the last year (2010), the Sino-Argentinean ties were severely affected by trade, political, and diplomatic issues, a situation that left a pall of doubt over the future of these links, and questions about Chinese behavior as a world power. Between them, the two countries have accumulated significant economic, political, technological (with important agreements in the space, nuclear and biotechnology industry), and military development, which one would expect as the natural product of the "strategic relationship;" yet this relationship was clouded by shadows of doubt and uncertainty during 2010. As measures to protect domestic production, the Argentine government implemented anti-dumping policies restricting imports of some products of Chinese origin. Dumping charges were already being directed at China by the Ministry of Economy of Argentina since the end of 2009.

China reacted to these measures by applying rules related to the presence of certain compounds of soybean oil and the maximum allowed.[15] According to Oviedo, at a meeting of the Chamber of Commerce for Import and Export of Foodstuffs of China, organized in the Dongcheng District of Beijing by China's Ministry of Commerce in late March 2010, a decision was made to implement strict control on imports of crude soybean oil from Argentina as of April 1st 2010. Similarly, provincial governments ceased the issuance of import permits, returning that power to the Bureau of Permits and Fees Affairs of the Ministry of Commerce to make new requests.[16]

The implementation of this measure resulted in the complete suspension of shipments of Argentine soybean oil from 1 April 2010, affecting 46% of Argentina's total production of that product. In 2009 exports of soybean oil to China had reached US$1,400 million. With reference to this, a leading Chinese scholar said at a seminar in Buenos Aires that "protectionist measures imposed by Argentina in the bilateral trade with China could, at first, benefit the domestic market in the South American country, but in the long run, it will end up being injured", adding that "what happens is that Argentina is the Latin American country that has imposed more restrictions in the past 18 months with the arrival of Chinese products" (Oviedo, 2010c). As an Argentinean analyst said then, "the Chinese government's decision to apply the BT 1535/2003 standard, which sets a ceiling of 100 parts per million residues of hexane for crude soy oil shipping, lit a warning light in the Argentina-China relations" (Oviedo, ibid.).

The suspension of Chinese imports was central to the agenda of the visit that President Cristina Fernández made to China during the second week of July 2010, but, in her interviews with the President and the Chinese Premier, she could not unlock the impasse, although sales agreements were signed in railway equipment from China for US$1,200 million along with other commercial agreements and financing for about US$8,000 million.

This embargo, which represents an act of reprisal for Argentinean analysts and diplomats, has caused serious damage to Argentina's economy and has created the perception that Argentina is suffering the impact of the practice of *realpolitik* on the part of China, an attitude contrary to the spirit of South-South relationship and "strategic partnership."

Argentina and China had been the main partners in the soy sector (grain and oil) during recent years. 75% of soybeans and 31% of soybean oil exports from Argentina[17] had China as their destination up to the moment of China's unilateral suspension of trade. Argentina's place in Chinese consumption can be understood in light of the figures: 78% of Chinese soybean oil, and 22 of soybean imports had Argentina as source (Ibid.).

For Argentina, the domestic economic impact was enormous: soybean processing represents 8.6% of state tax revenue, while the soybean complex exports generated revenues of US$14,014 million in 2009, representing 25% of total Argentine exports (Ibid.). The closure of the Chinese market affected the milling plants that had invested US$1,000 million in recent years. Argentina partially found other import markets to replace the Chinese, but, because of the conflict, the price of Argentine soybean oil suffered a discount, in contrast to other markets such as Brazil, of up to US$75.5 per ton.[18]

Political and diplomatic problems began after the Argentinean president suspended the planned and announced official visit to China[19] in January 2010 only a few days before the trip due to short-term domestic political problems. According to Chinese analysts, the Argentine government would not have made the same decision, to suspend an official visit, if it had been the U.S., and here, in this writer's opinion, is the crux of the matter, as it was a matter of the "prestige" of a great power at stake, a particularly relevant topic in Chinese perceptions.[20]

Even thoughduring her trip the president later publicly apologized to the Chinese President, the impact of the insult is difficult to quantify. Other issues were added to this one that did not reach public importance but certainly affected bilateral relations. Argentina began restricting the entry of Chinese nationals into the country via a reduction in the concession of visas, to which

China responded by making it more difficult for Argentineans to access information and communicate with their embassy and consular service.

It is clear that what has caused the failed relations, from Argentina's side, has been the low level of knowledge about Chinese culture and ignorance of the "diplomatic factor" (Labarca, 2009) as an advantage for the development of bilateral ties. There is no doubt that the suspension of Cristina Fernandez's presidential trip was a fact that predisposed China's political leadership negatively against the Argentine government. However, as discussed below, the political justification, appealing to diplomatic reasons, would be invalidated by the repetition of the Chinese practice of trade retaliation.

Given that in China, despite modernization, the links between economic and political power are still fuzzy, so that policy decisions directly affect economic opportunities (Labarca, 2009), we are witnessing a deteriorating "strategic relationship", because it is affecting the export trade that is so important for Argentina. At a seminar in Buenos Aires last May, Chinese scholars had spoken of a "good relationship, with *not harmonious* factors".[21] The Argentinean perception in this respect is that the relationship has not been on track, despite the recent presidential visit to Beijing.

China took commercial revenge against Argentina as an answer to the barriers imposed on the imports coming from this, and other Asian countries, with the aim of protecting the local production. As had happened the last time, it has been possible for the Argentine exporters to sell part of the soybean oil to other countries, though with significant losses due to lower prices. China again justified its curbs on imports citing the low quality of the product. But the truth is that the Chinese actions reconfirm the aggressiveness of its trade policy.

During a recent visit to Argentina (May 11 and 12, 2011) by China's Minister of Commerce, Chen Deming, the minister announced the purchase of 500,000 tons of soybean oil, which would resume the sales of 2009. He also said that the Chinese government's intention is to make investments in partnership with Argentine companies to jointly sell to third countries. He also reiterated the aim to increase bilateral trade in local currency, i.e., in Yuan and Argentinean pesos, and he affirmed that, in accordance with its five-year plan, China will increase direct investment in Argentina in primary and value-added products, citing as an example increased purchases of Argentine wine.[22] However, he warned that the purchases will continue "while enhancing the business environment in Argentina and product quality". [23]

However, the remaining question is why retaliation is applied to soybean oil and not to the grain itself, which has much less added value. Subsequently, China resumed imports of soybean oil. From the formal point of view there existed no public document about it, just as had happened when Beijing stopped importing Argentine soybean oil. There was only unofficial information, both in China and Argentina. In mid-October 2010, the Chinese Chamber of Importers announced that after six months it had begun buying contracts for soybean oil.

The resumption of exports was a good sign of getting the bilateral relationship back on track. However, despite the relative importance of bilateral ties, and their weight in relation to the whole region, voices have been raised in Argentina that call for a review of bilateral relations and the supposed benefits of a "strategic relationship" that has not worked on a bilateral basis.[24]

In Argentine sectors linked to international relations, public and private, it is considered that China has not been reciprocal to permanent political gestures that the Argentine government has made to Beijing. For example, although the issue of human rights has been a very important aspect in the government of Néstor Kirchner and Cristina Fernández de Kirchner, both agreed on the need to prioritize trade over political issues and thus backed China in this area, both within the United Nations, by keeping quiet and not ruling on the international demands to which the Asian power has been subjected, and also by appealing to the principle of non-intervention in the internal affairs of states (Oviedo, 2010a).

Similarly, the Argentine governments have strengthened their support to China on the Taiwan issue, restricting most of the political, economic, cultural and academic contacts, making them thus marginal in the international exchanges of Argentina (Oviedo, 2010a).

The announced Chinese investments have concentrated on the purchase of assets in the oil industry and have thus not contributed to the expansion of the range of direct foreign investment. From the Argentinean point of view, the overall bilateral relationship has entered a period of uncertainty about the future, even though the Argentine government insists that the bilateral relationship is of great importance for the country. Argentina has made efforts to bring bilateral relations to the highest possible standard. Although until late 1990 the bilateral relationship was relatively limited, Argentina, like Chile, had been able to maintain a positive policy, despite ideological differences, in part thanks to the silence of each country with regard to the internal politics of the other.

However, Argentina sees China as the only winner in bilateral trade (Oviedo, 2010c), and with the retaliatory measures taken on soybean oil exports, China has shown that it is willing to use the market as a discretionary source of power. In October 2010 China had made a small purchase of oil, which was shipped in December of that year. At the time of writing this chapter (May 2011), the Chinese government has been on a seven month suspension of soybean oil purchases, and, as a result, shipments from Argentina were discontinued, leaving the Argentine exporters in a complicated financial situation.[25] As happened last time, some of the exports have been relocated in other countries with significant losses due to lower prices.

Argentina has great export potential in other areas, such as mining, metallurgy and other foodstuffs produced out of soybeans. It also has commercial appeal as a market for Chinese manufactured goods, for the import of simple manufactures (textiles, footwear and toys), but also, increasingly, for the import of high value-added products such as cars, motorcycles, electronics, airplanes and trains. In terms of its intellectual infrastructure, Argentina was the first country in the Southern Cone to set up a Confucius Institute for teaching Chinese language and culture (Ellis, 2009), with an established program at the University of Buenos Aires that hosted the presentation of the latest and most important book on the Argentine-Chinese relations.[26]

c) Brazil

During the 1990s, the end of the Cold War and the beginning of an international restructuring process led to a redefinition of the international system and of the rules that could set a new pattern of international relations. In this context, Brazil proceeded to some adjustments in its strategies of international integration. East Asia was viewed as a special region due to the importance of its investment potential and its access to technology, and the region was increasingly seen as a market with high purchasing power. Politically, because of the growth of the perception that: a) the process of redefining the international order would require long and intensive negotiations; b) that difficulties would exacerbate global trends towards regionalism; and c) that South America would tend to remain in the U.S. sphere of influence; Brazil began to act strategically. In this it had two objectives: 1) to strengthen the South American region as a base for international integration and 2) to expand relations with the various regional centers. Despite the more traditional relationship with the United States and Europe, relations with Asia became a priority as a bargaining tool with the other two poles (Altemani de Oliveira, 2006).

Under the governments of Lula da Silva, Brazil adhered to the view that sees the international system as being in transition, that it has gone from "a period defined by polarities" characteristic of the Cold War to that of "indefinite polarities" (Lafer,2001) which is currently dominant. In this vision of a world of "indefinite polarities," there was a space for insertion by a Brazil rising in the global power structure. The perception of weakness was replaced by a re-evaluation of the role of Brazil which saw it as a middle power and emerging nation that needed a high-profile diplomacy suited to its abilities and needs (Pecequilo, 2008: 143).

However, this is not *pure* realism; it is rather combined with a *Grotian* vision of the international system by following the rules and institutions of the multi-lateral order while simultaneously promoting its redesign in every agenda, with countries seeking their own active participation in the mechanisms of global governance (Bernal-Meza, 2010).

Two groups of emerging powers came to dominate the instilling of their preferences in the mechanisms for the reformulation of the global order through multilateralism: the BRICs (Brazil, Russia, India and China) and IBSA (India, Brazil and South Africa). This last group reaffirmed Brazil's "return to Africa" from a strategic perspective of the southern hemisphere, while the former rep-resented the emerging global power group. Brazil's presence in these two groups lets us see that Brazil wants to be present at all negotiating tables of the world as it is in the WTO and the G20, and wants to be in the UN Security Council, where it seeks a permanent seat. These institutions constitute the sites where rules are made, many of which can affect Brazil either positively or negatively (Bernal-Meza, 2010).

For Brazil, membership among the BRICs is very important because, in the new vision of order and global power, this grouping will transfer to itself status in the hierarchy of international politics, and here BRIC countries agree on the desire to be influential, increasing their relative rank (Ibid.).

The country returned to *realism*, pushing its own vision of regionalism, and applying different strategies of power accumulation. It left the Kantian neo-ide-alism and utopian multilateralism of Cardoso's preceding period behind (Bernal-Meza, 2009), and also the policy that had promoted an alliance with the United States, predominantly during the Cardoso governments. Brazil returned to *selec-tive universalism*, reprising their partnerships and linkages with India and China, and strengthening new networks in South Africa and Russia.

Brazil became the only South (and Latin) American country to again adopt realism as the theory or paradigm of its foreign policy (since Brazil, like Argen-tina and Chile, had left the realist paradigm between the mid and late 1980s). Its foreign policy formulated a vision for defining its "spheres of influence," reject-ing the concept of "Latin America," and distinguishing between an area under U.S. domination (Central America and the Caribbean) and another under the predominant influence of MERCOSUR, whose axis was Brazil itself. However, despite the perception of failure that currently dominates the views of its rela-tionships and projects with the rest of South America, Brazil is returning to a broader perspective, closer to Central America, the Caribbean and Mexico.

The new foreign policy perceived the international system as a power game of conflict among the most powerful actors in the system. Multilateralism was stripped of utopian ideals and became the game of competing interests, and the spoils of which were to be distributed according to the outcome of trade negotiations. In order for multilateralism to succeed, it was essential to recover the importance of coalitions and alliances between similar countries. Returning to the thinking of Celso Lafer, the future of global scenarios is consistent with the vision of a world order in which the loss of unilateral hegemonic stability is perceived. It is believed that this may allow Brazil a space for action for its repositioning as a global player proceeding from the recognition of its status as an emerging world power.

The key instrument of that position, through its international re-insertion, would be the application of the ideal of Brazil as a "logistical state." Thus, in recent years Brazil has combined an active participation in multilateral forums with the promotion of its national interests from a *realistic* perspective. The novel element is that today, alongside its pursuit of power, as measured in terms of the accumulation of military capabilities, Brazil is pursuing a strategy based on a "reciprocal multilateralism" (Cervo and Bueno, 2008). This view suggests that Brazil has come to hold a progressively prominent place in the various domains of international relations, from regional security to the plane of finance.

However, there are concerns about Brazil's material capacity to become a world power. "Brazil, unlike the U.S., the EU or China, cannot hope to become a dominant power in any future global order, due to its scarce material resources. The country is not a great power". As Daniel Flemes has further argued: "[g]reat powers are able to exercise power globally by using their political, military and economic strength" (Flemes, 2010:143). The fact that Brazil does not have strategic nuclear development surely influences the Chinese analysis on bilateral political ties.

Brazil-China Relations

The Brazil-China agenda is, thematically, the most extensive that China has in Latin America. Even though trade plays an important role, the bilateral political relationship and its international projection may be seen as more important.

Since the changes in its external relations, during early 1974 China was the only country in Asia with which Brazil was able to establish significant ties in the context of South-South cooperation. And, after the restoration of diplomatic relations in August that year, Brazil and China shared an agenda of Third World solidarity (an event recognized by scholars observing South-South relations) (Altemani de Oliveira, 2006).

Contrary to what happened with other South American countries, Sino-Brazilian relations became politically strong, with many corresponding manifestations of this closeness visible in their interactions at the United Nations, though relations were modest in economic terms. In 1993 Asia was identified as a prior-

85

ity for Brazilian diplomacy because of its cooperative potential in scientific and technological fields and the importance of its market. Greater economic openness and trade integration of the two countries since the 1990s has favored the development of greater trade and economic ties. The declaration of a strategic "parcería" (association) between the two countries in 2004, as it was argued, would strengthen the strategic alliance between the two countries, capitalizing on earlier successes in the area of technical and scientific-technological cooperation, with the joint work for the development of satellites (CEBERS) having been signed in 1988 and then expanded in 1995 with the goal of producing four satellites in total. Bilateral cooperation continued in the areas of biotechnology, informatics, research on new materials, combating AIDS, production of generic drugs and traditional medicines, and research into new medicines (Ibid).

The Cardoso (1995-2002) and Lula da Silva (2003-2010) governments, under the foreign policy of *universalization* and *selective universalism,* accorded privileged status to relations with the so-called "emerging powers," which today form the clusters of BRIC and IBSA countries that coordinate their positioning strategy in negotiations in different international forums. So the relationship with China became essential in the context of world politics.

According to the Brazilian perspective, the closer link with China was justified because the eastern country was an essential partner of Brazil. This was especially true by virtue of China being a permanent member of the Security Council of the UN, but also because of the fact that both countries share similarities regarding their concerns and diagnoses of the world situation, around which they can build consensus and defend common interests. Moreover, this was because they have complementary economies and national development programs that offer many prospects for cooperation in all areas, including finance and investment.

Brazilian policy makers felt that their country and China had enough common goals to deepen bilateral ties. Those goals were manifested in the implementation in both countries of national autonomous projects, their openness to international cooperation based on domestic economic development, as well as in their foreign policies and independent international integration. Moreover, both shared an industrial vocation that joined them in common goals with respect to the global economic order.

Since the end of the Cold War, the two countries have collaborated with the forces that are against U.S. hegemony and favor the building of a multipolar international system opposed to the U.S. aspirations to establish a unipolar world. The difference was that China sought to become a strategic power while Brazil renounced the modern means of deterrence and defense (Becard, 2008).

For Brazil, the strategic relationship with China, as part of the group of emerging powers known as BRICs and by virtue of their integration into IBSA, is a tool for reshaping the global order through multilateralism. In particular, the BRICs comprise the clustering of global emerging powers. Together, become significant in the field of international politics, and, by their simultaneous desire to be influential in it they increase their country's relative ranks globally. Brazil shares with China a behavioral pattern of "shared leadership," in contrast to the prevailing pattern of hegemony in Brazil's relations with its neighbors (Bernal-Meza, 2010).

This shared leadership has been clear in the WTO negotiations and the formation of the G-20. However, the principle of "strategic *parcería*" that promotes such cooperation is also a controversial issue in Brazil, where the content of the concept is being discussed (Cervo, 2008; Becard, 2008). Also, the fact that China does not support reform of the UN, in particular in terms of the broadening of the Security Council with new permanent members (a place that Brazil aspires to occupy), raises doubts about the meaning of the strategic partnership with China.

Brazil and China agree on the effort to create, integrate and strengthen counter-hegemonic partnerships within their memberships among the BRICs, the G-20 (within the WTO frame), and as impetus-providers to the G-20 (which replaces the G-8). However, this effort implicitly involves Brazil and China's recognition of the hierarchical structures of global economic power. The two countries are not willing to defy the WTO and the IMF. In this regard, both countries are rebellious to the hegemonic order, seeking to strengthen multilateralism, but also conservative, as they do not aspire to displace international regimes.

The Sino-Brazilian relationship is based on three areas of attachment to strengthen the strategic partnership: 1) a strong bilateral trade that is overcoming the asymmetry of the initial structural inequalities,[27] 2) a technological cooperation based upon their respective specialization profiles that include highly-sensitive areas, such as space, aeronautics and engineering, 3) the interpenetration of productive enterprises and services, initiated by cross-investment and the establishment of industrial firm subsidiaries in each other's country (Cervo, 2008). From these perspectives, the Sino-Brazilian bilateral relationship has the greatest potential for deepening.

During the last decade, trade between China and Brazil soared, from just US$2,300 million in 2000 to US$36,100 million in 2009,[28] tripling in value over the past five years. Brazil had a trade surplus with China of $4.3 billion in 2010, reversing the deficit of the previous two years.[29] That year, China became Brazil's main market, taking precedence over the U.S., and this represents a qualitative change for foreign trade. What is questioned, however, is the bias of the center-periphery relationship. Currently, Brazilian exports to China consist of 74% commodities, 18% of semi-manufactures and 8% of manufactured goods.[30] Following the onset of the international financial crisis, in 2009 Brazil exported

42.1% less to the United States than in 2008; however, it exported 23.1% more to China. Yet the exports have been mostly limited to commodities, led by iron ore and soy.[31]

However, despite the size and diversity of the country's economy, Brazil's intellectual infrastructure to sustain its business in China is relatively modest. Surprisingly, there is no university in the country with a program devoted to Chinese studies. Likewise, the country has infrastructural deficiencies that affect its ability to expand its exports to China. The effort to partially overcome this difficulty is one aspect of China's cooperation with Brazil (Ellis, 2009).

The counterpart to this increase in bilateral trade is the fact that Brazilian exports to South America and Mexico are losing ground because of Chinese competition. According to FIESP (a business association in São Paulo), Chinese products reduced Brazil's global exports by US$12,600 million between 2004 and 2009[32].

Despite the "strategic relationship" and the fact that the two countries have jointly established a High Level Committee on Consultation and Cooperation, the only such committee that China has with any South American country, these factors, from the Brazilian perspective, have not helped to deepen the topics of the bilateral agenda in the global systemic context.

From the Brazilian point of view, it is considered that the country has done much, more so than China, in the pursuit of bilateral relations and strategic cooperation. Brazil has sought to transform China into one of its major trading partners; it has granted China the status of market economy, supported its entry into the WTO, and its admission as an observer in the Organization of American States (OAS), as well as its admission to the Interamerican Development Bank (IDB) and the Latin American Parliament; it has voted for China in the Human Rights Commission of the UN in 2004 and negotiated the lifting of trade barriers.

But China did not support Brazil's position in calling for the Security Council reform, nor to allow the entry of new permanent members, and this fact deepened Brazilian doubts about the meaning of the strategic relationship.

In general, both countries are rebellious to the hegemonic order, seeking to strengthen multilateralism, but also conservative, as they do not aspire to do away with international regimes. The two countries have been characterized by their strengthening of the functioning of the IMF, the international body perhaps most questioned by the developing countries. However, a pall of doubt is emerging on the horizon of bilateral relations. The fact that China's status of *great power* poses a problem for any attempt towards policy coordination beyond the legitimate aspirations in relation to the desire to deepen economic ties and technological/technical cooperation (Almeida, 2006), adds to the series of problems and misunderstandings that Brazilian diplomacy has had. Among these, those that stand out are the lack of Chinese support for Brazil's aspiration to occupy a permanent seat on the Security Council of the UN, and that Brazil's attempts to establish solid and permanent mechanisms with China to ensure political support at the multilateral level, both in the political (Security Council) and economic arena (G-20, G-8) have failed (Becard, 2008: 249-251). This demonstration of Brazilian confidence in the strategic relationship is not echoed by China. In addition, China's support to Brazil has not been unanimous and unqualified in the topics considered essential in Brazilian foreign policy and, despite the promising outlook, the political dialogue between the countries was concentrated on the defense of principles and general rules for developing countries rather than "global" political issues (Ibid.). The foreign policy efforts of the two countries do coincide in the use of global governance institutions to create new coalitions that may help them realize common interests (Flemes, 2010).

d) Uruguay-China Relations

Uruguay was the most recent of the MERCOSUR countries to recognize the People's Republic of China (Paraguay still does not) and to establish diplomatic ties, a decision adopted in 1988.

There is a close relationship between Uruguay's decision to approach the bilateral integration process that Argentina and Brazil had begun in 1986 and to conduct its decision-making process in foreign policy matters according to an outline heavily influenced by the foreign policy of its two large neighbors, Brazil and Argentina.

For Uruguay, the process of cooperation between Argentina and Brazil was a pivotal event on a regional level, the distinctive feature of which was the convergence of the democratic regimes of the two countries. This process gave Uruguay the possibility to act as an articulator of the regional agenda as a "small partner." When the democratic government took office, the "ordering criteria of foreign policy" which stressed the differences from the previous dictatorial regime became relevant, and led to changes in the international agenda. An example of this was the recognition of the People's Republic of China (Bizzozero, 2008).

Given the small geographical size and population of Uruguay, its undiversified economic structure and its greater distance from China, bilateral trade and economic relations are marginal in the country's external links. Uruguay exports agricultural products with a preferential concentration in wool, since the Chinese market consumes 40% of the total exports of this product. In addition, it exports leather and frozen fish. Meanwhile, its imports from China have historically been concentrated in textiles and other light manufactures.

89

Given its small domestic market, imports of Chinese goods have been relatively modest (Ellis, 2009).

These features point to the importance of the relevant political aspect of the relationship and bring Uruguay closer to the international profile of its great neighbors.

e) Paraguay-China Relations

Paraguay's diplomatic relations with Taiwan can be traced back to the era of the Cold War. The dictatorship of Alfredo Stroessner (1954-1989) and its political support structure the "Colorado" Party (with right-wing authoritarian tendencies) followed a conservative foreign policy of relative isolation, but the country was also relatively isolated by the international community at the regional level in different periods. These conditions allowed the country to maintain cordial relations with Taiwan, which provided Uruguay with economic assistance and cooperation. Over the years the two countries have developed relatively large networks and links of all kinds, supported by common ideological visions. Taiwan became a major donor of financial assistance, and this is the reason why the bilateral diplomatic relations were maintained even after the return of Paraguay to the democratic system and then continued despite the country's accession to MERCOSUR.

The combination of this policy, and the lack of access to a coast to facilitate the development of foreign trade beyond that with its immediate neighbors, have limited Paraguay's interactions with China. To Taiwan, maintaining its relationship with Paraguay is part of its struggle for national survival (Ellis, 2009). Paraguay is the only South American country that still maintains diplomatic relations with the island. The importance that Taiwan places in its relations with Paraguay has consequently increased as has Taiwanese financial aid to Paraguay. According to Ellis, in May 2006, as a demonstration of the importance that Taiwan assigned to Paraguay's diplomatic recognition, the Taiwanese government announced a package of US$250 million of investments in electronics, plastics and information technology in the South American country to be developed in the coming years.

The great success of Taiwan has also been to prevent MERCOSUR as a whole from having a FTA with China. For all these reasons, Paraguay's links with the Asian power are extremely modest. During 2006, Paraguayan exports to China reached only US$20 million (Ellis, 2009), a figure that has not changed significantly in subsequent years.

However, the current president of Paraguay, Fernando Lugo, has on some occasions stated his willingness to establish diplomatic relations with Beijing in order to establish similar external lines as its neighbors and MERCOSUR partners. However, the network of connections and relationships that Taiwan has developed over the decades with various groups and sectors of Paraguay's power elite, and the importance of economic aid and cooperation that Taiwan maintains, makes that decision difficult to achieve.

Conclusions

The countries studied in this document, and the whole region called Latin America and the Caribbean, are facing an enormous challenge in relations with China. The pluses and minuses of the relationship, and their impact on the international, economic and political relations of these countries, can be assessed from the case studies analyzed here. The growing ties between Latin America and China will not only affect the region itself, but also have an impact on its relations with the United States, since the concern is growing in Washington and the idea of the region as a "problem" for its safety is returning.

Despite the presence of political and diplomatic factors, the economic interests have been the ones that dominated the shaping of the course of China's relations with Latin America. The general evolution of the international economic relations of the region indicates that its member countries, to a greater or lesser extent, have shifted their economic relations to China. The case of the three countries studied here shows that. Moreover, this is closely related to the objectives of China in Latin America, which are primarily economic and only secondarily political.

In relation to the countries we have discussed here, the first conclusion concerns the difficulties in understanding MERCOSUR-China relations as part of South-South relations to the extent that resources, capabilities and potential power are strongly asymmetrical, even in the case of the Brazil-China relationship. Additionally, there is the absence of a uniform position within the South American block with respect to its relations to China to the extent that Paraguay keeps a distance by maintaining the diplomatic recognition of Taiwan. However, this does not seem to be an obstacle to the strengthening of MERCOSUR-China ties. The main obstacle is the importance that China actually assigns to the region.

The review of China's bilateral relations with the MERCOSUR countries show that countries like Chile and Brazil have managed to cultivate a special and stable relationship with the Asian power. However, this is not the case with Argentina, which in recent years has failed in assessing the importance that Asian values, for example, the diplomatic factor as a comparative advantage, have in the creation and projection of bilateral ties. The differences in political culture show how difficult it is even among Latin American countries to maintain politically sympathetic channels in China. However, Chinese trade retaliation, when applied to a product with higher added value (soya oil) but not the grain (soybean), is evidence of the Chinese attempt to transfer to its own industry a greater share of processing, thereby increasing its own local production, and thus concentrating in its hands the activities with higher added value in the production chain.

The Sino-MERCOSUR trade relationship has been a key factor for the deepening of bilateral ties. The growth rates of foreign trade have been a surprising fact. However, except for Brazil, there is the danger that the pattern of trade with China has developed the classic colonial features and resembles the unequal trade corridor of the North-South as reported 60 years ago by ECLAC. The Latin America-China economic relationship is not, as is often claimed, a South-South relationship, but rather reproduces the North-South trade corridor and the British investor pattern of the nineteenth century.

China's role in the process of trade with Latin America is crucial: the Asian country demands commodities, invests abroad according to the requirements for the extraction and transport of those commodities, and advances in its own import substitution and export, thus threatening Latin American alternative productions (Sevares, 2007).

China's demand for Latin American commodities (copper, soybeans, iron) has raised the international prices of these products. However, the increasing participation of China in the exports of MERCOSUR makes these countries particularly vulnerable to Chinese foreign trade policy, which increases the importance of continuing bilateral political dialogue in order to maintain channels of cooperative links.

When comparing the export baskets of the MERCOSUR countries, it can be seen that the signing of a free trade agreement, as was the case of Chile, has increased the number of export products, thus promoting diversification, even when the participation of the principal commodity, copper, is still very high compared to other products.

The synthesis of the foreign policies of the MERCOSUR countries shows that while Chile has a strategy of the international insertion of an open economy and seeks to increase the number of free trade agreements, Argentina has a neo-protectionist economic policy, though it is prepared to negotiate a free trade agreement with the European Union, through MERCOSUR, and has been a strong supporter of the negotiation of a FTA with China.

In turn, Brazil has changed its view on the importance of free trade agreements and currently believes that these are not functional for economic development or positive for the internationalization of its economy. Brazil is not, at the moment, an advocate of a free trade agreement between MERCOSUR and the European

Union nor of an agreement between MERCOSUR and China. The signing of free trade agreements is no longer of interest to Brazil because its policymakers believe that now it would deprive the nation the possibilities of integration into the global economy and regional and multilateral trade agreements.[33]

Politically, one of the problems that are found in the Sino-MERCOSUR relations, which have an impact on the entire Latin American region, is that China considers Latin America as a homogeneous area, and thus has stated a general policy,[34] without perceiving the profound differences that exist between Latin American countries in general and between the member-States of MERCOSUR in particular. Among these differences are important ones in the degree of openness of their economies, their respective views on free trade agreements and their objectives in relation to China, issues that are supposed to be of great interest to Beijing. At the same time, the specific characteristics of each economic and industrial structure of South American countries reveal the limits of one and the extensive possibilities of others in these relations. Brazil, followed far behind by Argentina, and with these two countries far ahead of Chile, forms the hierarchy of possibilities and interests that China's perceptions have not yet managed to clearly differentiate.

Despite China's modernization, the boundaries between economic actors/ activities and political power are still fuzzy, so policy decisions directly affect economic opportunities. If we add the difficulties resulting from the lack of knowledge about their respective cultures and diplomatic policies, we have a picture that shows how difficult it is even in Latin American countries to maintain comprehensive political channels with China.

The paradox is that while China gives priority to economic interests, keeping political relations with Latin America in the background, this may bring some political difficulties in the short and medium term. Despite the diplomatic efforts of China, Taiwan's presence in South America, a less favorable scenario than Central America for the island, remains important. Excluding diplomatic ties with Paraguay, trade relations with the other countries are relatively important. According to data provided by the Ministry of Economic Affairs of Taiwan, between January and August 2008, Chile accounted for Taipei's second largest trading partner in South America after Brazil and the largest exporter in Latin America to the island, with US$1.563 million.

Although it is clear that China has made a commitment to integration in a region historically marked by the legacy of American hegemony, the impact that this bilateral relation will have in the medium and long term is not so clear. Neither is it clear whether the pattern of specialization that is taking place in the China-Latin America relation will be an instrument to strengthen Latin American economic development, increasing wealth and optimizing the assignment of resources, or whether, on the contrary, the transfer of wealth and resource optimization at a global level will result in the spread of income inequality and the lack of well-paid employment in all Latin America (Ellis ,2009:286-287), in other words, creating a new pattern of specialization and dependence for the region. It is also striking that the policy of "properly solving trade frictions through consultation and cooperation", as declared in the guiding document of China's foreign policy toward Latin America and the Caribbean, was actually not implemented in the most important problem affecting commercial relations between Argentina and China.

Studying the two national cases of relations with China, those of Brazil and Argentina, one can draw lessons and warnings for the future of the relation, not only between these countries and China, but between Latin America and China in general.

Since Brazil is the largest South American country and has improved its capabilities to develop links at all levels and to address all the various issues of concern in the thematic agenda of international political relations with China, the perception that its leadership has of the results of these relationships is fundamental for the rest of the countries of the region.

To the decision-makers in Brazil, one of the major questions regarding its relations with China is the real sense, both concretely and that of possible future developments, of a strategic "parcería" (association). The Brazilian conclusion is that this is only a "cooperative partnership." Given the problems that have affected these relationships, it is not believed that the bilateral relationship has reached the category of "strategic" and, from this perspective, Brazil experiences a sense of failure regarding its relationship with China. This constitutes a warning for the other partners of China in South America, but also for China.

Whereas the idea of "strategic partnership" implies the convergence of efforts among partners with a view to realizing common political and economic objectives, and while the transition of world order involves negotiation on a number of agendas, there is no evidence of a political alliance based on particular political interests, including among South American countries. According to Altemani Henrique de Oliveira, in the commercial area there is no "strategic alliance," and the alliance that does exist focuses only on the field of scientific and technological cooperation, with the aim of breaking the monopoly of developed countries, and on the political-strategic field, correlating strategies of alliances in the sphere of multilateral forums (Altemani de Oliveira, 2006).

China does not share Brazil's overall main objective, namely to reform the United Nations Security Council. Given the importance that international institutions would have in a hegemonic world system in transition, this difference turns out to be extremely important.

Moreover, the trade *impasse* between Argentina and China, which impacts the overall bilateral relations, calls attention to the fact that the region has not devoted enough attention to the values in the Chinese world, which are still critical for the decision-making process. But at the same time, China does not seem to have realized the scope of its real impact, the weight that its decisions on trade and finance have on the economies of the countries of MERCOSUR. This shows that China's policy is no different from the practices of other world powers in relation to developing countries in applying reprisals and, ultimately, in having a clear *policy of power* which affects the conditions of economic development of less capable countries that are dependent on foreign trade for resources.

From the political point of view, China sought to discipline Argentina, i.e., it exerted the force of attraction of its market to change the behavior of the Argentine government. Without any doubt, this set for South America an example of the fact that China is also capable of disciplining the entire region in pursuing its need to maintain the North-South attributes of the relation such that they are favorable to China. China uses its market as a source of power, opening or closing it depending on the reciprocity of the counterpart's actions, implementing an effective policy of power that has been defined by Keohane as one of the four components of hegemony.[35] This Chinese behavior, essentially hegemonic, assumes that reciprocity in an asymmetric relationship is always favorable to the strongest. The Chinese government knows this and acts accordingly (Oviedo, 2010C).

China, Brazil and Argentina have held common positions in the framework of multilateral trade negotiations, from the formation of G-20 to the failure of the Doha Round, but this has failed to bring bilateral relations to a level of political equilibrium. This situation has led to a discussion over the need to reconceptualize the meaning of a "strategic partnership," understanding it rather as a harmonious relationship, but not necessarily as a relation between allies.

Seen from this perspective, China's strategy towards Latin America has focused on three key factors: 1) increasing its relative power by way of promoting multipolarity and democratization of international relations, in which the countries of the Latin American region can provide political support within the multilateral agencies, 2) containing the interests of Taiwan independence, and 3) strengthening ties and obtaining external resources for national development (Becard, 2008: 240). These factors are focused on the Chinese needs rather than those of Latin American and South American countries. While there are countries in the region that could take even better advantage of bilateral relations with China, in particular those that still can negotiate the establishment of diplomatic relations with Beijing, and despite the fact that Chile is satisfied with its links to the Asian power, this is not the spirit that now dominates the perceptions of the two major

South American countries: Brazil and Argentina. In Brazil, one of the main questions is the real meaning and the possible future of the "strategic partnership." The conclusion is that this is only a "cooperative partnership" and there is a sense of political failure. There is no evidence that there is anything like a *strategic partnership* between Brasilia and Beijing and between Buenos Aires and Beijing.[36]

The review of China's bilateral relations with the MERCOSUR countries shows that countries like Chile and Brazil have managed to grow a stable and special relationship with the Asian power; this has not been the case for Argentina, which has misjudged the diplomatic factor as a comparative advantage in recent months. The differences in political culture show how difficult it still is for some Latin American countries to maintain comprehensive political channels with China. However, Chinese trade retaliation, applied to a product with higher added value (soybean oil) and not the grain (soybean), shows the Chinese intention to relegate Argentinean exports to the category of primary goods and to transfer to its own industrial sector the larger share of the processing activities, concentrating on the higher added value activities of the production chain.

There is no doubt that the strengthening of bilateral relations has led to China's international integration, both in economic and political aspects. Without the changes in China's foreign policy and the development of links with key countries in the region, China's political presence in Latin America, including the Caribbean, would likely have been much more difficult. An event such as China's participation in UN peacekeeping operations in Haiti would have been simply impossible. The political counterpart is not observed in the situation of the countries of MERCOSUR, which raises the idea that this relation is becoming increasingly unequal. Thus, the strengthening of bilateral relations has led to China's international integration, both in economic and political aspects. None of the countries of the region have managed to establish with China a united front of countries in the South. While China's foreign policy toward the region espouses a shared belonging to the developing world and that the underlying principle of its policy is South-South cooperation, Sino-Brazilian and Sino-Argentine relations, because of the frustrations and problems that affect them, are being seen by these South American countries from a critical perspective. In short, they see that China applies to them a *realpolitik* or, simply, a *great power* politic. In this regard, China may be starting, if not to displace, at least to occupy part of the historical space of the United States in the international relations of Latin America and the Caribbean, but at the same time, to establish a pattern of economic specialization and unequal political relations similar to those that Great Britain historically imposed on the region in the nineteenth century and in the ongoing hemispheric hegemony of the United States in the twentieth century.

In conclusion, none of the region's countries, neither Argentina nor Brazil, have managed to establish with China a united front of countries in the South. Thus, this situation becomes an issue that China should consider with concern, given its growing role as a world power in order to avoid repeating the historical experience of the subjugation of Latin America to the hegemony of a global great power.

Notes

* English translation by Raúl Bernal Amitrano.

1 The MERCOSUR-China dialogue began in 1997 and continued until 2004, after Argentina and Brazil failed to persuade the government of Paraguay to diplomatically recognize the PRC.

2 Even though there were bonds between China and some Latin American countries before it was set up as the *Republic of China*, for example, Argentina had established diplomatic relations with Beijing in 1945, this document will refer to the contemporary period and the relations with the current P. R. of China, not considering the link with that since 1949 is called "Nationalist China" or "Republic of China".

3 Along with Venezuela and Mexico.

4 Opinions on the "China threat" are divided. According to Peter Lewis, the theory of yellow threat is exaggerated and it has been promoted mainly by a variety of different interests in the United States Congress, and by some academics and the media in that country. See Lewis (2007).

5 Considering China as "Third World" is the subject of debate. The political discourse of international relations of the Chinese state systematically tends to speak of P. R. of China as a developing country and, from this, to highlight the nexus of belonging to the South with the other semi-peripheral and peripheral countries. However, economic indicators do not identify the country as a developing country, except in the case of GDP per capita.

6 In order of importance, the main destinations for Chinese investments in Latin America are Brazil, Mexico, Chile, and Argentina.

7 PEOPLE'S REPUBLIC OF CHINA, Paper on China's policy toward Latin America and the Caribbean, in Xinhuanet, Beijing, November 5, 2008; http://www.spanish.xinhuanet.com/spanish/2008-11/05/content_755432. htm. We took the synthesis from Oviedo (2009b).

8 Ibid., p. 10.

9 Center-left alliance, which ruled the country between 1990 and 2010.

10 Ministry of Foreign Affairs of the People's Republic of China, http://www.fmprc.gov.cn/esp/wjb/zzjg/Idmzs/gjlb/3478/3480/t222248.htm., cited by M. Pérez Le-Fort.

11 Source: PROCHILE, http://rc.direcon.cl/files/bibliotecas/COMERCIO EX-TERIOR CHINA y HONG KONG,%202009,pdf

12 The top twenty products shipped to China in 2009 accounted for 97.6% of total exports. Among these, those that stand out are copper, cellulose and roasted molybdenum concentrates, which together amounted to 88.2%. Source: PROCI IILE, Ibid.

13 For example, as regards the promotion of globalization and its relation to the opening and deregulation of peripheral economies, environmental policies, transfer of nuclear waste to Third World countries, etc.

14 Source: "Desplazan al embajador argentino en China", in Clarin.com, January 20, 2011.

15 Publicly, the barriers to Argentine oil are due to a technical-health related issue, as Chinese authorities require that the product that enters its country has a limit of 100 parts of hexane (a solvent chemical) per million. However, sources from the Embassy of China explained that the unease was mainly due to the application of the barriers that the Argentine government imposed to a long list of Chinese imports, including some areas in which Argentina has no local production. Source: http://www.wattagnet.com/IA/15571.html

16 2010, 4, 3, Mi Na. Lifting of the trade dispute between Argentina and China, benefits from soybean oil. Information Network of China Edible Oils, in http://www.oil.com/article/2010/0403/article_13313.html.; Eduardo Daniel Oviedo, *Causas de la tensión comercial entre Argentina y China* (2010c).

17 Cfr. *"Fuerte castigo en el precio del aceite por las trabas chinas"*. Clarin, Buenos Aires, August 12, 2010, p. 18.

18 Ibid. Part of this oil has been for the production of biodiesel, which is also subsidized by the national government. Yet the cost to Argentina is important.

19 Argentina's President suspended the January 19, 2010 official visit to China, scheduled for the 25th of that month, justifying this decision on the need for preventing her vice-president from temporarily assuming the executive power which would give him the right of veto on issues related to the Central Bank.

20 Other authors are inclined to believe that the restrictive measures upon soybean oil by China was in retaliation to anti-dumping measures by the Argentine government on Chinese products, cf. For example, Eduardo Daniel Oviedo (2010 [a]). However, in my conversations with Chinese academics and consultants in Beijing, there was no mention that this was the real reason for China's reaction and they rather point out as relevant the importance that the Chinese government gives to the image of its country as a "world power".

21 See Julio Sevares, "Argentina-China: buena relación con *factores no armoniosos*", in Clarin.com, Economics, May 30, 2010.

22 "China comprará 500 mil toneladas de aceite de soja a la Argentina", in Ámbito. com, May 12, 2011.

23 Clarín.com, May 13, 2011.

24 For example, Argentina's largest daily broadcast, Clarin, published on January 4, 2011, section Tribune Review, an article in which it warned about the risk for Argentina in a relationship that does not seem satisfactory in the medium and long term, to the extent that China is investing in the purchase of assets, also Argentine, in oil and gas resources, the same resources on which there will be competition in no time.

The central criticism is that the equation that Peron's government established in the 70s, energy exchange for proteins, which must govern the pursuit of "strategic partners," has not been satisfied in the case of China. See Victor Bronstein, "China no es nuestro socio estratégico"; Clarín, Buenos Aires, January 4, 2011.

Meanwhile, another newspaper article warned against false promises about China's "big investment," stating that they were just a "Chinese tale" meaning something too farfetched, hard to believe. Cf. http://corredorbioceanico.wordpress.com/2011/01/06/se-acabo-el-cuento-chino/.

25 "Represalia china con la soja por trabas argentinas", in: *Ámbito Financiero*, Buenos Aires, April 11, 2011, p. 1.

26 This is the book of Eduardo Daniel Oviedo. *Historia de las relaciones internacionales entre Argentina y China. 1945-2010*. Buenos Aires, Editorial Dunken, 2010.

27 As evidenced by the various lines of technology cooperation and the purchase of 100 aircrafts to Brazil's Embraer.

28 Source: http://estrategiaynegocios.net/mundo/Default.aspx?option=9392

29 source: http://translate.google.com.ar/translate?hl=es&langpair=en%7Ces&u=http://www.reuters.com/article/

30 Source: http://www.iberoasia.org/blog/?p=651

31 Source: http://ipsnoticias.net/nota.asp?idnews=94701

32 Source: http://www.pymex.pe/noticias/mundo/4401-productos-chinos-restan-us-12600-mill-a-exportaciones-de-brasil.html

33 About this A. Cervo said "To the Brazilian project [it] is disgusting: the hemispheric integration (FTAA), bilateral free trade and even the Mercosur-EU agreement for the creation of a free trade area. From the Brazilian perspective, all these possibilities penetrate deeply into the domestic law and international integration, so they compromise the country's industrial vocation, the supreme good of political representation and the national interest" (Cervo, 2009a: 85).

34 As it is clear from the document "China's Policy Paper on Latin America and the Caribbean", op. cit.

35 Keohane believes that a hegemonic country should hold a large market for imports, control major sources of capital, access to essential raw materials, and competitive advantages in the production of value-added goods. In: Robert Keohane, *Después de la Hegemonía. Cooperación y discordia en la política económica mundial,* Grupo Editor Latinoamericano, Buenos Aires, 1988: 50-52.

36 For the Brazilian case, this view was raised by Amaury Porto de Oliveira, in mid1990 when that association was not yet declared, and taken up by authors such as Amado Cervo and Becard Danielly Ramos Silva, in the years of the past decade, after almost five years of existence of the link. Cf. Altemani de Oliveira (1996), Cervo (2008), Becard (2008). For the Argentine case, the doubts about the "strategic alliance" appeared in the press of Buenos Aires from June 2010 after the Chinese authorities' actions against Argentine exports of soybean oil.

References

Almeida, Paulo Roberto (2006) "Uma nova arquitetura diplomática? Interpretações divergentes sobre a política externa do Governo Lula (2003-2006)", *Revista Brasileira de Política internacional*, 49 (1): 95-116.

Altemani de Oliveira, Henrique (2006) "O Brasil e a Ásia", in H. Altemani and A.C. Lessa (orgs.), *Relações internacionais do Brail: temas e agendas*, São Paulo: Saraiva; 1: 169-210.

Baine, Nicholas &Woolcock, Stephen (eds.) (2007) *The New Economic Diplomacy. Decision-making and Negotiation in International Economic Relations.* Aldershot, Ashgate: Global Finance, 2ᵉ éd.

Becard, Danielly Silva Ramos (2008) *O Brasil e a República Popular da China. Política Externa Comparada e Relações Bilaterais (1974-2004).* Brasília: Fundação Alexandre de Gusmão.

Bernal-Meza, Raúl (1994) *América Latina en la Economía Política Mundial.* Buenos Aires: Grupo Editor Latinoamericano.

Bernal-Meza, Raúl (2000) *Sistema Mundial y Mercosur. Globalización, Regionalismo y Políticas Exteriores Comparadas.* Buenos Aires: Universidad Nacional del Centro de la Provincia de Buenos Aires y Grupo Editor Latinoamericano.

Bernal-Meza, Raúl (2003) "Política Exterior de Argentina, Chile y Brasil: Perspectiva Comparada", in José Flávio Sombra Saraiva (ed.) (2003) *Foreign Policy and Political* Regime. Brasilia: Instituto Brasileiro de Relações Internacionais.

Bernal-Meza, Raúl (2004) "Política Exterior de Argentina, Brasil y Chile: Perspectiva Comparada, in Denis Rolland & José Flavio Sombra Saraiva (eds.) (2004) *Political Regime and Foreign Relations. A Historical perspective.* Paris: L'Harmattan.

Bernal-Meza, Raúl (2009) "Latin American Concepts and Theories and Their Impacts to Foreign Policies", in José Flávio Sombra Saraiva (ed.) (2009) *Concepts, Histories and Theories of International Relations for the 21ˢᵗ Century. Regional and National Approaches.* Brasilia: IBRI.

Bernal-Meza, Raúl (2010) "International Thinking in The Lula's Era", *Revista Brasileira de Política Internacional*, 53 (special edition): 193-213

Bernal-Meza, Raúl (2010ᵃ) "El pensamiento internacionalista en la era Lula", *Estudios Internacionales,* (XLIII)167: 143-172.

Bizzozero Revelez, Lincoln (2008) *Uruguay en la creación del MERCOSUR. ¿Un cambio en la política exterior?* Montevideo: Universidad de la República.

Cervo, Amado Luiz (2008) *Inserção Internacional. Formação dos conceitos brasileiros.* São Paulo: Saraiva.

Cervo, Amado Luiz (2009a) "La construcción del modelo industrialista brasileño", *Revista DEP, Diplomacia, Estrategia y Política, Brasília,* (10): 74-86.

Cervo, Amado Luiz, and Bueno, Clodoaldo (2008) *História da Política Exterior do Brasil*. Brasília: Editora UnB.

CICIR, Latin American Research Group (2004) "Report on China's Latin American Policy", *Contemporary International Relations*, 14(4): 14-30.

Ellis, R. Evan (2009) *China in Latin America. The Whats & Wherefores*, Boulder, Co. & London: Lynne Rienner Publishers, Inc.

Flemes, Daniel (2010) "O Brasil na iniciativa BRIC: sofá balancing numa orden global em mudanza?" *Revista Brasileira de Política Internacional*, (53)1: 141-156.

Jiang, Shixue (2002) Sino-Latin American Relations: perspectives on the past and prospects for the future, *ILAS Working Papers* (1).

Jiang, Shixue (2006) "Recent Development of Sino-Latin American Relations and its Implications", *Estudios Internacionales*, (XXXVIII) 152: 19-42.

Labarca, Claudia (2009) "El capitalismo confuciano y la globalización: nuevas bases para construir *xinyong* y *guanxi*-enseñanzas para Chile", *Estudios Internacionales*, (XLII)163: 23-46.

Lafer, Celso (2001) *A identidade internacional do Brasil: pasado, presente e futuro*. São Paulo: Perspectiva.

Lafer, Celso (2002) *La identidad internacional del Brasil*. Buenos Aires: FCE.

Lewis, Peter M. (2007) "La presencia de China en América Latina. Un tema controvertido", *Estudios Internacionales*, (XXXIX)156: 27-54.

Li Xing (ed.) (2010) *The Rise of China and the Capitalist World Order*. Surrey, England & Ashgate Publishing Company, Burlington: Ashgate Publishing Limited.

Neves, Miguel Santos (2006) A China como potência global emergente: vulnerabilidades, tensões e desafios,*Política Externa*, (15)1: 7-21.

Oliveira, Amaury Porto de (1996) O prometo da China, *Caderno Premissas* (13).

Oviedo, Eduardo Daniel (2005) *China en expansión*. Córdoba: Editorial de la Universidad Católica de Córdoba.

Oviedo, Eduardo Daniel (2009) China-Mercosur, Conference, in *VIII Jornadas de Investigación de la Facultad de Ciencias Sociales de la Universidad de la República*. Montevideo, 7 de septiembre de 2009.

Oviedo, Eduardo Daniel (2009a) "The New International Role of China and its Relations with Argentina in Times of Crisis", *The Journal of Global Development and Peace*, (Spring 2010): 44-68.

Oviedo, Eduardo Daniel (2009b) "China, América Latina y la crisis global", *Observatorio de la Política China* (2009). Available at http://www.politica-china.org/imxd/noticias/doc/1235901864Oviedo_Vigo_Pca_exterior.pdf

Oviedo, Eduardo Daniel (2010) *Historia de las relaciones internacionales entre Argentina y China.* Córdoba: EDUCC.

Oviedo, Eduardo Daniel (2010a) *Historia de las relaciones internacionales entre Argentina y China. 1945-2010.* Buenos Aires: Dunken.

Oviedo, Eduardo Daniel (2010b) "Relaciones China-MERCOSUR", *Seminario Internacional: La construcción de vínculos económicos más estrechos entre China y Argentina a inicios del siglo XXI.* Buenos Aires: Universidad Nacional de Tres de Febrero (agosto).

Oviedo, Eduardo Daniel (2010c) "Causas de la tensión comercial entre Argentina y China debido a las restricciones fitosanitarias aplicadas a la importación de aceite de soja argentino durante el gobierno de Cristina Fernández de Kirchner", in *IX Congreso Internacional sobre Democracia: Los senderos de la democracia en América Latina: Estado, Sociedad Civil y Cambio Político.* Rosario: Facultad de Ciencia Política y Relaciones Internacionales, Universidad Nacional de Rosario y Secretaría de Cultura del Centro de Estudiantes; 18-21 octubre 2010.

Pecequilo, Cristina S. (2008) "A Política Externa do Brasil no Século XXI: Os eixos Combinados de Cooperação Horizontal e Vertical", *Revista Brasileira de Política Internacional,* (51)2: 136-153.

Pérez Le-Fort, Martín (2006) "Relaciones sino-chilenas bajo nuevas circunstancias", *Estudios Internacionales,* (XXXVIII)152: 123-136.

Roccaro, Isabel Esther (2009) Las relaciones comerciales entre MERCOSUR y China, *Sumario* (52)segunda quincena, noviembre: 12-13.

Sevares, Julio (2007) "¿Cooperación Sur-Sur o dependencia a la vieja usanza? América Latina en el comercio internacional", *Nueva Sociedad,* (207): 11-22.

Simonoff, Alejandro (2009) "Regularidades de la política exterior de Néstor Kirchner", *Confines,* (5)10: 71-86.

Simonoff, Alejandro (comp.) (2010) *La Argentina y el mundo frente al Bicentenario de la Revolución de Mayo.* Buenos Aires: Editorial de la Universidad de La Plata.

van klaveren, Alberto (1997) "América Latina: hacia un regionalismo abierto", in Alberto van Klaveren (ed.) *América Latina en el mundo.* Santiago: PROSPEL.

van Klaveren, Alberto (1997a) "América Latina: hacia un regionalismo abierto", *Estudios Internacionales,* (XXX)117: 62-78.

Zhang, Xinsheng (2006) "El entendimiento sobre el Tratado de Libre Comercio entre China y Chile", *Estudios Internacionales,* (XXXVIII)152: 113-121.

Chapter 3

The Struggle for Modernization and Sino-Latin American Economic Relations

Introduction

The following study stratifies the global economy according to Pareto's principle and confirms the trend toward global economic de-concentration in the first decade of the twenty-first century. This de-concentration is related to the rise of Asian countries in the world economic structure, which, based on modernization processes, show that it is possible to ascend and occupy positions in the global Directory of major economic powers. Nowadays, the main examples of this process are China, Japan, India and also Russia. At the same time, the access of these nations into the Directory generates a counter-trend which tends to the re-concentration of economic powers. Therefore, de-concentration and re-concentration combine the contradictory economic forces of nations in the early twenty-first century, bearing in mind that the "Pareto optimal" has not yet been reached and there is a margin to expand the trend towards economic de-concentration.

The access of China into the global Directory is a special case in this group of nations. In fact, the characteristic of authoritarian modernization, based on a one-party political system, caused a real disturbance in Latin America's political systems and exposed the failure of Latin American leaders in promoting modernization in the region, with the one exception of Brazil. Hence, this research has focused on the internal and external factors that propelled China's modernization and that may be important to Latin America, a region that is characterized by non-consolidated democracies which have formed, in almost all of its countries, an anti-authoritarian consciousness opposed to the Chinese political system.

The research also pays attention to Chinese interests which enter into harmony or tension with Latin America's interests and create a Chinese-Latin American network of common and contradictory interests. This network is based on tangible and intangible capacities of power, which determine the status of each political unit in the international structure and build "power relations". As a result, it confirms the "North-North model" for Sino-Brazilian interaction and the "North-South model" for China linking with the rest of Latin American countries. Within this framework the "dilemma of non-renewable resources" appears; renewable resource complementation, the turning point of Chinese investment in the region; competition in third and local markets, where dumping and the recognition of China as a market economy face anti-dumping barriers.

These factors, combined with the political will of the governments, show that there are political units satisfied with their primary economies and also with the new international division of labor. In contrast, there are also some units who aspire to reach economic de-primarization, promote industrialization and add value to their products. In the first case, cooperation exceeds tension; in the second case, tension will appear alongside cooperation. However, because of the incipient stage of industrialization in Latin America, harmony and tension over interests will co-exist in the short and medium term.

De-concentration of world economic power

Table 1 stratifies the major economies by size, estimated according to their Gross Domestic Product (GDP) and Purchasing Power Parity (PPP). Following Pareto's principle, 80% of Gross World Product (GWP) should be concentrated in about 20% of the units. In 2000, however, that 80% was exceeded with only 14 countries of the 181 listed in the "World Development Report" by the World Bank. As a first conclusion, the statistics in 2000 reveal the concentration of the global economy in a few states, a recurring tendency in the last few decades of the twentieth century.

Applying the same criteria to the conglomerate of these nations (i.e. the top 14), it is possible to create a line of demarcation between large and medium-sized economies, drawing 80% to 80% of GWP. Thus, in the year 2000 the Directory of major economic powers was composed of six units (the United States, Japan, Germany, the United Kingdom, France and China) and the remaining eight, located outside it, in middle power status.

Table 1: World economy stratification

Status	Year 2000			Year 2009		
	Countries	GDP	PPP	Countries	GDP	PPP
Great	United States	1	1	United States	1	1
powers	Japan	2	3	China	2	2
	Germany	3	5	Japan	3	3
	United Kingdom	4	7	Germany	4	5
	France	5	6	France	5	8
	China	6	2	United Kingdom	6	7
				Italy	7	10
				Brazil	8	9
				Spain	9	12
Middle or	Italy	7	8	Canada	10	14
Semi-Peripheral	Canada	8	12	India	11	4
Powers	Brazil	9	9	Russia	12	6
	Spain	10	13	Australia	13	17
	Mexico	11	11	Mexico	14	11
	India	12	4	South Korea	15	13
	South Korea	13	14	Netherlands	16	19
	Netherlands	14	16	Turkey	17	15
				Indonesia	18	16
				Belgium	19	26
Small or	Argentina	15	21	Poland	20	18
Peripheral Powers	Turkey	16	15	Sweden	21	30
	Russian	17	10	Switzerland	22	34

Source: The World Bank, World Development Report 2002 and 2010.
      Exclude the Republic of China (Taiwan). China includes Hong Kong.

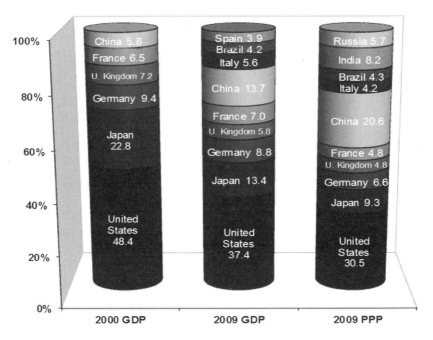

Graphic 1:
Percentage of participation of each director in the oligopoly of economic power

However, if we apply similar criteria during the year 2009, the great and middle powers increased from fourteen to nineteen, while the Directory grew from six to nine major economies (Italy, Brazil and Spain), without counting India and Russia which, in terms of PPP, are part of the oligopoly and exclude Spain and Italy. Irrespective of measurement in terms of GDP or PPP, more nations participated in the 80% of GWP. As a result, we can say that at the end of the first decade of the twenty-first century, the trend toward global economic concentration has been reversed to de-concentration, as an effect of the contraction of the great economies such as the United States, Japan, the United Kingdom, Italy, Spain and Canada. This economic "democratization" was mitigated, in part, by the rapid rise of China, India and Russia; although they are actors that enter or reenter the Directory of major economic powers to open up the oligopoly to the participation of more nations, at the same time they tend to re-concentrate the world's wealth. On the other hand, according to Pareto's principle, there is scope to expand the decentralization of economic force because 20% of the 181 nations listed in the report are represented by 36 units, while in 2009 only 19 economies were the ones that accumulated 80% of that wealth. To sum up, there is still enough margin to expand economic decentralization to reach the Pareto optimal[1].

China's appearance in the oligopoly of big powers redistributed the economic power accumulated by the United States among its directors. However, without falling into the debate between advocates of unilateralism or apologists of multipolar reaction, the de-concentration of economic power (the main characteristic of the Westphalian system) was expanded in the first decade of the twenty-first century. Thus greater participation in the administration of international affairs was given to actors that, in the historical evolution of the system, have been marginal and passive units, objects of the foreign policy of great powers rather than subjects of international law (China, India and Brazil). Such participation in the Directory allows some units to acquire the "privileges" of great power and share responsibilities in the administration of international order. As a result, they have an important role in the management of world politics and, therefore, of international relations.

The struggle to rise in the international structure

In 2009, the World Bank facts show China and Japan as the second and third world economy, respectively. India ranked eleventh (and fourth in terms of PPP) followed by South Korea, Turkey and Indonesia, while Russia recovered its traditional place among the major economies. Other East Asian countries that until World War II were colonies, such as Taiwan and Vietnam, also rose in the world economic stratification. In contrast, no country in Latin America has changed its traditional role of middle power since the mid-twentieth century, except Brazil (ranked among the major economic powers) and Mexico (in fourteenth place in 2009), while the remaining nations were located below the top twenty economies. Therefore, the historical evolution of the world economy shows the rapid rise of these Asian powers in relation to humble or nonexistent post-war international roles, while Latin American countries, except Brazil, remain in their traditional positions.

These facts verify the wisdom of political decisions that have been taken by the political classes in Asian countries and the failure of Latin American leaders to find the path to continuous growth that will catapult the countries of the region into a higher stage in their socioeconomic development. At the same time, the success of modernization in East Asian countries and India causes a disturbance[2] in the Latin American systems. This demand also tends to be satisfied by economic modernization policies implemented in order to achieve a better position for these nations in international politics. Thus, the patterns of socialization and competition of the international system[3] have a strong influence on Latin American political systems, assimilating experiences from other political systems and shaping its behavior, under pressure from the competition of modernization among nations and the struggle to rise in the international structure.

Nonetheless, the socialization of political unity does not mean falling into mere imitation of the Asian model of modernization. In fact, taking into account that the experiences of nations are historical and therefore peculiar, unique and not reproducible, it is unacceptable to transplant this model to Latin American countries. This may be explained by their belonging to other civilizations, with different political regimes and economic practices. That is, the success of Asian modernization exposed the inability of Latin American leaders to achieve native processes of growth, while the "import" of alien models would cause the failure of them because they assimilate to different realities. However, it is possible to recover certain patterns of political behavior that led to the Asian countries and China in particular reaching more important economic levels. Therefore, the Asian experiences, rather than being understood as an Asian model, lead us to discover the promoting factors of modernization adaptable to the Latin American economies, understanding that the "import of model" is not the key for developing the countries of lower relative power.

Authoritarian modernization versus modernization in democracy

Asian modernization is clearly represented in the sequence of economic growth known as the "Flying Geese Paradigm", initiated by Japan in the seventies and followed by the "Four Little Dragons" (Singapore, Hong Kong, Taiwan and South Korea) in the next decade. These economies were benefiting from the modernization led by the United States in the Asian periphery of the Western bloc in the framework of the bipolar order. Once the Soviet Union disintegrated, China appeared in a new phase of the same sequence, followed by Vietnam, which moved in that direction after consolidating its independence. Therefore, China's modernization was not independent of the modernization process in Europe since the seventeenth century and expanded to different regions of the world, aspiring to be ecumenical, until arriving in East Asia after the Second World War. Thus we can say that there is no modernization *of* China but modernization *in* China (Oviedo, 2005: 93-97).

The quest for economic modernization has been a constant in the Communist leadership since the formation of the PRC (People's Republic of China). The military alliance and economic and financial relation with the Soviet Union gave support to the First Five Year Plan (1953-1957), based on the Soviet model of growth. Then, with the tension that caused the breakdown of relations with Moscow having just started, Mao Ze Dong proposed the "Great Leap Forward" (1957-1962) or the rapid industrialization of the economy to reach the level of Western Europe countries in a short time. After its failure, the pragmatic line of the CPC (Communist Party of China), whose two main personalities were Liu Shao Qi and Deng Xiao Ping, set up the "Moderate Restoration" (1962-1965), reestablishing rationality, planning and the import of grains, measures to facilitate economic recovery (Fanjul, 1999: 73-103). However, the distrust of Chairman Mao (who saw his leadership being displaced from the political scene) promoted the "Cultural Revolution", isolating China from the international community in an autarchic vision of the economy. This process, limited in time by the official documents between 1966 and 1976, completed its most critical stage in 1969, maintaining certain basic relationships of autarchy and import substitution until the death of the leader. After a two-year political transition, the Chinese revisionist line returned to power in the CPC and decided to reform the economy in December 1978, based on Zhou En Lai's school of thought relative to the "four modernizations" (agriculture, industry, defense and science and technology). With a long-term vision and different environmental conditions, China's leadership guided the modernization of the economy from the "import substitution model" to the "production-export model", with gradual integration into the world economy. This situation has been characterized in post-Maoist China as "capitalist restoration" in reference to revived features of economic and social order prior to 1949 (Bailey, 2002: 212).

China presents a new challenge to Latin American countries, as it modernized its economy with a "stabilized one-party totalitarian regime" (Oviedo, 2005: 76), different from the other cases mentioned above[4]. In the process, Chinese totalitarianism has been functional to economic modernization, coercively overcoming the social obstacles that had challenged it. Its repressive character has ignored the socio-political demands that economic reforms have raised as a consequence of the whole process. This aspect can be observed not only in human rights issues but also in those that come up daily in the country and are linked to economic growth (see Sorman, 2007).

For the last twenty-five years, constitutional regimes of Latin America have on the contrary implemented modernization at the same time respecting individual freedoms and human rights in a society increasingly aware of the respect for such values. While the views of different social actors are considered in the Latin American process, the Chinese regime imposes submission to other groups. These are two different kinds of modernization: China implements a *monistic and authoritarian model,* coercively imposed from top to bottom; Latin American countries put forward the *pluralistic and democratic model,* based on dialogue and negotiation with diverse social actors. Of course, not everything is coercion in one-party regimes, because in recent years, "political control depends less on terror than on persuasion and organization" (Almond, 1999: 113), especially when the Chinese government validates its "legitimacy of exercise" by the high rates of growth of its economy. As Bailey stated, "The fact remains, however, that CPC rule is justified on the grounds that it alone guarantees social stability and economic progress" (Bailey, 2002: 225).

The challenge for Latin American countries is modernization in democracy. In this region constitutional governments predominate and there is a minority of totalitarian regimes (i.e. Cuba). These governments emerged as a result of transitions to democracy in the eighties of the last century, removing military regimes and creating an anti-authoritarian consciousness in the region. However, these political transitions, included in the third wave of democratization in the late twentieth century[5] (Huntington, 2007), remain to be completed by "new transitions" or "second-generation transitions" (O'Donnell, 1988: 3-11), not political but economic and social, to consolidate political democracy with economic modernization absent in the region[6].

Totalitarianism has the inverted form of this problem. China faces the challenge of the pressure of economic modernization on the political regime because political development is not limited to mere economic reform, but requires political openness and institutionalization. Indeed, since the start of China's reform, the use of coercive measures was not reduced and greater consensus in the political system did not arise from free and voluntary expression (Oviedo, 2005: 93). It is, therefore, a modern political system with low institutionalization.

This problem has been observed by the Chinese leadership. President Hu Jin Tao, during his visit to the United States in 2006, in a conference at Yale University, announced the reform of the political system which would take into consideration foreign experience but without copying any foreign model[7]. The Chinese political system would be their own. If this were so done, China's experience would be evidence of the expansion of modernization into the political arena precisely because modernization as a historical process involves innovation and not simply the repetition of existing models. As Bobbio, Matteucci y Pasquino (1995: 988) say, modernization is not merely the diffusion process of the institutions, European values and techniques, but also an open and continuous interaction between different institutions, different cultures and different techniques. However, since that speech of President Hu no substantial changes in the political regime have been verified and the question about how the Chinese government will perform its political transition still has no response. The case of India is different: it has executed a democratic praxis since the founding of the state, which, although precarious, is based on economic growth and does not require political transition. The case of China demands the arduous task of improving its political regimen and the orderly management of its economy.

China's modernization patterns to be considered in Latin America

The economic competition generated by this Eastern power after three decades of continuous growth has been analyzed extensively by economists, paying less attention to the policy variable. Therefore, this subpart analyzes the patterns of political behavior that affected Chinese growth and that might be adopted in Latin America as a consequence of the success of this Asian experience.

These patterns corresponded to both levels of political reality: the internal and external. Internally, China's leadership experienced the producer-exporter model and created the Chinese market which was incipient there. Modernizing leadership was orientated by the CPC which regionalized the reform process and reduced the ideological distance among its main members, with implications for the stability of political leadership, autonomy of decisions and rapid crisis resolution. Externally, the basic factors are foreign policy functional in the modernization process, strategic cooperation with the hegemonic powers and the use of the import of market as a plausible source of introverted hegemony.

- *Production-export model and market creation.* China created a virtuous circle of "investment, production and market" under conditions of macroeconomic stability, investment protection and peaceful environment similar to nineteenth century liberalism. It attracted foreign investment to formed joint venture or exclusive capital companies to produce in special zones of China and export overseas. With foreign investment and an international market it created the "world's factory", at same time giving life to the domestic market (and civil society) where the relationship between supply and demand exists in potential victims of planning and state property. The key for this creation was the gradual liberalization and marketization of the economy (Wu, 2003: 1-49), choosing the producer-exporter model and the accumulation of international reserves.
  These reserves are used to stimulate internal demand and stabilize the virtuous circle in times of disruption, such as the subprime mortgage crisis in the United States. That is, the Chinese government still maintains the producer-exporter model and applies Keynesian measures, injecting financial reserves into local markets through infrastructure plans to counter the adverse effects of the global economic crisis. There is uncertainty about the capacity of the Chinese market to be the driving force for reviving the process because it is tied to depend-

ence on international trade. However, non-economic factors, such as the political regime and consciousness of the past, explain China's attitude to the crisis. For example, it is common for the Chinese to consider this type of crisis as "light cold", because in the collective memory there are still vivid memories of the real hardships that the Chinese people had to overcome: for example, the civil war and the Japanese invasion in the thirties of the twentieth century, World War II, the failure of the Great Leap Forward, famine and confrontation with the United States and the Soviet Union in the sixties, among others.

- *Modernizing leadership and regionalization of the reform process.* Modernization has been imposed by the CPC leadership, traditionally formed by urban members and the Han majority. According to the 2001 census, this ethnic group represents 91.5% of the population and started the economic boom in their natural habitat: eastern China. Its rapid economic growth led to imbalances in the backward western and central regions of the country, so it was decided to promote the integration of both areas into national development. This experience takes up again the idea of what political and social sector will be responsible for leading modernization in Latin America and the need (in a first phase and in states with large territories such as Argentina and Brazil) to regionalize the process that leads to the concentrated application of scarce resources and then progress towards integration. The political party system differs from Chinese totalitarianism in that it requires reaching agreement (tacit or explicit) among the modernizers on the general direction in which to guide the process.

- *Reduction of ideological distance and stability in political leadership.* In exercising its monopoly of political mediation, the CPC eliminates the political competition of the party system. Consequently, the competition of democratic regimes becomes an intra-party competition among political leaders in the Politburo Standing Committee. The achievement of the revisionist leadership, after the 1976 coup, was to remove the radical Maoist line and the hegemony of the party following Deng Xiaoping's thinking on the "economic reform and opening-up". Thus, the narrowing of the ideological distance between the current nine members that have political control of the party has been functional to the continuity of political orientation. This transformation had the party as the main actor, maintaining stability through peaceful negotiation and punishing dissent, as happened with former general secretary Zhao Zi Yang in 1989. The conflicting interests were solved inside the party and each of these leaders represented a true trend of thought that revolves around the greater or lesser extent of political orientation. For instance, during the nineties in the last century, Li Peng represented the most closed, hard and orthodox in the group, while Zhu

Rong Ji was the man in favor of modernizing and opening up the political party, but both agreed on the reform model. Thus the narrowing of the ideological distance appears, resulting in increased regime stability. To this most important aspect was united the consensus to eliminate the life tenure system in government official posts and the gestation of the political succession process that has been successful in the transfer of power from Jiang Ze Min to Hu Jin Tao and is expected to act normally in the next political succession.[8]

In contrast, Latin American regimes show that the ideological distance between political parties (or within a political party) has been a factor of instability which obstructs the formation of the harmonious political orientation conducive to modernization in the long term. The political clash in Mexico during the 2006 elections announced political problems with an impact on the economy. The cycles of liberalization and nationalization of Argentina's economy show the lack of a national project for modernization like that achieved, compulsively, by the Chinese Communist Party. The political division of society, such as happened in Chávez's Venezuela and Morales's Bolivia, expressed lack of agreement on creating a pluralist project of modernization. Therefore, the shortening of ideological distances among political parties in Latin America (in order to harmonize the national long-term goals and transform them into political agreements as has happened in Lula's Brazil and the Chilean coalition) is fundamental to any process of modernization.

- *Political autonomy and rapid crisis resolution.* The autonomy to use pressure from social groups is characteristic of strong political institutions. In China it appears in the decisions taken at a domestic level before the crises of Tian An Men (1989), Fa Lun Gong (1999) and Uyghur's ethnic (2009), and various at external level, from the crisis in the Taiwan Strait to the repeated ones that emerge in the relationship with the United States. However, pressure from the economic system (with the objective process of globalization and the world economic crisis) put conditions on China for opening up the political system which cannot remain closed as it did during most of its contemporary history. So, the political regime has greater autonomy than subordination to domestic and external influences and disturbances, but requires transformation. For example, the accumulation of unsatisfied demands overwhelmed the political system in 1989. It showed that, besides the increase in the political dissenters' thinking against reform, social conflict arose in spite of police control. However, this police regime served to quell social and political demands. The crisis had an impact on economic interactions and the country was vacillating till 1992. They were years of slow expansion until, once the crisis was overcome and the system was stabilized, Deng Xiao Ping re-launched a new phase of totalitarian modernization with constant and accelerated growth up to the present.

- *Foreign policy functional in modernization.* Foreign policy has been an important instrument for maintaining the expansion of the political system in harmony with its environment and to ensure that external conditions accompany domestic economic transformations. Its habitual mechanisms were: peaceful negotiations; multilateral, bilateral and "people to people" diplomacies; the abandoning of permanent alliances; the rejection of the recovery of traditional isolationism. These instruments of foreign policy are to be seen within a long-term framework; ancestral political realism; the state-centric view and integration into the global economy. These variables confirm the voluntary socialization of this political unity in the international system.

  For example, civilizational time influences foreign policy decision-making. The statesmen designed external actions based on notions of time different from the Western countries, inserted in the historical continuity of one of the oldest human civilizations. Comparatively, the short-term view seems to belong to young countries, such as Latin American nations, where foreign policies are outlined to be implemented in each phase of government, without reaching a consensus on long-term external continuity, which goes beyond the political alternation.

- *Cooperation with the hegemonic powers.* In its strategic *entente,* the Chinese government prioritizes the relationship with the United States and other great powers. Indeed, in the recent processes of modernization in Asia, foreign policy (and especially trade policy) fixed its attention on the relationship with the global hegemonic powers. This external factor is considered normal in the cases of Japan, the Republic of Korea and Taiwan, because during the Cold War these countries maintained military alliances with the United States, a situation continuing to the present day. This policy continued in China's experience since its Communist government associated the superpower to its economic growth, being a main trading partner and foreign investor. The cases of India and Vietnam are similar. Therefore, these cases confirm the hypothesis that in the Asian experiences of modernization it was necessary to maintain cooperative ties with the hegemonic power. Thus they differ from the traditional view of opposition and antagonism to the United States that has emerged in Latin America's public opinion and governments since the later nineteenth century and are still in force today. The achievements of China's leadership have been associated with the United States, European countries and Japan with its economic growth, although its natural habitat (the Asian continent) continues to occupy the highest percentage of foreign trade and investments.

- *The market as a source of introverted hegemony.* This remains a critical resource for its foreign policy. The use of it by so-called "popular diplomacy" should be remembered: attractive economic potential was offered to countries that did not recognize the PRC so as to change their position after the 1949 revolution. With a mixture of realism and marketing, China sells to the world the image of the imperative necessity of its economic ties and persuades foreign leaders of the importance of its 1,340 million people market. Differing from traditional hegemony, China exercises an "introverted hegemony", keeping the "ideological clothing" on its domination, but centripetal action (centered on China) and economic interests are the ties that bind it to the international community (Oviedo, 2006).

Certainly, from the four sources of power, considered by Keohane as fundamental to the exercise of hegemony in the world economy, China has reached only one: the existence of a large import market. The other three sources are: 1) to have access to crucial raw materials; 2) control major sources of capital; and 3) competitive advantages in the production of high value goods (Keohane, 1988: 50-52). China has competitive advantages in the production of intermediate goods, but not in the high value-added goods that could generate high wages for its population. There is no control over global supply chains, which produce cheaply, but much of the value added of these products is gained by the distributors of such products. Besides, China does not control the major sources of capital, but has significant reserves in U.S. dollars and little in gold (1% of global reserves), though in 2007 it surpassed South Africa as the world's largest producer (Mueller, 2008). In addition, China seeks to stabilize the supply of raw materials, being Africa and Latin America reservoirs of energy, minerals and agricultural products. That is to say, it is incorrect to speak of full hegemony in economic terms, but it is possible to assert its transition to the same.

Chinese interests and pattern of relations with Latin America

China deploys its action on two levels of political reality. Internally, it continues and actualizes economic modernization to increase material and immaterial power capacities and consolidate the legitimacy of the CPC, which is supported by economic achievements. Externally, the core issue is to resolve the "Taiwan question" as a political factor that exclusively positions the PRC with respect to the international community. However, while this dispute remains a priority, the external strategy aims to continue the design of functional foreign policy toward modernization. Therefore, China will not interfere in its successful strategy to resolve a dispute that develops in favor of its interests, because of greater asymmetry with Taiwan, unless a sudden change transforms the Strait situation and requires its intervention[9]. Thus, domestic and foreign policies are interrelated and they are seen from Beijing as joint deployment areas of political behavior,[10] although the core presupposition of China's interest is to guarantee the existence of the PRC and a one-party totalitarian regime[11].

The "Taiwan question" has special characteristics for Chinese foreign policy and the Sino-Latin American relationship. This region does not have a homogeneous policy towards the PRC and it is the place where Taiwan concentrates its most widespread support in the diplomatic battle with the Taipei authorities. Latin America is the bastion of Taiwan in the world, since more than a half of the countries that recognized it are in this region[12]. Besides, the role of Latin American countries at the United Nations is important, because they form a group of coordinated action in areas important to the PRC. Therefore, economic modernization and the "Taiwan question" are significant factors in preserving political unity.

So the Chinese national interest is defined by the following priorities:

1. Preserve the PRC and its political system under the leadership of the Chinese Communist Party;
2. Continue, improve and deepen modernization, ensuring access to markets and raw materials in order to maintain the virtuous circle of "investment-resources, production and market" which tends to keep the process of economic transformation in the context of international crisis;
3. Resolve the "Taiwan question" as part of its national strategy to consolidate the recognition of its political power in the community of nations[13].

Those interests are in harmony or tension with Latin American interests and create a network of "common interests, concurrent or complementary, and contradictory" (Friedrich, 1968). These are highly dependent on tangible and intangible capabilities of the states, factors which, in turn, determine their relative positions in the international structure (Waltz, 1979: 119) and form different "relations of power". For example, the positions of China and Argentina in the international structure define an asymmetrical power relationship, as a "North-South model"; that is, a major economic power (China) and one country that still does not become a middle power (Argentina) from the economic point of view. In contrast, the Sino-Brazilian relations express the "North-North model", because both nations are members of the Directory of great powers, as shown in Table 1.

Table 2: Sino-Latin American relations of power (from international relations)

Country	Model
Brazil	North-North relations
Other country	North-South relations

Criteria: According to the asymmetries of power and position in the international structure.

This way of defining the "model of relations" can be criticized by economists because the components of the Sino-Brazilian trade still appear as a "North-South model": high percentage share of primary products in Brazilian exports against imports of Chinese industrial goods, which show variability on the in-dustrialization level of the states and, hence, different levels of modernization. However, from the perspective of international relations (whose object of study is the international political reality), these "power relations" between the system units are highly influenced by the asymmetries, formed by power capabilities and the position that they occupy in those international structures. In this scheme, the links with other Latin American countries follow the "North-South model", not only due to the asymmetries, capabilities and positions in the international structure, but also to the components of their exports.

Table 3: Sino-Latin American relations of power (from economy)

Country	Model
All Latin American countries	North-South relations

Criteria: According to the component of trade.

Interests and political will in Sino-Latin American relations

Those interests are closely linked to the Latin American growth model, be-cause, according to how we define the model, the content of economic exchange will vary. However, the political will of each unit appears within the immaterial capabilities, externalized in the behavior expressed through products or political decisions to endorse a particular model. In this matter, there are two trends: 1) the countries that want to deploy relations with China under the "North-South scheme" and adapt their economies to the new international division of labor; 2) those political units that want to support the "de-primarization"[14] of their economies to overcome this traditional model. In the first case, cooperation will be greater than conflict; in the second, tension will clearly coexist with cooperation.

Complementary interests are more likely to appear in the "North-South model": especially with Latin American raw material exports to China, the import of

Table 4: First three products exported to China by the Latin American and Caribbean countries - 2006-2008

Country	Product 1	%	Product 2	%	Product 3	%	1+2+3
Argentina	Soybean	55	Soybean oil	24	Crude oil	10	89
Bolivia	Tin ore	27	Tin ore	19	Crude oil	17	63
Brazil	Iron ore	44	Soybean	23	Crude oil	6	73
Chile	Copper	50	Copper ore	31	Wood pulp	6	87
Colombia	Oil crude	50	Ferroalloys	40	Nonferrous waste	5	95
Cuba	Nickel metal	71	Raw sugar	20	Common mineral	7	98
Ecuador	Oil crude	94	Nonferrous waste	3	Non-coniferous wood	1	98
Mexico	Integrated circuits	13	Copper ore	8	Office equipment parts	7	28
Paraguay	Cotton	31	Coniferous wood	26	Leather	24	81
Peru	Copper ore	39	Offal	16	Crude oil	10	65
Uruguay	Soybean	46	Wood pulp	13	Wool	9	68
Venezuela	Crude oil	51	Iron ore	9	Spiegel	2	62

Source: CEPAL, *La República Popular China y América Latina y el Caribe: hacia una relación estratégica,* Santiago de Chile, 2010.

Chinese industrial products and the Chinese investments in non-renewable resources sectors. This is the present situation of the economic relationship that turned China into the one of the main trade partners of all Latin American countries. However, tensions emerge in the relationship when these countries increase industrialization, add more value to their exports and try to ensure local labor. In that sense, the "dilemma of non-renewable resources" in the rivalry between Chinese and Latin American modernizations, the investment attraction from third regions, the export competition over third markets and the protectionist reaction against offensive Chinese products in the region indicate a more contentious relationship that the one that has been maintained until now, except in those countries that are backing the "primarization" of their foreign trade.

Hence, cooperation or conflict between Latin America and China emerge according to the will of each political unit in the face of the growth model, but coexist in the short and medium term because of the incipient industrialization of regional countries. In both cases, non-renewable resources are essential for the modernization of the region. They will produce a dilemma in defining the interests of nations in the short and long term, at least until the trend to "de-primarization" has been consolidated, without ignoring the viability of cooperation on renewable resources. In that sense, the agenda of interests in the Sino-Latin American relationship shows the following aspects:

- *Complementary interests and "the dilemma of non-renewable resources".* China's economic diplomacy creates channels for direct access to raw materials so as to continue with its economic growth and achieve the goal of modernization. However, if the objective of the Latin American region is also to modernize and to achieve economic development, in the future these economies will need more energy and minerals. If the region transfers these non-renewable resources, it will obstruct its future modernization and it will need those resources from other regions, as does China today after plundering its own.
  This "dilemma of non-renewable resources" emerges when we classify national interests as short, medium and long term, according to scope. It is clear that the Latin American governments aspire to concrete benefits in the short term, as a result of the export of its non-renewable natural resources. However, because these are finite, they simultaneously alienate long-term interests needed for their own modernization. The present plunder of these resources constitutes an obstacle to the future growth and development of these nations. So from a long-term perspective, this sector of the economy should be protected on account of its potential strategic value, although there are contradictions in mineral exporting economies (such as Bolivia, Colombia, Cuba, Chile, Ecuador, Peru and Venezuela, as we can see in Table 4), whose exports to China are dependent on these productions. The trade policies of the states in this region should at least find a balance between the interests of the short and the long term.
  It is reasonable to note that the protection of non-renewable resources does not imply rejecting cooperation on renewable resources. This is the area where the above-mentioned "economic complementarity" comes to life. However, if we look at table 4, most exports are concentrated in non-renewable resources (oil, tin, iron, copper, nickel, ferroalloys, etc.) and, to a lesser extent in renewable resources (soybean, soybean oil, raw sugar, cotton, coniferous wood, leather, etc.).

- *Latin American "de-primarization" and trade tensions.* Complementation is viable insofar as Latin America's exports are based mainly on commodities and China's demand remains constant. However, when governments seek to add value through industrialization, trade tension appears as the main factor. As a result, the "de-primarization" of export increases the possibility of friction with China. A significant example of this tension to be found in Argentine-Chinese relations was when China banned the importations of crude soybean oil from this country. In the last decade, Argentina's trade policy decided to process soybeans giving added value to their exports, while China persisted in buying the soybeans in order to industrialize them

119

in Huadong, a core region for grain processing, as was revealed in the trade crisis of 2010.

Argentina as an exporter of raw materials for food deems China an important partner, especially because of its need to maintain food security. Dependence remains in the field of renewable commodities, where the soybean and its byproducts occupy 80% of the total exports to China. However, the recent crisis has not caused the expected vulnerability, because Argentina's trade policy was able to mitigate the Chinese ban by selling soybean oil to alternative markets or processing it into biofuels. In the case of imports, there are no Chinese products that cannot be acquired in other markets. Moreover, although China is an important partner of Argentina's (representing around 10% of its sales abroad), exports are decentralized, except in trade with Brazil, where the exports to this market surpass more than 20% of them. Therefore, from the point of view of the theory of interdependence, vulnerability was not observed when the disruption of Chinese purchases occurred because there was no change in the policy framework (Keohane and Nye: 1988).

- *Economic growth and competition on third markets.* To these tensions another variant is added. While the Latin American nations tend to develop their export capacities, competition from China in third markets is emerging. An example of this is the challenge to Mexican industrial products in the United States, despite the geographical proximity to that country and a free trade agreement (FTA) like NAFTA. In South America, Brazil began to find competition from China in the world. In the case of Argentina, despite their geographical proximity and being benefited by the FTA with Brazil under the MERCOSUR framework, China has displaced it from the top position as provider to the Brazilian market.

- *Dumping, antidumping and market economy.* There is also competition in domestic markets, where China's dumping policy faces anti-dumping barriers and other local restrictions on the access of Chinese products, except in countries that have signed FTA with China and support the "primarization" of their economies in the new international division of labor (Chile, Peru). The "threat" of the dumping of Chinese products distorts domestic markets, although it is impossible to apply this concept to all countries in the region. For example, the "threat" becomes "salvation" to consumers in the depressed Cuban economy, due to deficient industrialization and shortages of goods because of the sanctions imposed by the United States and the European Union. However, we must bear in mind that this is a special case.

The persistent anti-dumping measures applied by Latin American governments to Chinese products have, since the middle of the first decade of the century, prompted Beijing's government to implement an offensive diplomacy towards the countries of the region to obtain the recognition of China as a market economy. In the effort to deepen relations with China and under pressure from the threat of losing the Chinese market, several countries (including Argentina, Brazil, Chile, Jamaica, Peru, Trinidad and Tobago and Venezuela) recognized that status, as well as a total of 97 members of the World Trade Organization (WTO), except major economies like the European Union, the United States, Japan and India.

However, when China was aspiring to gain that recognition (especially in the context of the international crisis and the rise of Keynesianism measures), it came to light that such a principle clashes with local economic interests. A report on the Latin American and Caribbean Economic System (SELA) states: that the countries that granted such recognition took the initiative to open dumping investigation from the fourth quarter of 2008 to the fourth quarter of 2009 (SELA, 2010: 29-30). Such measures expose the conflicting interests that arise between Chinese products and local industrialization, making this kind of commitment meaningless.

- *Turning point in Chinese investments.* Initially, Latin America is an important destination for Chinese investment. In 2009, the region accounted for 13% of the total Chinese FDI abroad, coming second after Asia, a continent which represented 71.5% of the total investments in the world.

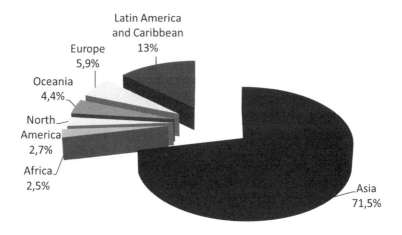

Graphic 2: Distribution of Chinese FDI by regions and continents - Year 2009

This percentage drops sharply to 0.6% of that total when excluding two "tax havens" (the Cayman Islands and the Virgin Islands) which as a whole reached 95.2% of the total for Latin America out of a total investment amounting to 6.978 US million dollars. Apart from these two destinations, only the remaining 4.8% corresponded to Chinese investments in the region, i.e. 350 US million dollars, of which 116 were destined to Brazil and 115 to Venezuela, leaving only 120 US million dollars to be distributed among the other nations, which represented 1.6% of the total for the region.

It is worth noting that Chinese investments have a similar tenor in all the countries, except in those which recognize the Republic of China, where more political influence appears than in the others. However, in contrast to Taiwan, the PRC has developed a strategy not for financial but rather for commercial attractiveness to those countries. Moreover, while Chinese investments in the region are still small, they grew slowly in absolute terms between 2005 and 2009, as shown in the following table:

Table 5: Main destinations of non-financial foreign direct investment of the People's Republic of China in Latin America - 2005-2009

Country and region	2005	2006	2007	2008	2009
Argentina	0.35	6.22	136.69	10.82	-22.82
Bolivia	0.08	18.00	1.97	4.14	18.01
Brazil	15.09	10.09	51.13	22.38	116.27
Chile	1.80	6.58	3.83	0.93	7.70
The Cayman Islands	5162.75	7832.72	2601.59	1524.01	5366.30
The Virgin Islands	1226.08	538.11	1876.14	2104.33	1612.05
Mexico	3.55	-3.69	17.16	5.63	0.82
Paraguay	-	-	-	3.00	6.47
Peru	0.55	5.40	6.71	24.55	58.49
Venezuela	7.40	18.36	69.53	9.78	115.72
Latin America and the Caribbean	6.466.16	8.468.74	4.902.41	3.677.25	7.329.90
Total world	12.261.17	17.633.97	26.508.09	55.907.17	56.528.99

Source: State Administration of Foreign Exchange, National Bureau of Statistical and Ministry of Commerce of the People's Republic of China, *2009 Statistical Bulletin of China's Outward Foreign Direct Investment,* Beijing, 2009: 36-37.
Unit: millions US dollars.

The political instability caused by the world economic crisis seems to influence the decision of the CPC to invest greater resources in the region. In fact, in 2010 several Chinese companies invested in Latin American or in foreign capital companies, especially in South America. Brazil received 17,170 million dollars of which 14,340 went into petroleum, natural gas and minerals[15]. Argentina was another major recipient. Chinese investments have changed the pessimistic expectations of political leaders and public opinion since the visit of Hu Jin Tao in 2004. In March 2010, the China National Offshore Oil Corporation (CNOOC) bought 50% of the Bridas Energy Holding. In November, British Petroleum sold 60% of Pan American Energy, acquired by Bridas and CNOOC at 7.059 million dollars. At the end of 2010 the Chinese state company Sinopec announced the purchase of Occidental Petroleum in Argentina for 2,450 US million dollars. These financial transactions are added to the Chinese investment in the production of urea on the island of Tierra del Fuego.

Table 6: Main destinations of non-financial foreign direct investment of the People's Republic of China in Latin America – 2010

Country and region	Realized investments		Announced investments
	1990-2009	2010	Since 2011 start
Argentina	143	5550	3530
Brazil	255	9563	9870
Colombia	1677	3	....
Costa Rica	13	5	700
Ecuador	1619	41	....
Guyana	1000	....	....
Mexico	127	5	....
Peru	2262	84	8648
Venezuela	240	....	....
Latin America and the Caribbean	7336	15251	22724

Source: United Nations Economic Commission for Latin America and the Caribbean (CEPAL), 2010.
Unit: millions US dollars.

This change in China's strategy has been so abrupt and unexpected that in late October 2010 a report of SELA predicted that "In the short and medium term it is unlikely that Latin America and the Caribbean will capture important volumes of China's total investment abroad...." (SELA, 2010: 28). Probably the turning point of Chinese investment policy is associated with three causes: 1) the expected growth of China's economy during and after the world economic crisis; 2) the intensification of the struggle between the powers for strategic raw materials like oil, gas and minerals and the need to control sources of supply; 3) the volatility of the dollar requires changing the United States' reserves for influence and control of business assets.

Chinese investments in the region show themselves as an area of cooperation rather than conflict. Latin American governments welcome Chinese investors, even in the field of non-renewable resources. Most Chinese investments are in that sector and have generated a Chinese lobby which is increasingly influential in political decision-making at national and subnational levels. In addition, more Chinese investments expand the flow of migrants that has risen sharply in number in recent years with growing influence in the region as in the rest of the world.

In short, the struggle between development models, levels of economic openness and interests of the parties give rise to some prospects for cooperation and tension in the relationship with China that we try to classify as follows:

Table 7: Complementation and tension from the Latin American perspective

Kind of external action	Complementation	Tension
Non-renewable resources exports	x	x
Renewable resources exports	x	
Export value-added products	x	
Attracting investment from other regions		x
Chinese capital exports to Latin America	x	
Competition in third markets		x
Competition in home markets		x
Latin America "de-primarization"		x

This table shows that the exportation of non-renewable resources, renewable resources and Chinese investment in the region are cooperative actions. In contrast, the exportation of value-added products to China; the Chinese capacity to absorb foreign direct investment; the competition in third and domestic markets present a new phase in Sino-Latin American relations, characterized by the increase of tension. However, several Latin American countries are comfortable with the exportation of primary goods, including non-renewable resources. Other countries, though, like Argentina, Brazil and Mexico, are struggling to add value to their exportations and the tension with China arises when this commercial policy clashes with its productive capacities.

It is no coincidence that the Chinese government had published its "China's Policy Paper toward Latin America and the Caribbean" in November 2008. In fact, the Chinese hunger for natural resources forces it to deploy "omnidirectional diplomacy" which it needs to ensure these resources and continue the modernization process. The time when the paper was published seems quite opportune, because Latin American countries, accustomed from the beginning to political life being subject to the hegemony of one or several great powers, nowadays witness the erosion of hegemonic power, without knowing the extent of the damage it has caused and its consequences for the region. The Chinese government takes into account the regional situation and it understands that the United States economic contraction generates higher margins of autonomy and greater viability than the Latin-American countries have had during the "Cold War" and the "Washington primacy order". In addition, European countries are suffering the economic crisis and focus on their internal problems, opening up a favorable scenario for Chinese incursions in the region.

Therefore, the document disguises the new mechanisms of domination, from which it can be inferred that the Chinese influence is seeking to transform itself into a hegemony. Even so, it has to be said that China still lacks three of four elements outlined by Robert Keohane in order to reach the position of hegemonic power. However, the current situation represents an opportunity for it to increase its political influence. In a world fueled by the economic crisis and a high degree of unrest, where the redistribution of economic power affects the balance of power, it is quite possible that China will be able to reduce the gap with the superpower sooner than foreseen by the academic world, as is shown in table 1.

Conclusion

The recent experiences in East Asia and India show that it is possible to rise in the global economic stratification and to achieve leadership positions in the world economy. On account of this, a big number of the Latin American nations which have already made the transition to democracy have to face "second generation transitions", not political but socioeconomic ones, to consolidate democratic processes with economic modernization. Moreover, it is imperative to create autonomous modernization models which take into account the political behavior patterns of successful experiences and, undoubtedly, China's is one of these. In the absence of this substantial change, Latin American nations will continue to hold the power roles that they have had in the past half century or be overtaken by other countries in the international struggle, with the only exception being Brazil.

Like India, Latin American countries are in a better position than China, because the PRC still has to make the political transition. This process is different from economic reform. In fact, due to the experiences of the former Soviet Union and other Communist countries, this political transition involves a traumatic change, with an impact on the economic system. Therefore, the challenge to modernize democracy excludes the Chinese political regime, because it suffers pressure from its economic modernization to transit to a pluralist, democratic and participative regime. Sorman, however, questions the mechanistic theory that China's economy will engender the middle class which will demand democracy (Sorman, 2007: 148). As for the Chinese government, it is aware of the necessary process of change and intends to move in the direction of creating a more participative political system, though evidence of this still cannot be observed in reality. Probably China's agenda will prioritize the resolution of the "Taiwan question" before political change, because there is a competitive political power on the island, which, although diplomatically cornered, presents a de *facto* situation that diminishes international recognition of the PRC.

If modernization has spread in East Asia and India, it might also come to be anchored in Latin America. So it is necessary to define who will guide the process and where it will start geographically. The model to be adopted might be "monistic", that is, from top to bottom. However, the region is immersed in pluralistic and democratic regimes, which implies involving them as actors in the negotiations for decision-making processes. In fact, what is required is that the modernizing elites reach some kind of commitment (tacit or expressed) which permit the reduction of ideological distances and harmonize partisan interests. Thus basic agreements on the orientation of modernization can be established so that political alternation will not prove to be an obstacle to political regime stability, generating the continuity of orientation in time. Obviously, this aspect involves political autonomy and the rapid resolution of the crises that the resultant modernization will bring about.

According to China's experience, foreign policy needs to be functional to modernization to ensure favorable environmental conditions. Aiming at this objective, its function is to maintain a pacific external environment, using peaceful conflict resolutions and to form an economic *entente* to avoid isolation and integrate the state into the international community. Indeed, foreign policy goes together with economic expansion and resolves, quickly and peacefully, emerging crises in order to ensure the stability of the political system in times of growth. Association with the hegemonic powers is essential to the initiation and development of modernization, similar to the PRC and the other successful experiences of East Asia and India. In turn, the Chinese market has been important in attracting FDI and orientating world exports which, in the case of Latin American countries, generate economic consensus and conceal differences with China on human rights.

China's interest in Latin America prioritizes the need to obtain essential raw materials to continue its modernization. Given the size of the population, China has plundered many of the non-renewable resources in its territory and is now venturing into other regions to obtain them and stabilize its access channels. This is one of the objectives of the "omnidirectional diplomacy" in the context of the North-South scheme (except Brazil). However, in these countries the "dilemma of non-renewable resources" brings into conflict short and long term interests. National and subnational governments are optimistic as to continuing to export more to China, although it is clear that these resources are important for use in the modernization of Latin America rather than in serving the modernization of others. Obviously this policy does not apply to renewable resources, where so-called "complementarity" appears. On the other hand, significant Chinese investments in non-renewable resources, particularly in Argentina and Brazil in 2010, produced a major change in the financial strategy toward the region and they predict the continued export of these resources to China.

The Chinese factor is relevant to Latin American trade. However, according to which model of growth governments assume, the prospects for developing relations with China tend to follow two different paths. Those who accept the "North-South relations" and the current international division of labor will find a path to sustainability in their cooperation with China. By contrast, those who adopt the "de-primarization" of economies (with the consequent export of industrial products to third markets and the protection of domestic markets) will increase the tension with China as their industrial capacities grow. However, as several Latin American countries are in the process of "de-primarization", logically both cooperation through the export of raw materials and the tension of incipient industrialization will coexist for many years. If, however, Latin American economies aspire to consolidate their modernization, the relationship will not be as pleasant as it has been so far.

Notes

1   The Pareto Optimal is based on criteria of utility: if something generates or produces profit, comfort, achievements or interest without damage to others, it awakens the natural process of optimization that will allow the achievement of an optimal point (Moreno, 2010).

2   A disturbance is an influence that another political system or extra-societal system exerts on the political system, often causing tensions (Easton, 1982: 224-226).

3   The socialization process limits and shapes the behavior of states in the same way that society sets rules of conduct that limit the behavior of individuals. In contrast, competition is between states, adjusting their relations through acts and autonomous decisions (Waltz, 1979: 119).

4   A gentler version of this model has been used in South Korea, where modernization is associated with the military coup of General Park Chung Hee, while the Republic of China has modernized the island of Taiwan under the dictatorship of Chiang Kai-shek and his son, Chiang Ching -kuo. Similarly, the Liberal Democratic Party governed Japan without political alternation for more than four decades.

5   The "third wave of democratization" includes Portugal, Spain and Greece, the Latin American countries and also Taiwan.

6   Modernization involves increasing the operating variable of the political system, comprising the rational orientation, structural differentiation and capacity. Its effect is an increase in the dominion that the political system has on the environment, which means greater control of the means (resources). (Oviedo, 2005: 92).

7   "From now on, we will continue, according to the desire of Chinese people and the situation in China, to advance with stability and security in a positive way in the reformation of the political system, developing socialist democracy. We will further enrich formal democracy; expand orderly political participation of our citizens by implementing a strategic project of the legal state, ensuring that citizens agree with the laws, take part in democratic elections, democratic policy making, democratic management, democratic control. We wish to note the useful experience of political construction in foreign countries, but not copy the model of the political systems in foreign countries" (Hu, 2006).

8   This logic of party excluded political dissent, which has promoted democracy as a "fifth modernization" since 1979 and operates clandestinely and illegally. However, the dissent was losing leadership because of economic expansion and the nationalist attitude of the emigrants who would not affect, with their opposition, the strengthening and promotion of the People's Republic of China in the international system.

9   The "White Paper" on relations with Taiwan proposed three uses of force scenarios: 1) if a grave turn of events occurs leading to the separation of Taiwan from China in any name, 2) if Taiwan is invaded and occupied by foreign countries, or 3) if the Taiwan authorities refuse, sine die, the peaceful settlement of cross-Straits reunification through negotiations. In República Popular China, Consejo de Estado, Oficina de Asuntos Taiwaneses, *El principio de una sola China y el problema de Taiwan*, Beijing, 21 de febrero de 2000.

10 Political behavior "is the behavior as a response to a particular situation which confronts the actor involved in a political relationship" (Melo, 1983: 171).

11 The survival instinct of the political unit is common to all states. This state of need of the political unit has originated in two of the main features of the international system: the de-concentration of power and the absence of a supreme authority. As Duroselle stated (2000: 124): "We must put aside security, because in essence it is

a common goal to all states, all political units, in the sense that any community is primarily proposed to survive."

12 In 2010 a total of 23 nations recognized Taiwan. 12 of them are in Latin America: eleven in Central America (Belize, El Salvador, Guatemala, Haiti, Honduras, Nicaragua, Panama, Dominican Republic, San Cristobal and Nevis, Saint Lucia and Saint Vincent and the Grenadines) and one in South America (Paraguay).

13 François Godement says: "The challenge is to find out what China needs and cannot get by its own means. First, despite its useful approach towards multilateral institutions, China needs the international system. The international monetary rules, the system of trade, security and access to resources are essential for its development. Secondly, it requires tangible assets such as commodities, including oil, technology, market access and national and overseas security, including security for financial assets. It is particularly vulnerable in Africa, where its assets are growing at a phenomenal rate but has little influence on security matters. Thirdly, we must bear in mind that China has intangible needs such as international recognition. As the tributary system was once a source of amour-propre for the Chinese bureaucracy, the current regime depends to some degree on international recognition as a sign of legitimacy to their citizens."

14 Pierre Salama (2008: 836) says: "There is no scientific definition of "primary", but we can say that an economy is primary if the exports of primary products dominate the total and it is in process of primarization if this segment tends to increase significantly." Inversely, you can asseverate the concept of "de-primarization", when the prevalence of primary products decreased compared to their share in total exports in previous times.

15 *Brasil: 84,5 por ciento de las inversiones chinas se destina a metalurgia y minería,* in Información y análisis de América Latina, Río de Janeiro, april14, 2011, en http://www.infolatam.com/2011/04/14/brasil-845-por-ciento-de-inversion-china-se-destina-a-metalurgia-y-mineria/

References

Almond, Gabriel A. (1999) *Una disciplina segmentada. Escuelas y corrientes en las ciencias políticas.* México: Fondo de Cultura Económica.

Baisley, Paul J. (2002) *China en el siglo XX.* Barcelona: Ariel Pueblos.

Bobbio, Norberto; Matteucci, Nicola and Pasquino, Gianfranco (1995) *Diccionario de Política.* Madrid: Siglo XXI.

CEPAL, Comisión Económica para América Latina y el Caribe (2010) *La República Popular China y América Latina y el Caribe: hacia una relación estratégica.* Santiago de Chile: Naciones Unidas.

Domenach, Jean-Luc (2006) *¿Adónde va China?* Buenos Aires: Paidós.

Duroselle, Jean Batipte (2000) *Todo imperio perecerá. Teoría sobre las relaciones internacionales.* México: Fondo de Cultura Económica.

Easton, David (1976) *Esquema para el análisis político*. Buenos Aires: Amorrortu.

Easton, David (1982) *Enfoques sobre teoría política*. Buenos Aires: Amorrortu.

Fanjul, Enrique (1999) *El dragón en el huracán. Retos y esperanzas de China ante el siglo XXI*. Madrid: Política Exterior, Biblioteca Nueva.

Fiedrich, Carl J. (1968) *El hombre y el gobierno. Una teoría empírica de la política*. Madrid: Tecnos.

Godement, François (2010) "Por una política global de la UE hacia China", *Estudios de Política Exterior*, 24 (137). Available at http://www.politicaexterior.com/articulo?id=4352

Huntington Samuel P. (1994) *La tercera ola. La democratización a finales del siglo XX*. Buenos Aires: Paidós.

Hu, Jintao (2006) "President Hu Jintao's speech at Yale University", April 24th. Available at http://news.xinhuanet.com/politics/2006-04/24/content_4466624.htm

Keohane, Robert O. (1988) *Después de la hegemonía: Cooperación y discordia en la política económica mundial*. Buenos Aires: Grupo Editor Latinoamericano.

Keohane, Robert O. and Nye, Joseph S. (1988) *Poder e interdependencia. La política mundial en transición*. Buenos Aires: Grupo Editor Latinoamericano.

Melo, Artemio Luis (1983) *Compendio de Ciencia Política*. Buenos Aires: Depalma.

Moreno, Marco Antonio (2010) "¿Qué es el Óptimo de Pareto?". Available at http://www.elblogsalmon.com/conceptos-de-economia/que-es-un-optimo-de-pareto

Mueller, Marion (2008) "China se reafirma como 1° productor mundial de oro en el 2008". Available at http://www.fxstreet.es/fundamental/mercado/boletin-semanal-del-precio-del-oro/2008-11-18.html

O'Donnell, Guillermo (1988) "La transición en Brasil: continuidades y paradojas", in Instituto de América Latina de la Academia de Ciencias Sociales de China, *Colección de Ponencias del Simposio Internacional "América Latina en el Umbral de los Años 90"*. Beijing: China Construction Press.

Oviedo, Eduardo Daniel (2005) *China en Expansión. La política exterior desde la normalización chino-soviética hasta la adhesión a la OMC (1989-2001)*. Córdoba: Educc.

Oviedo, Eduardo Daniel (2006) "China en América Latina: ¿influencia o hegemonía?", *Dialogo Político*, 23(2): 199-220.

Oviedo, Eduardo Daniel (2011) "La proyección de la ZICOSUR en el mundo: el horizonte de cooperación y rivalidad económica con China", Observatorio de la Política China. Available at http://www.igadi.org/

Oficina de Asuntos Taiwaneses del Consejo de Estado de la República Popular China (2000) *El principio de una sola China y el problema de Taiwan,* Beijing, 21 de febrero.

Ministry of Commerce of the People's Republic of China, *Statistical.* Available at http://www.mofcom.gov.cn/

State Administration of Foreign Exchange, National Bureau of Statistical and Ministry of Commerce of the People's Republic of China, *2009 Statistical Bulletin of China's Outward Foreign Direct Investment,* Beijing, 2009.

Salama, Pierre (2008) "Argentina: el alza de las materias primas agrícolas, ¿una oportunidad?" *Revista Comercio Exterior,* 58(12): 836-851.

SELA, Sistema Económico Latinoamericano y del Caribe (2010) *Evolución reciente de las relaciones económicas entre la República Popular China y América Latina y el Caribe. Mecanismos institucionales y de cooperación para su fortalecimiento,* Caracas: SELA.

Sorman, Guy (2007) *China. El imperio de las mentiras.* Buenos Aires: Sudamericana.

Waltz, Kenneth N. (1979) *Theory of International Politics.* New York: Random House.

Wu, Yu-shan (2003) "La reforma económica china en una perspectiva comparativa: Asia vs. Europa", *Universidad Nacional de Chengchi, Estudios y Publicaciones,* 4(2): 1-49.

World Bank (2002-2009) *World Development Report.* Washington: The World Bank.

Chapter 4

The Return of the Dragon
China's Transformation and Its New International Role and Expansion in Latin America

We know we have to play the game your way now.
But in ten years we will set the rules!

Chinese Ambassador to the WTO
during the negotiations on China's entry
(Quoted in Bergsten, 2008: 65)

Many analysts of political economy and international relations agree that, for the last quarter of the 20th Century, there has been a remarkable process of reallocation of the global economic epicenter from the North Atlantic to East Asia (Frank, 1993; Arrighi, 1996; Hobsbawm 2008, Martins, 2009). Undoubtedly, the People's Republic of China (PRC) is a key player in this global shifting of power. In fact, the heritage left by ancient China's celestial empire and its population of over 1.3 billion have led to the common assumption that China is bound to become the next superpower.

On the verge of this emerging international structure, it is necessary to understand the features and implications of China's global rise and the domestic sources driving it (e.g., its stages of reform), as well as to attempt to estimate the present and future impact of the PRC on Latin American countries, highlighting the opportunities and challenges that these circumstances may entail. This paper seeks to understand such implications and impacts through an analysis of China's global rise and its impact on Latin America.

The Inner Transformation

An old Chinese proverb states that "the best closed door is the one that can be left open". China's transformation during the last 60 years depicts this wisdom, indeed. Unexpectedly for many, after nearly three decades of tight state control over the economy, under the leadership of Mao Zedong, the ruling elite that succeeded him in power decided at by the end of the 1970s to "open a closed door" and undertake an ambitious process of modernization, liberalization and economic openness. The Chinese government, headed by Zhou Enlai, and after him by Deng Xiaoping, embarked on the task of modernizing the country in four strategic areas: agriculture, industry, science and technology, and national defense.

The central concern behind this transformation was to narrow the development gap between China and the most advanced countries, specifically neighboring countries like Japan, South Korea, Taiwan and Hong Kong. For Deng, China could only become a great power through a policy of systematic modernization, with emphasis on economic development while maintaining the structure of political control over the Communist Party (CP) (Wilhelmy and Soto, 2005: 52). The challenge ahead was to leave behind an impoverished, stagnant, closed, and planned economy, and to move forward to a competitive market economy.

According to journalist Li Datong (2009), the reform policy had two very clear stages. In the first one, which took place between 1978 and 1989, the impetus for change was placed upon reducing rural and urban poverty. In the second one, which began in 1992 with Deng's famous trip to the South of the country and culminated in 2001 with the entry of China into the World Trade Organization (WTO), the government focused its efforts on promoting economic growth in close partnership with business sectors.

The main decisions were: the collectivization of agriculture and the authorization of private use of communal lands (the Household Responsibility System); the lifting of the ban on private business activities; the opening to foreign capital inflows for the first time since the Revolution of 1948; the creation of Special Economic Zones (there are currently twenty SEZ among cities, provinces and coastal areas); the privatization of many enterprises (with the exception of a few large monopolies linked to energy and the banking system); the decentralization of the national government control in favor of the provincial governments; the general reduction in tariffs and trade barriers; and finally, the legal recognition of private property in 2005.

These reforms made possible the so-called "Chinese miracle", namely, such great economic performance since 1978. Between that year and 2006, the PRC maintained an annual average growth of 9.7%—a trend that was interrupted only after the events of Tiananmen Square in 1989 and during the last regional crisis in 1997 and 1998 (Zhao, 2006: 3). While the initial expectations were to quadruple the GDP by the early 2th Century, from 1978 to 2006, the actual GDP performance showed an impressive growth of thirteen times. Foreign trade has increased fivefold in the last ten years, while its share in world trade over the same period has more than doubled, reaching in 2007, 9% in exports and 6.8% in overall imports. China increased its market penetration in developed economies and simultaneously became a major export destination, especially for the economies of the Asian region, thus turning itself into a new hub of global trade—the largest exporter and third largest importer in 2007—and striving to overtake the United States, European Union and Japan (D'Elía et al., 2008: 67-8).

One of the main sources of this trade expansion has been the growing number of foreign firms in the country that rely on low production costs for their operations. In fact, the participation of such firms in Chinese exports rose from 10% in 1990 to almost 60% in 2004 (Blonigen and Ma, 2010: 475). This phenomenon, called "processing trade," shows that China became the largest recipient of foreign direct investment (FDI) among developing countries for the first time in 1993, and one of the world's top three between 2003 and 2005 (Cheng and Ma, 2010: 545). Furthermore, the commercial success and the big attraction of capital bolstered its international reserves: while in 1992 the reserves were US$19 billion, equivalent to 4% of GDP, fifteen years later they had reached US$1.4 trillion, corresponding to 50% of GDP (Truman, 2008: 169).

It should also be noted that the Chinese structure of exports has changed dramatically since 1992. Along with a steady and significant decline in the share of agriculture and light manufacturing, such as textiles, it has shown a significant growth in advanced manufacturing, in such areas as mechanics, consumer electronics, appliances and computers. This change also confirms that its comparative advantage continues to be the specialization in labor-intensive goods (Amiti and Freund, 2010: 35).

The lag in agricultural exports and indeed, the transition from exporter to net importer of these kinds of goods, is due to the unprecedented process of opening up the sector, conducted by means of a large reduction in tariffs and the elimination of export subsidies, in order to institutionally bolster the country in the face of its coming entry into the WTO. Along with its voracious demand for raw materials, large Chinese purchases of agricultural commodities have brought significant revenue especially for the agricultural-primary exporting economies. It is worth noting, however, that China's agriculture has grown rapidly in recent years (Huang et al., 2010: 397).

Table 1: China: GDP evolution and its share of world GDP

Current GDP in US$billions	Percentage share of world GDP	World Ranking
388	1,7	10
1.198	3,8	6
2.244	5	5
2.645	5,5	4
3.251	6	4

Source: D'Elía et al., 2008: 68.

Table 2: China's position in world trade

20	19
14	9
13	16
11	12
7	8
3	3
3	3
2	3

Source: D'Elía et al., 2008: 71.

The main domestic transformation has been the gradual establishment of a "socialist market economy." Its progress is quite evident: by 1979 all industries were state-owned or "collective," and the state controlled the prices of 97% of the products in circulation; while in the late 1990s less than 30% of the companies remained under state control and market forces determined 97% of prices. Since 2001, these margins have remained largely constant.

But this economic rise has its own obstacles, challenges and weaknesses, which will test its potential for future growth. On the one hand, China is still a poor country in terms of *per capita* income, estimated in 2010 at US$4,260 per year, equivalent to only 10% of income in the U.S. and Europe. This low score is combined with a severe revenue concentration, in which 90% of the wealth is accumulated by the richest 1% of the population (Datong, 2009). The reason behind this social burden lies in privatization, liberalization and the sharp contrast between the interior and the most dynamic coastal and industrial areas—57% of the GDP is produced in eastern China, 26% in the central region and only 17% in the west (D'Elía et al., 2008: 69). Consequently, this explains why economic growth is mainly driven by exports and investment rather than by domestic consumption.

On the other hand, environmental problems have become truly pressing. The PRC recently replaced the U.S. as the largest emitter of greenhouse gases. As a consequence of increasing car ownership and of polluting industries (and the many coal processing plants), air quality has deteriorated in major cities. For example, the concentration of toxic particles in Beijing in 2008 exceeded by 80% the tolerable standard set by the World Health Organization (Jacobs, 2010). In rural areas, the use of fertilizers and pesticides *en masse* to bolster agricultural productivity has contaminated much of the watersheds.

Concerning the challenges, it must be added that the PRC is not a democracy. The political system is essentially an authoritarian government, ruled by actors that are imposed through intra-party and bureaucratic struggles, waged behind closed doors in Beijing (Wilhelmy and Soto, 2005: 53). Far from being a "harmonious society," there have been major social conflicts based on different claims: a cry for greater democracy, better living conditions, recognition of political autonomy in the case of Tibet, among others. Since the days of Deng, the rule has been to contain domestic dissent with a "strong fist", as evidenced by the Tiananmen Square episode in 1989. In September 2003, Human Rights Watch reported that more than three million people participated in various protests in just one month and that, in more than one hundred cases across the country, these demonstrations escalated into violent clashes with local security forces and the destruction of governmental buildings (Becker, 2006: 169). Therefore, it remains to be seen whether the political system will would be able to adapt to the radical social changes already under way, and how it will open the game to new actors in the struggle for power.

The New International Role of China and Its Expansion in Latin America

Despite these challenges, there is a strong global consensus on the ongoing rise of China to great power status. Napoleon's famous prediction—"Let China sleep, for when she wakes, she will shake the world"—seems to be finding confirmation (Kynge, 2006). In fact, according to Susan Shirk, who was responsible in the State

Department for bilateral relations with the PRC during the Clinton administration, China is "reemerging as a major power after one hundred and fifty years of being a weak player on the world stage - a brief hiatus in China's long history" (2007: 4). Considering its structural position, a recent estimate of China's comprehensive power compared with other major powers in the international system gives the following results (Table 3).

Table 3: Early 21st Century State Power Structure for China, France, Britain, Russia, Japan, Germany and India

	China	France	Britain	Russia	Japan	Germany	India
Military Power	Strong	Strong	Strong	Strong	Weak	Weak	Strong
Political Power	Strong	Strong	Strong	Strong	Weak	Weak	Weak
Economic Power	Strong	Weak	Weak	Weak	Strong	Strong	Weak

Source: Yan, Xuetong (2006: 21)

Here, we see that the PRC is the only power with a strong status in each of the three dimensions analyzed, and thus the principal strategic competitor behind the American superpower. This has triggered a major debate about the potential conflict between these two actors in which there are at least two positions to distinguish: the "unpeaceful rise" of China under an intense security competition and contention for hegemony (Mearsheimer, 2006, 2010), and the "accommodation" of this rise in the *Liberal international order* led by the United States (Ikenberry, 2008; Rosecrance, 2006).

It is also necessary to look at the new Chinese international protagonism in a more dynamic way. In this regard, the country is increasingly playing critical roles in various global issues - from non-proliferation to climate change - besides being a subject of controversy in the West on issues related to unemployment, trade deficits, and human rights. In the last decade, the PRC has combined its economic dynamism with pragmatic policies on security and defense, and strong diplomatic outreach. As a result, it has begun establishing strong relationships not only in Asia but also in Europe, Africa and South America. "While these developments predate September 11, 2001, they have unfolded at a time of strategic preoccupation on the part of the United States, both in military operations in Afghanistan and Iraq and in the global counterterrorism campaign. This last, in turn, has opened strategic space for China to expand its influence at both regional and global levels" (Gill, 2007: 1).

It is noteworthy that historian Paul Kennedy has once again stated his thesis on the long-term decline of United States, identifying current weaknesses in the capacity to project its soft power and in its economic performance - severely beaten by the last economic crisis. In his conclusions, he wrote:

> [T]he ebb and tides of history will take away [the American] hegemony, as surely as autumn replaces the high summer months with fruit rather than flower. America's global position is at present strong, serious, and very large. But it is still, frankly, abnormal. It will come down a ratchet or two more. It will return from being an oversized world power to being a big nation, but one which needs to be listened to, and one which, for the next stretch, is the only country that can supply powerful heft to places in trouble. It will still be really important, but less so than it was (Kennedy, 2010: 11).

A central process in this trend, following the theoretical proposal of Immanuel Wallerstein (2001), is the ongoing transfer of production capacity from North America (and Europe) to China. Large corporations, like General Electric, Emerson, Honeywell, and Rockwell, have moved most of their manufacturing plants to China. Even a part of the American defense industrial base has been reallocated abroad or relies on inputs from China and its neighbors, which consequently represents a serious threat to the American national security, according to a recent report sponsored by AFL-CIO (Yudken, 2010). Also, the American productive displacement can be observed by simply examining the latest Fotune *500* ranking, for instance (CNN Money, 2011), where only two U.S. companies are among the worldwide top-10: WalMart (1st) and Exxon Mobile (3rd), while there are already three Chinese firms - Sinopec (7th), State Grid (8th) and China National Petroleum (10th). If these trends continue, recent estimates (The Economist, 2010) indicate that by 2019—or by the first half of the next decade - Chinese GDP will exceed the American one for the first time in history.

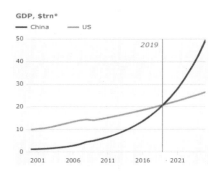

Graphic 1: China vs. U.S. (GDP)
Source: The Economist, December 16, 2010.

It must be added to these considerations that the U.S. is financing its military supremacy and costly war in Afghanistan by means of its fiscal deficit and thanks especially to China's credit. Beijing is now the largest creditor in the world and the largest creditor to the U.S., owning US$800 billion in U.S. Treasury bonds, while Washington continues enlarging its condition as the biggest global borrower with US$14.3 trillion in public debt. The picture gets even worse due to the sustained current account imbalance between the two countries and particularly in the trade balance, which in 2010 registered a surplus of US$273 billion in favor of the PRC (U.S. Census Bureau, 2011).

Although "China still lags behind the United States on many other indicators of power, [and] it's far too soon to talk about a fundamental transfer of power from Washington to Beijing" (Walt, 2011), it must be said that, as Gideon Rachman indicates:

> China's spending on its military continues to grow rapidly. The country will soon announce the construction of its first aircraft carrier and is aiming to build five or six in total. Perhaps more seriously, China's development of new missile and anti-satellite technology threatens the command of the sea and skies on which the United States bases its Pacific supremacy. In a nuclear age, the U.S. and Chinese militaries are unlikely to clash. A common Chinese view is that the United States will instead eventually find it can no longer afford its military position in the Pacific. U.S. allies in the region—Japan, South Korea, and increasingly India—may partner more with Washington to try to counter rising Chinese power. But if the United States has to scale back its presence in the Pacific for budgetary reasons, its allies will start to accommodate themselves to a rising China. Beijing's influence will expand, and the Asia-Pacific region—the emerging center of the global economy—will become China's backyard (Rachman, 2011).

This is just a part of what China's rise can generate geopolitically in relation to the U.S. Perceiving this potential future, recently, John Mearsheimer has again recommended Washington to quickly adopt the strategic option of *off-shore balance*, noting that "the United States should concentrate on making sure that no state dominates Northeast Asia, Europe or the Persian Gulf, and that it remains the world's only regional hegemon. [...] We should build a robust military to intervene in those areas, but it should be stationed offshore or back in the United States" (2011: 31).

In the case of Latin America, the nature of its current ties with China goes back to the end of the Cold War. Before that, during the height of the Cold War in the

1960s and 1970s, Beijing had an ideological approach toward the entire region, considering it as one of the main battlegrounds in the competition for hegemony between the United States and the Soviet Union. This attitude was seen in statements like the following, made by Chinese premier Zhou Enlai in 1972: "The Chinese government and the Chinese people firmly support the just struggle of the Latin American people and believe that a united Latin America, through its struggle, will win a greater victory over the expansionary influence of imperialism [in the form of] new and old colonialism" (as cited in Jiang, 2008: 29).

But both the de-ideologization of China's foreign policy and the worldwide spread of the globalization process provided a framework for strong economic expansion of Sino-Latin American relations (Cesarín, 2006: 52). Some figures illustrate this phenomenon. Exports from Latin America and the Caribbean to China increased suddenly from US$1.5 billions in 1990 to nearly US$3 billions in 1995 and US$5,4 billions in 2000. Between 2000 and 2004 exports grew 42% annually, reaching over US$21 billions. In 2003, primary goods accounted for 45.5% of the basket (Davy, 2008: 4). For its part, China's exports to the region during the 1990's grew more than five times, achieving a global trade surplus that lasted until 2002. However, with countries rich in resources, like Brazil, Argentina, Chile and Peru, the trade balance represented a deficit for Beijing (Cheng, 2006).

A key point in the contemporary China-Latin America relations is to analyze both the opportunities and challenges that this rising power entails to the region. So far, in many Latin American countries there has been a dominant enthusiasm - driven by governments, business communities and some academics - that has overshadowed the negative outcomes. In this sense, there is an urgent need for our societies to understand the stakes at work in the increasing and complex relations with China.

With regard to opportunities, it is possible to identify four positive effects of the Sino-Latin American relations. The first one is a growing political cooperation and coordination at the international level. Here it is important to note that, starting with the Cuban Second War of Independence (1895-1898) and for many decades, the region had been under the regional hegemony of Washington, which considered it as its own backyard. In addition, other great powers like Great Britain, France and Germany tried to keep a certain amount of political and economic influence, particularly in the Southern Cone. Thus, Latin America became what historian Tulio Halperin Donghi called "an arena for hegemonic struggle" (1980). But this situation has been changing in accordance with recent international power shifts. Nowadays, the region is more politically autonomous than before due to the leadership of middle powers such as Brazil and Mexico, and especially due to the process of economic and political integration (through

MERCOSUR, CAN and UNASUR) involving most of the countries. In parallel, the international power structure is moving away from the American unilateralism of the 1990s towards a *rise-of-the-rest* scenario in which China overpasses other great powers, as mentioned above. This trend gives Latin America the opportunity to promote its own interests and values and contribute to a more multipolar and multilateral international system. The common ground with China lies in the fact that in the last two decades Beijing's diplomatic activities have increasingly emphasized the importance of multilateralism, seeking to develop global, regional, and sub-regional organizations. The potential *South-South* cooperation towards these goals hitherto is materialized in instances like the G-77 or the United Nations system—the humanitarian mission in Haiti (MINUSTAH), where China has sent 155 police officers, is a clear example—but also in the direct dialogue between the region and the Asian country. This dialogue has begun an institutionalization process through the participation of the PRC as observer in existing organizations, including the Latin American Integration Association, the Organization of American States, the Inter-American Development Bank, and the Agency for the Prohibition of Nuclear Weapons in Latin America and the Caribbean, and also through new political or consultation mechanisms between itself and existing bodies, such as the Andes Community, the Rio Group, and MERCOSUR (Teng, 2007: 98; Hirst, 2008: 97).

A second opportunity is economic cooperation in the form of trade and investments. As a market opportunity, developing Asia was, to a large extent, a missing piece in the Latin America pie charts of trade. North America and Europe, and Latin America itself, were traditionally the places to be (Devlin, 2008: 112). But starting in 1990's and according to an ECLAC study (Rosales, 2009), China's trade progress in the region has been fast and relatively steady. Comparing the years 2000 and 2007, the position of China among major trading partners of the region changed as follows: Argentina from 6th to 2nd, Bolivia 18th to 10th, Brazil 12th to 2nd, Chile 5th to 1st, Colombia 35th to 6th, Costa Rica 26th to 2nd, Cuba 5th to 2nd, Mexico 25th to 5th, and Peru from 4th to 2nd. If we consider the regional ranking of major trading countries with China, the first place is occupied by Brazil with a total of US$42 billion in trade, followed from a distance by Chile with US$17.4 billion, Mexico with US$17 billion, Argentina and Venezuela with US$7.7 billion and US$7.1 billion respectively (Infolatam, 2010).

China's interests in the countries of the subcontinent has become clearer in the last decade: Latin America is an important reservoir of raw materials, food and natural resources needed for sustaining its growth—China currently imports 30% of its oil, 45% of its iron ore, 44% of other non-ferrous metals, and an increasingly high proportion of agricultural products. The pattern of trade and investment established in recent years reflects these interests: forestry (Peru and Chile), fishing and oil (Argentina and Venezuela), iron ore and steel (Brazil), food production (Brazil, Chile, Argentina and Peru), and mining (Peru, Colombia, Chile) (Cesarín, 2006: 52-3).

A controversial point in relation to investment was President Hu Jintao's statement in 2004 about a US$100-billion ten-year investment plan for Latin America. As Juan Gabriel Tokatlián points out, "Such an offer could hardly be refused, and although it has yet to materialize, Latin American leaders increasingly see the PRC not only as a key commercial partner but also as a potential source of much-needed infrastructure investment" (2008: 60).

Thirdly, technological and scientific cooperation can be an important asset in Sino-Latin American relations. The most notable example of cooperation was the joint launch of two satellites by China and Brazil in 1999 and 2003 and also the satellite deal with Venezuela that led to the launching in October of 2008 of Venesat-1 (also named *Simón Bolívar*), the first Venezuelan communications satellite. Under this deal, 90 Venezuelan specialists worked on the satellite. These engineers acquired basic knowledge at the Beijing University of Aeronautics and Astronautics, and also received professional satellite engineering training (NasaSpaceFlight.com, 29/10/2008).

China has also established agreements and joint commissions on scientific and technological cooperation with Brazil, Mexico, Chile, Argentina, Cuba and more recently Colombia and Ecuador. This cooperation also extends to agriculture, forestry, fisheries, animal husbandry, medicine, earthquake prediction, manufacturing, information technology, biology, geology, and aerospace (Jiang, 2008: 37). According to Osvaldo Rosales, head of the International Commerce and Integration Division of the ECLAC, the reason behind all this collaboration is that "China intends to become a technological power by 2015 so it is looking for know-how in our region by signing bilateral agreements" (SciDev.Net, 1/6/2011).

There is certain consensus that another opportunity for Latin America, the fourth here, lies in the example of the successful Chinese economic model. "As China continues to expand its economic interests beyond the Asia-Pacific region, affecting more and more of the developing world, the term "Beijing Consensus" (*Beijing Gongshi*) has evolved from a theoretical idea to one which is increasingly taken more seriously in analyses of both the PRC's foreign policy and its growing economic footprint on a global level. Many developing states are considering emulating China's economic success by using some of the same policies" (Lanteigne, 2009: 42). The Consensus can be summarized on three assumptions. First, innovation is the key to economic growth; second, a gradualist approach to economic reform is better than a single and deep reform and better than a shock therapy; and third, nation-states need to develop by using their own methods, free from unwelcome international interference

(Ibid: 43-5). The centrality and strategic role of the State in the development process, in opposition to the concept of "minimal State", is another key feature that should be added to this consensus, which seems quite attractive for Latin American governments after the failed experiments of neoliberalism in the last decades. In brief, the PRC offers numerous lessons and some of them—not all—can be learnt and adapted to the region's own characteristics. One of the most important learnings in this sense is that free trade and macroeconomic stability are not sufficient to guarantee success. What is required is the use of mechanisms and policies to allow for technological upgrading and long-term development goals (Jenkins and Dussel Peters, 2009: 12).

In relation to challenges, there are also four topics to point out. The first one is the economic impact generated through the ongoing trade and investment patterns with China. Although the Asian power offers a great opportunity for Latin American natural resources and commodity exports, as highlighted above, it is also a big source of problems because of the competition with the region's own manufacturing sectors in two different types of markets: the domestic markets and the high-income consumer export markets (this is the case of Mexico in relation with the United States). Those countries whose production structure and exports resemble China's, that is, countries dominated by unskilled, labor-intensive manufacturing, will compete for markets and incur losses due to strong Chinese competitiveness (González, 2008: 151).

But a more pressing problem than the mere productive competition may also appear. On the rhetorical level, the Chinese government seeks to promote the idea of South-South cooperation in its dealings with Latin America, but in practice it is becoming apparent that the trade pattern with the region resembles more a *North-South* model, with trade and investment heavily tilted toward energy and natural resources. Quoting Professor Lanxin Xiang:

> The fact remains that Chinese trade and investment in the region cannot escape the stigma of a neocolonial pattern, especially given China's very narrow commodity needs. The historical precedent of success in this framework is, ironically, not the United States, but Great Britain. From the sixteenth to the early twentieth century, Britain invested heavily in South America to extract primary materials and agricultural goods to sustain its enormous industrial manufacturing capacity. Today 75 percent of Brazil's total exports to China is limited to five primary and agricultural products. Likewise, the most important Argentine export to China is soy beans, and Chile and Peru rely on exports of one product to China: copper. Whether this trade pattern is sustainable and for how long remains a key question" (2008: 55).

144

Precisely, a second challenge is the social and environmental impact of the relation with China. There is an increasing number of environmental conflicts in which Chinese companies are being questioned for their lack of environmental awareness. One of the clearest examples is the Marcona iron ore mine in Peru, where labor exploitation is compounded by the destruction and contamination of the surroundings and water sources. Also in Peru, *Chinalco* has bought the rights to open a copper mine in Mount Toromocho (86 miles from Lima), but in order to dig out the copper ore, the company has to shift 7,000 inhabitants of Morococha town and move them across the valley (BBC News, 17/6/08). Similar conflicts can be found in the community of Loncopué (Neuquén Province) in Argentina or in southern Bolívar State in Venezuela where *Las Cristinas* gold extraction project is under way with Chinese capitals. But it is not only mining that is endangering the sustainability of regions and locals. China's strong demand and investment in soybean production is also threatening many parts of the Amazonian rainforest in Brazil and, more recently, the fertile valleys of Río Negro Province in Argentina, where the state firm *Heilongjiang Farms* has reached a controversial agreement to grow 320,000 ha. of genetically-modified soybeans (Tiempo Argentino, 13/7/11).

In general, all these trends imply a strong pressure on ecosystems, depletion of natural resources on Latin American territory (agricultural soils, biodiversity, water resources, fisheries and energy resources), a detriment to the sovereignty of local communities over their natural resources and territories, and the services they provide (food, water, etc.) (Aedo et al., 2005: 14).

A third unresolved issue between the PRC and Latin America is the "Taiwan puzzle". Professor Marc Lanteigne explains:

> Like Africa, Latin America has been a diplomatic battleground between Beijing and Taipei, as Taiwan had made considerable economic inroads in the region and was able to secure much diplomatic support in the region. As of 2008, twelve Latin American states recognize Taiwan and have no official diplomatic ties with China, including El Salvador, Haiti, Honduras, Nicaragua, Panama and Paraguay. In recent years, Dominica (2004), Grenada (2005) and Costa Rica (2007) switched recognition from Taipei to Beijing, while the tiny Caribbean island of St Lucia, after recognizing Beijing in 1997, decided ten years later to reverse that decision and reopen relations with Taipei, illustrating the still unpredictable nature of the diplomatic shell game between the two sides in the region" (2009: 139).

What seems quite clear is that isolating Taiwan is a key political objective for China in Latin America and that both countries have competed fiercely with each other throughout the region, mobilizing substantial diplomatic resources to achieve their national interests (Teng, 2007: 102).

Finally, a fourth challenge stems from questions about the possible U.S. reaction to its diminishing influence on its self-ascribed "backyard". This scenario has been closely followed by strategic think tanks in Washington for the last decade. Two positions must be distinguished here: one is the fear of those who see the PRC's new presence in the region as the opening move toward a large-scale diplomatic offensive to challenge the U.S. in the Hemisphere; and the other, a more benign perspective, involves perceiving the increasing linkages as an opportunity, rather than as a threat, and as a natural manifestation of the energy and resources the Asian country needs, without an explicit or inevitable clash with the superpower (Roett and Paz, 2008: 1). The latter view is in keeping with the idea of the "peaceful rise," publicized by President Hu Jintao. According to Zheng Bijian, one of its main ideologues, "China does not intend to challenge or subvert the existing political and economic international order [...]. China does not seek hegemony now, nor will it do so in the future. We have already made it a basic state policy of contemporary China that we will never seek hegemony" (Zheng, 2005). China's historic reemergence should therefore run by compliance to international rules, multilateralism, peaceful resolution of disputes, and tolerance towards other nations.

But up to now, using a nonideological approach, Beijing's main concern in the Western Hemisphere has been to avoid any geopolitical consequences resulting from its expansion. However, evidence so far shows that it has failed to convince the United States that its intentions are nothing but benign. "Given the importance of Sino-U.S. relations and the geopolitical implications of this reality, there is an urgent need for both Beijing and Washington to openly recognize the triangular nature of Sino–Latin American relations and to engage in dialogue about trilateral strategic interests" (Xiang, 2008: 57).

Conclusions

China's rise in the international system is in fact the return of one of the greatest powers and civilizations that humankind has seen. Through a complex domestic transformation, Beijing has flexibilized its socialist economic policy - but not its political system - in order to implement market reforms, allowing the arrival of foreign capitals and the full integration of its economy into international trade flows. As a result, in the last three decades it has shown an impressive performance in many indicators (GDP, total trade, FDI, international reserves), condition that have been called the "Chinese miracle". But in parallel with this success, the country faces a number of internal issues ranging from social inequality, to environmental degradation and human rights violations.

In the international arena, China clearly overshadows the rest of the great powers—Japan, Great Britain, France, Germany, India, etc.—in terms of political, economic and military might. China still qualifies far behind the United States in these variables, but there is a growing consensus that there is a closing gap between these two countries. If one relies on history, it is possible to assure as Kennedy does that "the ebb and tides of history will take away [the American] hegemony" and everything indicates that the PRC is the best-suited country to take its place.

These facts and trends are of critical importance for Latin American countries. Indeed, the regional economic boom in this early century is, in part, due to the strong Chinese demand for commodities and natural resources that has been pushing up international prices. In this sense, China entails both opportunities and challenges for our countries. On the positive side, a robust relation with Beijing offers the chance to boost political, economic, scientific and technological cooperation. The Asian country also offers the region an alternative and fruitful example of economic reform - known as the Beijing consensus - in which the state is the driver of socio-economic transformations, and that is certainly different from the neoliberal proposals that failed in the region (Cesarín, 2010: 8).

But this scenario, which at first sight seems quite attractive, needs a more cautious consideration of the challenges. One of the most important challenges is the economic impact spreading in two directions: the harmful effects that cheap Chinese imports have had on Latin American manufacturing sectors, and the commodities boom that "conceals the risks of relying on a volatile and largely unskilled sector for the maintenance of a long-term economic growth and prosperity" (Davy, 2008: 2). In this sense, behind the siren's song lies the danger of an asymmetric trade leading to new ties of dependence and a new subordinated insertion of Latin America under the dictates of a distant great power. Certainly, Professor Julio Sevares (2007: 12) is right when he does not see a *South-South* logic as characterizing the Latin America-China economic relationship, but rather a more classic *North-South* trade pattern and a British-like extractive investment trend, as in the 19th Century.

Also worrying is the socio-environmental impact of the expansion of Chinese economic interests in the region. Despite Beijing's socialist and progressive rhetoric, there have been accounts of worker mistreatment, community degradation, and over-exploitation of natural resources by Chinese firms in many Latin American countries. These situations make it clear that China does not represent a legitimate alternative to the extractivist and unsustainable model of development currently in force in the region. On the contrary, China seems to reinforce it.

The other two open-chapters that may fuel instability into China-Latin America relations are the Taiwan issue and, perhaps more importantly, the potential collision with the fading United States influence in what once was its "own backyard." Ultimately, the movement towards an open strategic challenge between China and the United States—not just in Latin America but also in Africa, and all of Asia—or towards respectful relations between both powers, will depend on one of the following factors affecting their mutual interaction: a zero-sum game product of structural changes in the international system, or a positive-sum game resulting from converging interests and perceptions.

In any case, Latin American countries and their leaderships must quickly realize what is at stake if the PRC's influence continues to grow in the region. Clear strategies should be developed and a strong negotiation attitude maintained in order to successfully deal with a great power that is returning to the forefront of history.

References

Aedo, M. Paz, Sara Larraín and Pablo Sepúlveda (2005) *China y América Latina. Comercio e Inversiones. Obstáculos y desafíos para la Sustentabilidad.* Programa Chile Sustentable, Fundación Heinrich Böell.

Amiti, Mary and Caroline Freund (2010) "The Anatomy of China's Export Growth", in Feenstra, Robert C. and Shang-Jin Wei: *China's Growing Role in World Trade.* Chicago: The University of Chicago Press.

BBC (2008) "Peru's 'copper mountain' in Chinese hands", *BBC News* website, June 17. Available at http://news.bbc.co.uk/2/hi/americas/7460364.stm.

Becker, Jasper (2006) *Dragon Rising. An inside look at China today.* Washington D.C.: National Geographic.

Bergsten, C. Fred (2008) "A Partnership of Equals: How Washington Should Respond to China's Economic Challenge", *Foreign Affairs*, 87(4): 57-69.

Blonigen, Bruce A. and Alyson C. Ma (2010) "Please Pass the Catch-Up. The Relative Performance of Chinese and Foreign Firms in Chinese Exports," in Feenstra, Robert C. and Shang-Jin Wei (eds.), *China's Growing Role in World Trade.* Chicago: The University of Chicago Press.

Cesarín, Sergio (2006) "La relación sinolatinoamericana, entre la práctica política y la investigación académica", *Nueva Sociedad*, (203) Mayo/Junio: 48-61.

Cesarín, Sergio (2010) "China y Argentina: Enfoques y recomendaciones de política para potenciar la relación bilateral", *Serie Aportes* (8). Available at http://www.fes.de/cgi-bin/gbv.cgi?id=07560&ty=pdf.

Cheng, Joseph Y. S. (2006) "Latin America in China's Contemporary Foreign Policy", *Journal of Contemporary Asia*, 36(4): 500-528.

Cheng, Leonard K. and Zihui Ma (2010) "China's Outward Foreign Direct Investment", in Feenstra, Robert C. and Shang-Jin Wei (eds.), *China's Growing Role in World Trade.* Chicago and London: The University of Chicago Press.

CNN (2011) "Global 500", an article from *CNN Money* blog. Available at http://money.cnn.com/magazines/fortune/global 500/2010/full_list/index.html.

D´Elía, Carlos, Carlos Galperín and Néstor Stancanelli (2008) "El rol de China en el mundo y su relación con la Argentina", *Revista del CEI*, (13): 67-89.

Davy, Megan (2008) "¿Qué presagia el crecimiento de China para América Latina?", *Panorama del Desarrollo Internacional* del *American Enterprise Institute*, (2) Julio. Available at http://www.aei.org/docLib/20080811_DPOJulio2008.pdf.

Devlin, Robert (2008) "China's Economic Rise", in Riordan Roett and Guadalupe Paz, (eds.) *China's expansion into the Western Hemisphere.* Washington D.C.: The Brookings Institution.

Frank, André Gunder (1993) "América Latina al margen del sistema mundial. Historia y presente", *Nueva Sociedad*, (123): 23-34.

Gill, Bates (2007) *Rising Star. China's New Security Diplomacy.* Washington D.C.: Brookings Institution Press.

Giovanni Arrighi (1996) "The Rise of East Asia: world systemic and regional aspects", *International Journal of Sociology and Social Policy*, 16(7/8): 6-44.

González, Francisco E. (2008) "Latin America in the Economic Equation—Winners and Losers: What Can Losers Do?" in Roett, Riordan and Guadalupe Paz (eds.), *China's expansion into the Western Hemisphere.* Washington D.C.: The Brookings Institution.

Halperín, Donghi, Tulio (1980) *Historia Contemporánea de América Latina.* Madrid: Alianza.

Hirst, Mónica (2008) "A South-South Perspective", in Roett, Riordan and Guadalupe Paz, (eds.) *China's expansion into the Western Hemisphere.* Washington D.C.: The Brookings Institution.

Hobsbawn, Eric (2008) "Después del siglo XX: un mundo en transición", *Letras Libres*, julio: 16-22. Available at http://www.letraslibres.com/revista/convivio/despues-del-siglo-xx-un-mundo-en-transicion

Huang, Jikun, Yu Liu; Will Martin and Scott Rozelle (2010) "Agricultural Trade Reform and Rural Prosperity. Lessons from China," in Feenstra, Robert C. and Shang-Jin Wei (eds.), *China's Growing Role in World Trade.* Chicago and London: The University of Chicago Press.

Ikenberry, G. John (2008) "The Rise of China and the future of the West", *Foreign Affairs*, 87(1): 23-37.

Infolatam (2010) "Aumenta superávit de América Latina con China", an article from Infolatam's news website, September 2. Available at http://www.info-latam.com/2010/09/02/america-china-speravit/.

Jacobs, Andrews (2010) "In China, Pollution Worsens Despite New Efforts", *The New York Times,* July 28. Available at http://www.nytimes.com/2010/07/29/world/asia/29china.html?_r=1.

Jenkins, Rhys and Enrique Dussel Peters (eds.) (2009) *China and Latin America. Economic relations in the twenty-first century.* Bonn-Mexico City: Deutsches Institut für Entwicklungspolitk and Centro de Estudios China-México UNAM.

Jiang, Shixue (2008) "The Chinese Foreign Policy Perspective", in Roett, Riordan and Guadalupe Paz (eds.) *China's expansion into the Western Hemisphere.* Washington D.C.: The Brookings Institution.

Kennedy, Paul (2010) "Back to Normalcy. Is America really in decline?" *The New Republic,* December 30: 10-11.

Kynge, James (2006) *China Shakes the World: A Titan's Rise and Troubled Future—and the Challenge for America.* New York: Houghton Mifflin Harcourt.

Lanteigne, Marc (2009) *Chinese Foreign Policy. An Introduction.* New York: Routledge.

Li, Datong (2009) "China's stalled transition", *Open Democracy,* February 19. Available at http://www.opendemocracy.net/article/chinas-stalled-reforms.

Martins, Carlos Eduardo (2009) "A Teoria da Conjuntura e a Crise Contemporânea", *Polis, Revista de la Universidad Bolivariana,* 8(24). Available at http://redalyc.uaemex.mx/src/inicio/ArtPdfRed.jsp?iCve=30512210017.

Mearsheimer, John J. (2006) "China's Unpeaceful Rise", *Current History,* 105(690): 160-162.

Mearsheimer, John J. (2010) "The Gathering Storm. China's Challenge to US Power in Asia", *Chinese Journal of International Politics,* 3(4): 381-396.

Mearsheimer, John J. (2011) "Imperial by Design", *The National Interest,* (111): 16-34.

NasaSpaceFlight.com (2008) "China launch VENESAT-1 – debut bird for Venezuela", an article from *NasaSpaceFlight* news website, October 29. Available at http://www.nasaspaceflight.com/2008/10/china-launch-venesat/.

Rachman, Gideon (2011) "Think Again: American Decline", *Foreign Policy,* Jan/Feb. Available at http://www.foreignpolicy.com/articles/2011/01/02/think_again_american_decline.

Roett, Riordan and Guadalupe Paz (eds.) (2008) *China's expansion into the Western Hemisphere.* Washington D.C.: The Brookings Institution.

Rosales, Osvaldo (2009) *China, EU and Latin America: Current Issues and Future Cooperation.* Shangai: ECLAC, F. Ebert Stiftung & Shangai Institutes for International Studies, April, 27-28. Available at http://www.eclac.cl/comercio/ noticias /noticias/5/35965/presentacion_Shangai_2009.pdf.

Rosecrance, Richard (2006) "Power and International Relations: The Rise of China and its Effects", *International Studies Perspectives*, 7(1): 31-35.

SciDev.Net (2011) "China boosts Latin American science ties", an article from Science and Development Network news website, January 6. Available at http://www.scidev.net/en/news/china-boosts-latin-american-science-ties-1.html.

Sevares, Julio (2007) "¿Cooperación Sur-Sur o dependencia a la vieja usanza?" *Nueva Sociedad*, (207) Enero-Febrero: 11-22.

Shirk, Susan L. (2007) *China: Fragile Superpower.* New York: Oxford University Press.

Teng, Chung-chian (2007) "Hegemony or Partnership: China's Strategy and Diplomacy Toward Latin America", in Eisenman, Joshua, Eric Heginbotham and Derek Mitchell (eds.), *China and the developing world: Beijing's strategy for the twenty-first century.* New York, M.E. Sharpe, Inc.

The Economist (2010) "We invite you to predict when China will overtake America", December 16, 2010. Available at http://www.economist.com/blogs/dailychart/2010/12/save_date.

Tiempo Argentino (2011): "Barcesat: "El acuerdo sojero de Río Negro con una empresa china es nulo", an article from Tiempo Argentino's news website, July 13. Available at http://tiempo.elargentino.com/notas/barcesat-acuerdo-sojero-de-rio-negro-con-una-empresa-china-es-nulo.

Truman, Edwin M. (2008) "The Management of China's International Reserves: China and a Sovereign Wealth Fund Scoreboard", in Goldstein, Morris and Nicholas R. Lardy (eds.) *Debating China's Exchange Rate Policy.* Washington: Peter G. Peterson Institute for International Economics.

U.S. Census Bureau (2011) *Trade in Goods with China.* Available at http://www.census.gov/foreign-trade/balance/c5700.html.

Wallerstein, Immanuel (2001) *Después del Liberalismo.* México: Siglo XXI.

Walt, Stephen M. (2011) "In the war of American decline, should we fight battles at home or abroad?" *Foreign Policy*, May 12.

Available at http://walt.foreignpolicy.com/posts/2011/05/12/the_choice.

Wilhelmy, Mandfred and Augusto Soto (2005) "El proceso de reformas en China y la política exterior: de Deng Xiaoping a Hu Jintao" in Cesarín, Sergio and Carlos Moneta, *China y América Latina. Nuevos enfoques sobre cooperación y desarrollo. ¿Una segunda ruta de la seda?* Buenos Aires: BID-INTAL.

Xiang, Lanxin (2008) "An Alternative Chinese View", in Roett, Riordan and Guadalupe Paz, (eds.) *China's expansion into the Western Hemisphere.* Washington D.C.: The Brookings Institution.

Yan, Xuetong (2006) "The Rise of China and its Power Status", *Chinese Journal of International Politics*, 1. Available at http://www.irchina.org/en/pdf/yxt06.pdf.

Yudken, Joel S. (2010) *America's Manufacturing Crisis and the erosion of the U.S. Defense Industrial Base. A report for the AFL-CIO Industrial Union Council*, September. Available at http://www.ndia.org/Divisions/Divisions/Manufacturing/Documents/119A/1%20Manufacturing%20Insecurity%20ES%20V2.pdf.

Zhao, Min (2006) *External Liberalization and the Evolution of China's Exchange System: an Empirical Approach*. Final Draft, The World Bank Beijing Office. Available at http://siteresources.worldbank.org/INDIAEXTN/Resources/events/359987-1149066764594/Paper_MinZhao.pdf.

Zheng, Bijian (2005) "Diez puntos de vista sobre el ascenso pacífico de China y sobre las relaciones entre China y Europa", *Real Instituto Elcano*. Available at http://www.realinstitutoelcano.org/analisis/867/867_DiscursoZheng.pdf.

JØRGEN DIGE PEDERSEN

Chapter 5

China Rising – India Responding

Introduction

The rise of China has meant an increase in its economic weight, its military might and its political influence, and these developments have been a source of anxiety for its greatest neighbour, India. But it has also created opportunities and a rapid increase in mutually advantageous economic relations. In addition, India has, on a large variety of international political issues, seen rising China as a potential ally rather than an adversary and potential competitor. China's close friendship with Pakistan and outstanding border conflicts with India still continue to define the relationship between the two great Asian nations, but at the same time, and despite the historically rooted animosity, the two nations have expanded their mutual cooperation. This chapter will trace the evolution of these partly contradictory trends in the relationship between China and India and provide an assessment of their implications for future developments.

Theoretical Context

The financial crisis and the severe economic problems faced by the US and the rest of the developed world have happened at the same time as strong economic growth continues in China. This has fuelled speculations and theorizing about a change in global political and economic power relations and a rapid move away from the US-led world of the 20th century. In the long-term historical perspective, these events are often interpreted as signs of yet another transition in the world system and a possible change of the global economic hegemony, with historical parallels discernable in the transition from the Dutch to the British hegemony or that of the British to the US hegemony. Changes in global economic hegemony have often been accompanied by or maybe even caused by deep-rooted transitions in the dominant economic regime or form of capitalism, from commercial to industrial capitalism or from unregulated free market capitalism to the Fordist/Keynesian forms of regulated capitalism. A system-wide dominance of financial capital, which could be a plausible way of characterizing the current global economic system, has according to some observers always been signalling the "autumn" of major phases of world capitalism (Arrighi and Silver, 2001) and announcing the coming of a new major techno-economic transition (Perez, 2002). In a similar vein, the debate on the rise and decline of great powers in the international system also has tended to see in current developments an on-going process of decline of US world dominance and give rise to speculations over the future configuration of world power, as exemplified by the work of Paul Kennedy (Kennedy, 1989).

All these debates have had a common difficulty in providing a convincing prediction as to who would be the new international hegemon or what would characterize a possible new phase of global capitalism. Leaving aside speculations over the nature of future capitalism and focusing only on the question of US decline and the emergence of new potential hegemons, China is an obvious candidate to replace the US due to its size and its rapid economic growth. The country has both economic and political weaknesses, however, that in the eyes of many make it an unlikely candidate to become a new hegemon (Bardhan, 2010).

The rise of China may perhaps be better seen in a centre-periphery context as a move away from a partly self-imposed place at the extreme periphery of the global economic system towards a position more appropriate for its size, but stopping short of real hegemony at the centre - hegemony being more about setting the rules of the game than about size. But to the extent that size does matter, China is a natural contender for great power status, possibly in the long term even global dominance, but there is another country whose economy is growing fast and has a size comparable to China's. That country is India; and while clearly not in an equally important position as China in the world system, India is nevertheless sufficiently important to be of special interest to the debate on the implications of the rise of China.

The relationship between India and China, and in particular India's reaction to the rise of China, is neither simple nor one-dimensional. It is a highly complex relationship, with many facets and diverging trends in the different areas where the impact of China's rise interacts with India's own development dynamics. It is also a relationship that is heavily influenced by the historical chain of events that has given their relationship a strongly antagonistic character. To fully understand today's India-China relations, it is necessary to briefly recapitulate its historical evolution.

The Historical Background

The traditional story of post-independence relations between India and China is one of mutual distrust, war and permanent hostility, especially after the brief, and for the Indian side, disastrous war along the two nations' disputed borders in late 1962. The war was in all likelihood not the result of any deliberately planned hostility on either side but had its origin in disagreements over the status and fate of Tibet, with India failing to understand the intensity of Chinese attachment to the area, and China mistrusting India's intentions and actions such as the granting of asylum to the fleeing Dalai Lama.[1] During most of the 1950s the disagreements over Tibet had co-existed with a general feeling of commonality and friendliness between the two newly independent Asian countries, both having young and ambitious new leadership. *Hindi-Chini-bhai-bhai* ("India and China are brothers") became almost an official designation of the relationship as did the five principles of peaceful coexistence commonly declared by both countries: *Panch Sheel*. This cordiality of relations changed dramatically and permanently when the Chinese decided to "teach a lesson" to the Indians and inflicted a humiliating defeat to the Indian military forces in a conflict over the exact demarcation of the borderline between the two countries.[2] The Indian defeat was even more humiliating because the conflict ended with the Chinese forces unilaterally withdrawing to what subsequently became a "Line of Actual Control" after having made their point. This humiliating outcome of the military conflict made it practically impossible for Indian governments to agree to any future compromise on the border issue that might be interpreted by the Indian public as a concession to what was now universally seen as the Chinese enemy.

The military defeat, combined with China's subsequent nuclear test in 1964, was probably the key event that led to a dramatic increase in India's defence expenditures from the 1960s onwards, including the strong determination from then on to pursue the path towards nuclear weapons capability. The Indian victory in the 1971 war with Pakistan over Bangladesh and the "peaceful" detonation of a nuclear device in 1974 probably resulted in a certain reduction in the Indian feeling of inferiority towards their northern neighbour. In any case, by 1976 diplomatic relations were re-established when the Congress government in New Delhi decided to send an ambassador to Beijing, and China, in return, dispatched an ambassador to Delhi. In 1979, the Foreign Minister in the new non-Congress coalition government and a prominent leader of the right-wing nationalist party, Bharatiya Janata Party (BJP), visited China, thus signalling the broad political

155

support among Indian political parties to a gradual normalization of relations with China. The process of normalization was derailed for some years, however, as a result of China's (failed) attempt to once again 'teach a lesson' to a neighbouring country, Vietnam, whom India regarded as a friend and ally.

A turning point in India-China relations came in 1988 with the Indian Prime Minister Rajiv Gandhi's visit to Beijing. The visit resulted in the setting up of the Joint Working Group to deal with the border issues. This made it possible to set the controversial border issue aside in order to promote collaboration on political, economic and civilian issues and generally to normalize and expand friendly relations between the two nations.[3]

The early 1990s were marked by a deepening of political ties with several high-level visits including presidents and prime ministers from both nations and the signing of agreements on future peaceful cooperation in various areas. The steady improvement of relations during the 1990s received a temporary setback with India's decision in May 1998 to take "a nuclear leap forward"[4] when it openly tested five nuclear devices. This declaration of its status as a nuclear power was accompanied by scarcely veiled arguments that pointed to the threat from China as the most important motive for going nuclear.[5] Not surprisingly, the Chinese leaders protested strongly over being cast as India's enemy, but apart from this the Chinese reaction was subdued and after a few years the process of normalization of relations continued. It may even be argued that the nuclear tests, together with India's advancement in its independent missile programme, contributed to a virtual elimination of India's inferiority complex vis-à-vis China and paved the way, for India at least, to see Indo-Chinese links as a relationship between equals (Mohan, 2003:149). 1998 can thus be seen as the most recent watershed in India-China relations. It is also around this time that China began in earnest to be widely regarded as a true rising power, especially in the economic field, and the late 1990s will thus be a convenient approximate starting point for a discussion of India's reaction to the rapid rise of China.

In what follows, I will proceed by discussing three broad arenas of engagement between India and China since the 1990s and assess both changes and continuities in their relationship resulting from (or coinciding with) China's rapid rise in international affairs. The bilateral and regional security arena is the traditional scene for India-China relations. The emerging bilateral economic relations are direct consequences of China's economic rise as are the two countries' increasing engagement in the international economy. Finally, a new and exciting arena for India-China interactions is found within various new international political organizations and, most importantly, within both new and already existing global economic governance institutions. Here a pattern of collaboration (and some rivalry) between the two countries has emerged in recent years. While the three arenas each have their own dynamics, they are not isolated from each other and at times their mutual interdependencies come out very clearly.

Figure 1: Three arenas for contemporary India-China interaction

The Bilateral and Regional Security Arena- A Ceremonial Dance of Peacocks?

India's security policy has for natural reasons always been centred on the South Asian region and, since the 1962 armed conflict with China, its main concern has been relations with Pakistan and China – the three countries together forming what has been termed "The South Asian Strategic Triangle".[6] For India the most pressing security problem has been its adversarial relations with neighbouring Pakistan and India's security problem has been especially aggravated by the strategic alliance between China and Pakistan, and the close relationship of first Pakistan, later also China, with the US. India's position in this strategic triangle has constituted a highly precarious situation, especially since the collapse of its faithful ally, the Soviet Union in 1991. The collapse of the Soviet Union left India with a feeling of being left alone surrounded by dangerous enemies. It probably also formed an important part of the backdrop of India's decision to act unilaterally and declare its major power ambition through the 1998 nuclear detonations.

While the 1998 tests resulted in a reduction in India's feeling of insecurity towards its strongest adversary, China, and the nuclear response by Pakistan to some extent achieved the same for Pakistan (vis-à-vis India), it did not fundamentally change the nature of the security game in the region. China's firm alliance with Pakistan, and especially its perceived role as a key aide for Pakistan's nuclear and missiles programme, was seen by India as part of a Chinese balancing strategy in South Asia whose aim was to ensure that India would never become dominant in the region. Together with the inability of both sides to find a final resolution to the border issues, despite the efforts of the Joint Working Group, the firm Chinese alliance with Pakistan has resulted in India being permanently suspicious of China's regional intentions.

The fast rise of China's economic and military capabilities has only strengthened the Indian fear of being encircled by China. The possibility of a simultaneous two front conflict with Pakistan and China has for this reason been a driving force behind the country's military strategy and its own expanding military capability. For China, India's role as host to the Dalai Lama and the Tibetan government in exile has remained a cause for concern and irritation, while falling short of constituting any real threat to China's territorial security.

For India, the rise of China has been very visible through its increasing presence in the South Asian region, and India has responded by trying to expand its own role in East and South East Asia. China has expanded its political and economic ties not only with Pakistan but increasingly also with India's smaller neighbours: Nepal, Sri Lanka, Burma and Bangladesh. New ports and related infrastructure facilities on the rim of the Indian Ocean are being constructed by Chinese companies in Burma, in Pakistan and in Sri Lanka, and China has been an important weapons supplier to Bangladesh. This has given rise to Indian concerns over being challenged in what it considers its own waters by this small "string of pearls" (Athwal, 2008: 44ff). The Chinese motivation for the expansion of activities relevant for naval power projections is probably a mixture of military strategic aims and more mundane commercial aims of ensuring some protection to the commercial trading routes through the Indian Ocean, especially to the oil and gas supplies from the Persian Gulf. The expansion of port facilities is, by India, often seen in the context of the rapid expansion of China's naval capabilities. At the same time, and partly in response to this, India has itself begun an expansion of its own naval capabilities with the ultimate aim of being capable of operating far beyond Indian shores, if necessary with nuclear arms (Athwal, 2008: 50ff). India has increasingly "shown the flag" not only in the Indian Ocean but also in the South China Sea, and as far away as Taiwan and Japan with whom India is trying to expand military (in this case: naval) ties. These initiatives form a part of a larger Indian "Look East" perspective (Mohan, 2005: 207ff; Athwal, 2008: 63ff).

China has also expanded its role in the South Asian region by constructing key infrastructure facilities, mostly roads, in Burma, Nepal and Pakistan, and its increased construction activities along its border with India has led to similar (counter-) initiatives from India, including plans for improving the security-related infrastructure on its side of the eastern parts of the Line of Actual Control. The construction of infrastructure facilities has also, for both parties, been combined with commercial motivations, namely a desire to improve local conditions for development in these often remote areas and also to improve commercial links to the South-East Asian region in particular.

While these military and security related changes can be interpreted as mutual balancing acts – like a ceremonial dance of peacocks - prompted by security dilemma-like motivations, they also reflect on the increasing military capabilities of both China and India as their economic resources have increased dramatically as a result of their economic advances. It is not fully clear whether either side attaches very high security priorities to these developments. To some extent they seem to routinely act to mirror the advances and actions of the other part and most of the time India has been the party reacting to the Chinese actions.

The most important security-related friction between the two countries remains China's strong alliance with Pakistan. Traditionally this alliance meant that China always was ready to support Pakistan whenever this country needed some assistance to be able to balance India, for instance in the supply of military equipment or delivery of crucial nuclear or missile technologies. While this pattern of competitive rivalry still exists, a new element has been introduced as a result of the improved relationship between India and the US and the strains in US-Pakistan relations. When the US, for instance, refused to provide Pakistan the same access to (civilian) nuclear technologies as India had been granted, China immediately stepped in with offers to supply nuclear reactors and other technologies to Pakistan. There are signs, however, that China has become more cautious in its support for Pakistan and more concerned with improving ties with India. It has been less vocal in its support for Pakistan in the conflict over Kashmir and its recognition of the tiny state of Sikkim as an integral part of India has also done much to lessen tensions. On the other hand, India still views China's growing ties with Nepal with suspicion, along with its continued refusal to recognize citizens from Kashmir and Arunachal Pradesh – the two regions bordering Tibet – as full Indian citizens when they visit China.[7]

A final, but less important, source of security-related tension between China and India comes from the activities of the Chinese Communist Party (CCP). The CCP continues to maintain very friendly party relations with the Indian communists. In earlier times, when the Indian communists had more revolutionary inclinations than they possess today, these links could be seen as a potential danger to the domestic political order to be used strategically by China. Today these party-to-party links can probably be seen as useful back-door contacts to be used whenever the official channels are blocked. A related concern that sometimes crops up in India is linked to the growing "Maoist" armed uprising in parts of India and the suspicion that these movements may receive assistance from China. Similar allegations have been raised earlier with regard to the many small insurgent groups operating in the northeastern region of India. From an ideological point of view these allegations may make sense, and perhaps earlier may have had some substance. Today there is no solid evidence that points to any significant attempts by the Chinese to undermine the political stability of India, and, with the decline of revolutionary ideology in China itself, it is hard to see any motive for the CCP in doing so.

Summing up, the development in recent years of the relationship between the two countries within security-related areas is one of continued tensions and increasing build-up of strategic capabilities within a largely intact "strategic triangle"; but at the same time important efforts to isolate the difficult border issue have been made and both countries have made efforts to reduce tensions. A formal agreement in 2005 on the key principles behind a future resolution to the border issue through peaceful means has probably also reduced tensions, without really bringing a substantial resolution to the border dispute closer (Athwal, 2008: 122). Seen from the Chinese perspective, the rapprochement between the US and India has probably called for closer attention to the South Asian region and a firmer support for Pakistan. Seen in isolation, this may work to the detriment of Indo-Chinese relations, but, as we shall see in the next two sections, there are other developments pointing in a different direction.

Both countries probably have their hard-line and moderate voices with regard to their mutual relationship. In India, certainly, members of the military and strategic establishment are mostly hardliners while the Ministry of Foreign Affairs and the ministries of various economic affairs are more moderate and supportive of diplomatic settlements and the expansion of mutual ties. Recently, the Indian national security advisor asked the Indian media, which is often quite belligerent towards China, to "learn the virtues of moderation" with respect to their coverage of China-India relations to avoid any Chinese misunderstanding of India's peaceful intentions (*Economic Times*, 2011). This is a clear indication of the current domination of a moderate approach, which has been helped by developments in the other arenas outside the narrowly conceived security affairs.

The Economic Challenge from China: Competition and Collaboration

The most remarkable element of the rise of China has been its rapidly growing economy, and it is hard to imagine its increase in military might and political influence without this economic background. The economic rise of China has, since the late 1990s, been felt by India both directly and indirectly. The indirect impact on India has mainly come through China demonstrating that a poor developing country of a size equal to India can succeeding in achieving rapid economic development and a sizeable reduction in the level of poverty (Bardhan, 2010). These achievements have impressed many Indians and have led to demands for India to imitate China in order to repeat its economic success. The Indian government has indeed taken some actions intended to copy some of China's successful policies, for instance, in devising special economic zones and in inviting foreign companies to invest in export-oriented manufacturing activities. The success of these policies has so far been quite limited.

Despite superficial similarities, the differences in the two countries' economic models are many and important: democratic India's private capitalists are highly independent and politically influential, in contrast to the much stricter state-enforced discipline in authoritarian China and the generally much stronger state interference in the economy. Despite both countries having large state-owned enterprises, the Chinese state-owned enterprises are larger and much more closely linked to the political authorities. This has given the Chinese state a high level of influence over economic decisions whereas the Indian government has much less influence over both economic decisions and economic outcomes, and it is no surprise that similar policies may have very different effects in the two countries.

The direct impact on India from China's economic rise is that it has obviously interacted with India's own success in achieving rapid growth, especially after the turn of the century. The impact has been felt both in the increase in direct commercial exchange between the two countries and in the increasing presence of commercial companies from both countries in the international markets. Both domestic and international economic exchanges have been characterized by competition, mutual advantages, and by occasional collaboration giving rise to a complex and fluid picture.

The bilateral economic ties between the two countries have, for a very long time, been at an extremely low level. In 1984 a bilateral working group for promoting trade had been established (Athwal, 2008: 87), but its work did not result in any significant expansion of trade until many years later when political links had become more cordial. It was only in the wake of the visit by the Indian Prime Minister Vajpayee to Beijing in 2003 and reciprocal visits to India by Chinese officials that a firmer political basis for an expansion of trade was established (ibid.). A joint study group on trade and economic cooperation was set up and its report, which came out a few years later, identified a host of areas for mutually beneficial economic collaboration (Report, 2007). Parallel to the regular meetings of government officials from both sides, business representatives have also held regular meetings within the framework of a joint business council.

At the same time, India has expanded its economic ties with South-East Asia, in particular the ASEAN countries. The motives for a closer relationship with

ASEAN countries, and the forms of collaboration, have mostly been of a commercial nature, but the collaboration has from both sides also been motivated by apprehensions over the increasing economic influence of China in the region. Diversifying economic ties has been seen as a way to avoid potentially excessive economic dependence on China. To overcome any potential economic rivalry, India has increasingly supported the idea of an Asia-wide economic community including both India and China alongside the smaller Asian nations (Athwal, 2008: 73-75).

Since China entered the World Trade Organization (WTO) in 2001, both countries have been obliged to follow WTO rules for international trade and this has also worked to reduce trade barriers, especially tariffs and quotas; thus the membership in the WTO has facilitated an increase in bilateral trade. It should also be noted that economic reforms in both China and India have given local provincial governments in China and state governments in India much greater freedom to conduct commercial operations abroad than was possible earlier, and, as a result, there have been a number of examples of new cross-border economic ties being established through contacts between sub-state authorities (Holslag, 2010: 58-59).

In combination, all this has worked to facilitate bilateral trade and increasingly also investments by private and state-owned companies. At the same time there remain formidable obstacles to the expansion of mutual trade, not the least in terms of infrastructure facilities such as transport links. While a few mountain passes across the non-disputed border regions in the Himalayas have been opened for transit, most goods have to be transported by sea or by air (ibid.: 59-60).

As Figure 2 clearly shows, mutual trade has increased in importance during the last ten years. It has, however, been of concern to India that the increase in trade has not been fully symmetrical. While China has emerged as India's largest single trading partner (the EU collectively is still the largest), the trade has been skewed in China's favour. China's contribution to India's total imports has increased, especially since 2005, while its share of India's exports has stagnated for the last five years. In absolute figures, India has experienced a rising trade deficit with China, and while India's export to China mainly consists of iron ore and other raw materials, the Chinese export to India consists of a relatively broad spectrum of (mainly) consumer goods, including electronic goods.[8] The rising import of Chinese-made consumer goods was initially met with suspicion and concern by Indian businessmen who feared strong competition, and this competition has indeed put pressure on local producers. It is not only the rising import from China, however, but also the general opening of the Indian economy to imports from all trading partners, that has increased the level of competition in the Indian market. Yet, while clearly hurting some individual compa-

Figure 2: China's share of India's import and export

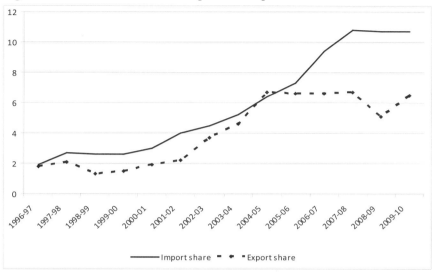

Source: Government of India, Department of Commerce, *Export-Import Data Bank* (accessed 9/8-2011, http://commerce.nic.in/eidb)

nies, the overall growth of the Indian economy has increased the playing field for all companies and most local companies seem to have been able to compete with the Chinese products.[9]

The Indian government has also tried to protect the Indian market against what they consider to be the unfair pricing of Chinese products. India has been an ardent user of WTO anti-dumping procedures and the majority of the anti-dumping cases brought forward by the Indian authorities has been directed against imports from China.[10] India has also within the WTO framework refused to grant China the status as a market economy, thus supporting the claims of many of its anti-dumping cases.

Mutual investments have also increased rapidly, and, while Chinese companies have made some investments in the Indian economy, the interest shown by private Indian companies in gaining access to the immense and rapidly growing Chinese market has been much greater. Investment figures are often unreliable and hard to obtain, so it is not possible to construct a fully accurate picture of investment relations. Investments into India are especially hard to decipher as many investments, for reasons of taxation, are routed through Mauritius and their original source is difficult to detect.[11] According to the official data on foreign investments into India, China has accounted for a very small amount of investments into India and an insignificant share of less than 0.1 per cent of all incoming investments during the period 2000-2011.[12] On the other hand, it is well known that large Chinese companies, like the computer manufacturer *Lenovo*, the telecommunications equipment manufacturer *Huawei,* and the domestic appliances manufacturer *Haier* all have had sizeable operations for some years in the domestic Indian market. This indicates that the rise of China has indeed led to some penetration of the Indian market by Chinese companies exporting goods and making productive investments. In addition, Chinese engineering and construction companies have won many contracts for constructing power plants, highways and telecom infrastructure (Report, 2007: 10).

For their part, Indian companies have shown an increasing interest in making investments and gaining access to the large Chinese markets. While not among the major destinations for Indian foreign investment, many of the large Indian companies working in the IT industry, and in a variety of manufacturing activities, have set up shop inside China. This has to some extent made the overall bilateral economic relationship more balanced than what the trade figures alone show.[13]

The increase in bilateral economic ties has not taken place in isolation from security issues and the general suspicion in India concerning China. Many Indians see the Chinese commercial activities as being closely linked to the Chinese state and thus see them as instruments of a strategic policy hostile to Indian defense and security interests. This has occasionally given rise to conflicts, such as when a Chinese company was refused permission to take part in a habour construction project close to an Indian naval facility in South India, or to suspicion and negative publicity, such as when *Huawei* established an advanced research facility that was rumoured to be off-limits to the company's Indian employees in the midst of India's IT centre, Bangalore. Cases like these illustrate the occasional link between the traditional animosity in India against China and the growing commercial ties; but in general economic ties have managed to grow without being unduly affected by security-related problems and concerns. The growing economic ties have, rather, led to a normal but complex pattern of simultaneous collaboration and competition in the marketplace.

A similar pattern of collaboration and rivalry has come as a direct result of the rise of both countries' relations with the international economy. Chinese companies have been very active in buying up energy assets abroad and securing long-term energy supply contracts. In Central Asia and in Africa especially, these Chinese activities have competed with similar, but less aggressive activities from Indian companies, in particular the Indian state-owned oil and gas companies.

For years, Chinese companies and the Chinese government have been very active in Africa in securing access to raw materials, and relations with China are often seen as an alternative to the long history of dominance of western commercial interests.[14] In 2008, India joined the game and arranged an India-Africa Summit in New Delhi. In this same vein, the Indian Prime Minister, Manmohan Singh, during his visits to several African states in early 2011, launched a diplomatic initiative to help Indian companies gain similar access to raw materials and local markets by offering large concessional loans to African governments. For some time Indian private companies have been active in Africa, and they have recently stepped up their commercial presence on the continent. Indian companies are active in telecomunications, in IT-related activities and in a broad range of industrial activities. The policies of India and China may be seen as a new "scramble for Africa" but so far there seems to have been room for both China and India to operate. As sources of raw materials and especially energy resources become increasingly scarce, the commercial competition may of course become more conflictual. It should be noted that there are also a few examples of collaboration between Chinese and Indian companies in, for instance, the oil sector in Sudan, and there have been negotiations between the two countries on mutual collaboration in the hunt for energy resources abroad (Holslag, 2010: 99-100). So far, competition seems to have prevailed over cooperation in the relationship between energy companies from the two countries, and both governments are active in support of their enterprises. While this need not necessarily lead to any serious conflicts, it is evident that the rise of China and its commercial expansion has brought an element of urgency and competition into India's relationship with Africa and other resource-rich regions of the developing world. In most of the cases of direct competition between companies from each country, the Chinese companies, being armed with much larger financial resources, have managed to secure the best contracts, but the Indian government is now considering ways to provide Indian companies with similar access to larger financial funds.

Overall, the commercial interactions between India and China – bilaterally and internationally – have been growing at a fast pace, and while there are clear instances of rivalry and competition, most of the exchanges have been peaceful and collaborative. A sober observer would conclude that increased economic interactions have contributed to making the relationship between the two countries less adversarial, but also that the economic rise of China has contributed very little to India's own economic advance, which has largely been internally driven.

Interactions in International Institutions: Alliances and Competition

The economic reforms and the country's opening up for participation and integration into the major multilateral organizations governing the world economy form an important part of the rise of China. It has also opened new avenues for both competition and collaboration with the other members of the international society, including an India that has been a long-standing, and most often founding member of most international organizations. Alongside their now common participation in existing multilateral organizations, both India and China have been active in establishing separate institutionalized forms of international collaboration, mainly in areas of common economic interests, but also, in limited ways, in more security-oriented forms of collaboration.

When, in 1998, the Russian Foreign Minister Primakov suggested a "strategic partnership" between Russia, China and India, both countries responded positively. The Russian initiative was widely regarded as an attempt to counter the global dominance of the US, as this was indeed a concern at the time in India, but subsequently this concern has diminished considerably as India has developed closer ties to the US (Athwal, 2008:114ff). Regular meetings of foreign ministers from the three states still take place, however, and this very first example of China and India collaborating internationally in a security-related area has been followed by several others. India has since 2005, for instance, been accepted as a permanent observer in the security-oriented Shanghai Cooperation Organization established by Russia and China and four Central Asian states, with which India has cultivated close links since their independence.

Despite these examples, the traditional security rivalry and conflicts between India and China has, for the most part, been a hindrance to a stronger international collaboration between the two Asian giants. China's response to India's intensely felt desire to obtain permanent membership in the UN Security Council has normally been polite, but not supportive. In particular, India's wish to obtain veto-right - like China and the other permanent members – is unlikely to be supported by China. This Chinese reluctance is probably partly due to the countries' mutual animosity in security affairs, partly due to China's alliance with Pakistan, which is strongly against Indian membership.

One of the more ambitious international efforts that has united a rising China with a similarly advancing India is the collaboration in the so-called BRIC coalition. Together with Brazil and Russia, India and China had been lumped together as a group of future economic powers in a study done by the international investment bank Goldman Sachs in the early 2000s.[15] This inspired the countries to form a loose alliance that has become more and more institutionalized with regular summit meetings, and the group has recently been expanded with the inclusion of South Africa. The focus of the group is mainly on global economic issues, in particular on their members' common interest in reforms of international institutions. All BRIC countries, not least China and India, are interested in reducing the dominance of traditional European powers in the global economic governance institutions and advancing their own influence.

These efforts have recently been met with some success and the group has been given increased influence in both the World Bank and the International Monetary Fund. The expansion of the earlier informal G8 group of dominant economic powers into a G20, including all BRIC countries in 2009, is also a testimony to the increased weight of the group in global economic governance institutions, and it has demonstrated to both India and China the fruitfulness of a close international partnership. Similarly, India and China have found common ground in global negotiations on climate issues. Together with Brazil and South Africa, the two countries now have regular meetings in order to coordinate their negotiating positions on climate issues in the so-called BASIC group.

Within the most important institution that is setting the rules for global trade, the WTO, India and China have also been cooperating more and more closely in their efforts to achieve a better deal for the poor and developing countries to which they see themselves as belonging. This is an area where for many years India, together with Brazil, has been among the most vocal advocates for the cause of developing countries, going back to the negotiations over the establishment of the WTO and more recently in the creation of the G20 coalition (not to be confused with the above-mentioned G20) of developing countries within the WTO in 2003. China has also joined this group, and both countries have increasingly collaborated in the Doha Round of trade negotiations (Holslag, 2010: 61-62). Overall, China has played a less prominent role than India within the WTO, probably due to its relatively recent membership in the WTO.

While the relationship between China and India in the field of international economic governance institutions mostly has been collaborative, there have been instances where the two countries have had a more conflictual or competitive relationship. When China in the mid 1980s joined the World Bank, including its arm for concessional loans, IDA, and also joined the Asian Development Bank, it did so as a potentially large recipient of concessional finance. India had for decades been one of the largest recipients of concessional loans from both institutions and was fearful of losing that position to China, especially if China's entry meant fewer resources available to India. It is difficult to determine whether China's entry into these international institutions and, more generally, its entry into the market for international aid, including bilateral aid, has deprived India of economic assistance. The fact is, however, that after the mid-1980s, and especially throughout the 1990s, China had received large amounts of concessional financial resources. At the same time India had experienced stagnation in its incoming aid flows and was overtaken by China as an aid recipient.[16] After the turn of the century, however, this situation seems to have changed somewhat and both China and India have now begun to contribute funds to international institutions, including the World Bank and regional development banks, and especially China is gradually receiving lower amounts of concessional forms of aid (while still receiving large World Bank loans).

To sum up, the rise of China has also meant an increasing participation in international governance affairs, and in this arena China and India have increasingly found themselves to have common interests, especially in confronting the developed countries. There are still some instances of rivalry and conflict, but the dominant trend has been towards increasing collaboration. Much of the impetus for this collaboration has come from the fact that both countries are rising economic powers with a common interest in making room for further advancement within the global economic governance system. As long as they have common aspirations in this field – and this is likely to be the case for many years to come – their interest in forming alliances will only increase.

Conclusion – Summing up

Writing on China-India relations, Garver (2001) was able to do this without mentioning economic ties and without considering the impact of China's economic rise for the relationship. This may well have been a correct assessment at the time, but ten years on it no longer seems possible to ignore all the new arenas for collaboration and conflict. The rise of China (and of India) has opened new arenas for collaboration and conflict between India and China. It has considerably broadened their mutual relationship and also made it less adversarial and more collaborative.

There is no doubt that the traditional adversarial relationship between the two countries still exists, but today it seems largely isolated to security-related areas and only occasionally does it affect their growing relationship in other areas. Within the global governance institutions, the relationship is mostly characterised by collaboration. In the economic arena, the two countries find themselves to be both in collaboration and competition with one another. While the traditional security arena remains largely conflictual, it is, however, less so than in earlier times and the security issues must today be considered of declining importance. This assessment is thus more optimistic than the judgement of a recent study that found that "distrust and rivalry still prevail" (Holslag, 2010: 165) and that "China and India will not grow without conflict with each another" (ibid.:1). That conflicts will occasionally still take place in the future does not imply that peaceful collaboration (and peaceful competition for that matter) will be of less importance. As the very same study also finds, "the general trend is that of accommodation due to intensifying economic interdependence" (ibid.: 33).

The rise of China has, precisely because it has happened alongside a similar rise of India, effected a broadening and deepening of the two countries' mutual relationship. The strengthening of their mutual economic ties may, to a limited degree, have been of benefit for both countries' continued economic progress. The most important effect has been the realization by both countries that they share large and growing common interests in many international issues and that they can collaborate on that basis. Similarly, they have found that their bilateral economic ties can be managed in a way that ensures mutually beneficial outcomes.

Returning to the speculations on the rise and decline of major powers, and in particular the possibility of China becoming a new world hegemon following a potential demise of the US, the investigation of India-China relations may contribute a certain scepticism regarding the future role of China.

The response of India to the rise of China, in combination with its own rise in the global system, indicates that China in all probability never will be able to become a global, or even a regional hegemon. China will always have India as a neighbour that will match it in size if not always in capability. India will gladly continue to collaborate with a rising China, but China will never be allowed by India to occupy a position by which it could dictate conditions to India. Probably the only useful outcome of the Indian nuclear tests was that it gave India a sufficient moral boost to see itself as an equal to China and act accordingly, for instance, in allowing the development of intense and growing economic ties. China's military superiority is of little use now, and in economic affairs India does have sufficient resources available to avoid becoming subservient to an eventual rise of a dominance-seeking China. In that sense the rise of India could be seen as a kind of insurance against China becoming too dominant – economically or militarily - in the future world system. But the rise of China to become one of the major powers, together with India, in a new world order characterized by many of the same types of governing rules as presently exist, is a scenario that is very much possible but by no means certain.

Notes

1   In a speech in the Indian Parliament in 1951 shortly after Chinese troops had marched into Tibet to "liberate" the country, the Indian Prime Minister Jawaharlal Nehru remarked that it was not clear to him "from whom they were going to liberate Tibet". Remarks like this clearly did not amuse the Chinese leadership. Nehru (1961: 303)

2   There is a long and probably never-ending debate over the exact chain of events that led up to the war including a variety of misperceptions and misguided individual actions. The debate has been based on interpretations of a plethora of published historical documentary sources, including the memoirs of key actors, mostly from the Indian side. For a brief recapitulation of some different interpretations, see Maxwell (1999) and Raghavan (2006).

3 See Hussain (1989) for a contemporary assessment of the visit.
4 See Mohan (2005: 1-28)
5 In a confidential, but leaked official letter to the US President, the Indian Prime Minister Vaypajee had pointed to the need to counter the nuclear threat from China. The "China threat"- argument was widely used by local commentators as well as by the outspoken Indian defense minister.
6 See Kapur (2011)
7 Indian citizens from these places are issued special visas different from those that other Indian citizens receive whenever they visit China.
8 The specific trade items are listed in Report (.2007), and updated lists can be found at the Ministry of Commerce website <http//commerce.nic.in>.
9 An early concern was the import of cheap Chinese batteries. According to spokespersons for Indian industry, local manufacturers quickly found that they could compete with the Chinese producers, especially in terms of quality. (own interviews in the Confederation of Indian Industry, June 2008)
10 Specific cases are listed on the website of the Ministry of Commerce.
11 According to official Indian data, Mauritius accounts for more than 40% of all direct investments into India after the year 2000. China is officially only no. 38 among foreign investors.
12 Data are published by the Ministry of Commerce & Industry, Department of Industrial Policy & Promotion http://dipp.nic.in
13 Indian FDI abroad is portrayed in Satyanand and Raghavendran (2010)
14 There is a rapidly growing body of literature dealing with China's growing ties with Africa. A brief exposé that also deals with India is Broadman (2008)
15 Wilson and Purushothaman (2003)
16 It is not easy to get a full overview of all the different kinds of concessional finance available to the two countries. The assessment given here is based upon data from the OECD, the World Bank, the Asian Development Bank and UNCTAD.

References

Arrighi, Giovanni and Beverly J. Silver (2001) "Capitalism and world (dis)order", *Review of International Studies*, 27(5): 257-279.

Athwal, Amardeep (2008) *China-India Relations. Contemporary dynamics.* London: Routledge.

Bardhan, Pranab (2010) *Awakening Giants, Feet of Clay. Assessing the Economic Rise of China and India.* New Delhi: Oxford University Press.

Broadman, Harry G. (2008) "China and India Go to Africa", *Foreign Affairs*, 87(2): 95-109.

Economic Times (2011) "Menon calls for restraint on reporting on China", August 12.

Garver, John W. (2001) *Protracted Contest. Sino-Indian Rivalry in the Twentieth Century*. Seattle and London: University of Washington Press.

Holslag, Jonathan (2010) *China and India. Prospects for Peace*. New York: Columbia University Press.

Hussain, T. Karki (1990) "India's China Policy: Putting Politics in Command", in Satish Kumar (ed.) *Yearbook on India's Foreign Policy 1989*. New Delhi: Sage.

Kapur, Ashok (2011) *India and the South Asian Strategic Triangle*. London: Routledge.

Kennedy, Paul (1989) *The Rise and Fall of The Great Powers*. New York: Vintage Books.

Nehru, Jawaharlal (1961) *India's Foreign Policy. Selected Speeches, September 1946-April 1961*. Bombay: Government of India, Publications Division.

Mazumdar, Arijit (2006) "India-China Border Dispute - Centrality of Tibet", *Economic and Political Weekly*, October 14: 4324-4325.

Maxwell, Neville (1999) "Sino-Indian Border Dispute Reconsidered", *Economic and Political Weekly*, 34(15): 905-918.

Ministry of Commerce website: <http://commerce.nic.in>

Mohan, C. Raja (2005) *Crossing the Rubicon. The Shaping of India's New Foreign Policy*. New Delhi: Penguin Books.

Raghavan, Srinath (2006) "Sino-Indian Boundary Dispute, 1948-60 - A Reappraisal", *Economic and Political Weekly*, September 9: 3882-3892.

Report (2007) *Report of the India-China Joint Study Group on Comprehensive Trade and Economic Cooperation*. New Delhi: Ministry of External Affairs.

Satyanand, Premila N. and Pramila, Raghavendran (2010) *Outward FDI from India and its policy context*. Columbia University, Vale Columbia Center on Sustainable International Investment: Columbia FDI Profiles.

Wilson, Dominic, and Roopa Purushothaman (2003) *Dreaming with the BRICs: The Path to 2050*. Global Economics Paper No. 99, New York: Goldman Sachs.

Chapter 6

Views from the "Periphery"

The Manifold Reflections of
China's Rise in the DR Congo[1]

Introduction

China's rise has produced a variety of impulses on the African continent. The understanding of these dynamics is essential for this book's endeavour to explore how China's rise impacts on semi-periphery and periphery countries. This chapter makes a contribution in this regard by means of a case study of one African country, the Democratic Republic of Congo[2] (DRC), a country which indeed could be labelled "periphery"[3]. While the current changes in China have been underway since 1978, as discussed in this book's introduction, Sino-African relations only started to gain importance from 2000 onwards (e.g. Alden et al., 2008). In the case of the DRC, ties with China started intensifying even later, after 2006. This was the year in which the DRC's elections, the first since 1965, ended the country's period of transition[4] after the 1996-1997 and 1998-2003 civil wars. Prior to this, war-torn DRC had been peripheral to China's foreign policy ambitions.

This chapter rebuts the common notion that "China's quest for resources is driving its significant presence in Africa", here formulated by Butts and Bankus (2009: 1). Indeed, China's need for resources is of great importance in this context, but the picture is more complex. The Chinese presence in Africa is equally driven by market seeking and diplomatic dynamics unrelated to the need for natural resources. This argument has indeed been made by a number of scholars (*e.g.* Brautigam, 2009; Mohan and Power, 2008; Snow, 2008) but has to date not been applied to the Congolese context. This is the gap that this chapter seeks to fill. It analyses each facet of the Chinese presence in the DRC and argues that whereas the Chinese activities are all propelled by China's rise, they both differ and converge in terms of their characteristics and drivers. The chapter contributes to this book's endeavour by showing how the Chinese activities in the DRC reflect the past decades' changes in China. It thus draws on Jiang's interpretation of the Chinese presence in Africa: "[M]uch of what the Chinese government, Chinese companies and individual entrepreneurs are doing today in Africa is an externalization of China's own modernization processes in the past decades" (2009: 585). A number of publications shed light on the different facets of the Sino-Congolese relation (Curtis, 2008; Jansson, 2010 and 2011; Jansson et al., 2009; Marysse and Geenen, 2009 and 2011; Mthembu-Salter, 2008; Okenda, 2010; RAID, 2009; Vircoulon, 2010a and 2010b). Yet, this chapter's contribution is novel, since none of the existing publications provide a holistic analysis of how the entire Chinese presence in the DRC reflects the changes in China. A number of the existing publications assess the implications of the Chinese activities in the DRC's mining sector, yet for this particular undertaking, the assessment of implications is left aside. Furthermore, the only significant aspect of the Chinese impulses in the DRC that does not form a part of the chapter's analysis is the sale and smuggling of Chinese weapons to the DRC (e.g. Hellström, 2010: 11; Curtis, 2008: 94). This is a complex and serious issue which there is not enough space to engage with here.

The chapter draws on field work conducted by the author in the DRC in September-October 2008, February-March 2009, October 2009 and February-May 2011. Interviews were conducted with Congolese respondents from government departments, civil society and the private sector; Chinese respondents from state-owned and private enterprises and the Chinese Embassy; and representatives from international governmental and non-governmental organisations, the diplomatic community and observers. For most of the interviews with Chinese stakeholders, the author collaborated with Professor Jiang Wenran of the China Institute, University of Alberta, Canada, whose contribution is gratefully acknowledged. The unique body of primary data gathered during approximately 130 interviews has been triangulated and complemented with a large body of secondary data: scholarly literature, news reporting and journalistic accounts.

The chapter proceeds as follows. A brief presentation of the analytical framework is followed by in-depth analysis of the characteristics and drivers of each Chinese activity in the DRC. A concluding discussion, summarising how the Chinese activities in the DRC reflect the past decades' changes in China, then closes the chapter.

Analytical Framework: Characteristics and Drivers of the Chinese Activities in the DRC

The analysis of the *characteristics* of the Chinese activities in the DRC consists of placing the activities on a continuum from state-level engagement to private sector activities (see Figure 1 below). The distinction is made on the basis of who the instigator is (in the case of trade, diplomatic, and political activities) and ownership (in the case of companies). Chinese *state-level engagement* with the DRC is related to the foreign policy ambitions of the Chinese government, although the link can be more or less direct depending on the activity at hand. Three groups of stakeholders are involved in the state-level activities: the Chinese government; China's state-owned enterprises (SOE); the People's Liberation Army (PLA); and the policy bank[5] China Export-Import (Exim) Bank. Chinese *private sector activities* in the DRC are carried out by small-scale entrepreneurs and private-owned companies. Admittedly, given the challenge of ascertaining exact ownership circumstances in China by means of interviews in the DRC, it is difficult to place the Chinese companies active in the DRC with certainty on the state-private continuum. Kaplinsky and Morris (2009) distinguish between four types of Chinese investors in Sub-Saharan Africa: central government-owned SOEs, provincial government SOEs, private companies incorporated in China, and private companies incorporated in Sub-Saharan Africa only. The data that this chapter draws on allows for a relatively certain placement of Chinese companies in the DRC on the state-private continuum. However, the data set is not detailed enough to make the distinction utilised by Kaplinsky and Morris within the groups of SOEs (central government- or provincial government owned) and private companies (country of incorporation) respectively. While most of the current Chinese activities in the DRC can be placed either at the state-led or the private sector end of the continuum, some of the Chinese activities in the DRC's mining sector are in between, as discussed in section 4.2 and illustrated in Figure 1.

The *drivers* of the Chinese presence in the DRC are in this chapter analysed both from a structure- and from an agency perspective. In terms of *structure*, the Chinese presence in the DRC is, fundamentally speaking, driven by China's rise. These developments have induced change in particular Chinese policy and commercial arenas, which in turn has given rise to the specific Chinese activities which occur today in the DRC. The specific structural dynamics driving each activity are analysed below. The *agency* notion enables the chapter to draw analytical attention to the agents involved in bringing about a certain Chinese activity in the DRC. In the context of this chapter, the group of agents largely comprise policy makers, state-owned- and private companies.

Figure 1: Characteristics of the Chinese activities in the DRC

State-level engagement   Private sector activities

MINING

- Mining activities: The joint ventures Sicomines, COMI-LU and COMMUS	**- Mining related activities:** Partly SOE-owned medium- and large sized companies in Katanga's mining sector pursuing both mining and processing activities	**- Mining related activities:** - processing plants in Katanga province - mineral traders in North Kivu and South Kivu provinces[a]

TELECOMMUNICATIONS

- Telecommunications: ZTE	**- Telecommunications:** Huawei

- Donations and credit lines - Chinese state-owned construction companies active as contractors for international tenders **- Peace- and army building activities**	**- Trade:** Import of Chinese consumer goods to the DRC and export of Congolese raw materials to China[b]

[a] As discussed in section 4.4, the little information that is available on these companies suggests they are private. However, I do not have complete information regarding their ownership structure. It is therefore possible that they are partly or wholly owned by Chinese SOEs.

[b] I have placed Sino-Congolese trade at the private sector end of the continuum since the Chinese state's foreign policy ambitions, as formulated in the Going Global Strategy, has not yet had any direct bearing on the commercial exchanges between the two countries. This is discussed further in section 5.

Table 1: Drivers of the Chinese activities in the DRC

Activity	DRIVERS	
	Structural drivers	**Agent drivers**
Donations and credit lines	The need to secure access to raw materials The importance of building strong political ties to developing countries	The Chinese government China Exim Bank The Chinese SOE CREC
Bilateral military exchanges	The need to maintain strong bilateral ties with the DRC	The Chinese government
Participation in UN peacekeeping mission	Global reconfigurations of power prompting China to be a "responsible international actor"	The Chinese government
Mining related activities	The demand for raw materials in the world economy	Private and state-owned Chinese companies
Import of Chinese consumer goods to the DRC	Competition in China ("push"); Opportunities in the DRC ("pull")	Chinese and Congolese traders
Export of Congolese raw materials to China	The demand for raw materials in the world economy	Trading networks and companies, mostly not Chinese
The construction sector	Market saturation in China and support from the Chinese government to "go out" ("push") Opportunities in the DRC ("pull")	Chinese SOEs The Chinese government
Telecommunications	Competition in China ("push") Opportunities in the DRC ("pull")	The companies ZTE and Huawei The Chinese government China Exim Bank

Donations and Credit Lines

The Chinese activities that are commonly understood as "aid" – donations and credit lines provided by the Chinese government – form part of Chinese state-level engagements with the DRC. On an agency level, this form of engagement is driven by the Chinese government and its foreign policy ambitions as formulated in China's January 2006 African Policy (MFA, 2006). However, the intensification of China's foreign policy efforts towards Africa, of which donations and credit lines form an important part, was and is propelled largely by structural imperatives: the need to secure access to raw materials and the strategic importance of having strong relations with developing countries as the power configurations of the global political economy change (e.g. Alden and Alves, 2008; Taylor, 2009:20 *et seq*). From 1972, when Sino-Congolese bilateral relations stabilised[6], until 2006, China only provided the DRC with six donations, one modest credit line and a small number of scholarships for Congolese students, as shown in Table 2. The donations were the kind of symbolic gifts also provided to many other African countries during this time (e.g. Brautigam, 2009: 34-35), such as a parliamentary building, a farm and a hospital. All the donations listed in Table 2 classify as official development assistance (ODA) as defined by the Development Assistance Committee (DAC) of the Organisation for Economic Cooperation and Development (OECD) (OECD, 2008).

The largest credit line extended to date was the loan provided to the Sicomines joint venture in 2008. After its renegotiation in 2009, the grant element7 is sufficiently low for the loan to be considered ODA. Yet, the loan classifies as Other Official Flows (OOF), not ODA, given that it is partly export-facilitating in purpose (OECD 2010:12. See also Brautigam 2011:213-215). The terms of the US$367.5 million credit line for the refurbishment of the Zongo II hydroelectric dam, extended in January 2011, are concessional, according to representatives for the IMF and for the Chinese Embassy in Kinshasa.[8] In terms of the credit lines extended prior to this, in 2000 and 2008 respectively, I have not been able

Source: Author's interviews with relevant stakeholders in the DRC in October 2008; February-March 2009; October 2009; February-May 2011; and in Beijing in November 2009. See also Jansson (2009).

[a] Projects are listed the under year they were announced, not the year they were delivered/implemented. The data covers the period until May 2011.
[b] However, it is not yet operational due to local circumstances.
[c] This is one of the pledges from FOCAC 2009, the only project the Chinese and Congolese parties had agreed upon at the time of the author's field research in 2011.
[d] At the time of the author's field research in 2011, the only known detail about the credit line was that it will be managed by the Chinese Ministry of Commerce.
[e] Negotiations not concluded at the time of the author's field research in 2011

Table 2: Chinese donations and credit lines to the DRC (1972-2011)[a]

Period	Year	Project	Financing	Nominal value	Delivered
1970s until today	1970s	Chinese medical teams dispatched (1973-)	Donation	N/A	Yes
		Training provided for Congolese professionals	Donation	N/A	Yes
		Farm project in N'Djili, Kinshasa producing crops and livestock (1970s-)	By an agricultural institute, Hebei, China; sale of crops	N/A	Yes
		Chinese government scholarships for Congolese students: 5-8 yearly (1985-2003); 11 yearly (2004-2006); 27 (2007); ± 30 yearly (2008-2011)	Donation	N/A	Yes
Pre-2006	1970s	Sugar factory in Kisangani (subsequently destroyed during the wars)	Donation	N/A	Yes
		Rice-planting technique promotion station	Donation	N/A	N/A
		Kinshasa mail distribution centre	Donation	N/A	N/A
	1979	The National Assembly building (Kinshasa)	Donation	US$42 mn	Yes
	1994	The Martyr's Stadium (Kinshasa)	Donation	N/A	Yes
	2000	Establishment of the company China-Congo Telecom (see section 7)	China Exim Bank credit line	RMB 80 mn	Yes
	2004	Hospital in N'Djili, Kinshasa	Donation	N/A	Yes
Post-2006	2006	Yearly donation of malaria medication	Donation (pledge from FOCAC 2006)	N/A	Yes, yearly 2007-
		3 schools, Kisangani (2); and Kinshasa (1)		N/A	Yes
		Malaria centre (Kinshasa)		N/A	Yes
	2008	Financing towards infrastructure refurbishment extended by means of the Sicomines agreement	China Exim Bank credit line	US$3 billion	Partly disbursed (US$478 mn)
		Next Generation Network (NGN) (Kinshasa)		US$32 mn	Yes[b]
		Fibre optic cable between Moanda and Kinshasa		US$32 mn	
	2009	Agricultural centre in N'Sele	Donation[c]	RMB 30 mn	Not yet
	2011	The Zongo hydroelectric dam	China Exim Bank credit line	US$367.5 mn	Not yet
		Refurbishment of Kinshasa airport	Credit line[d]	N/A[e]	Not yet

to assess whether or not they classify as ODA since I do not have access to the terms of the loans. Notwithstanding, they have all been extended by China Exim Bank and thus constitute state-level engagement. As further indicated by Table 2, there has been a marked increase both in terms of the donations made and the credit lines extended after 2006. The gap in value between the two is, however, significant: the credit lines provided are worth a great deal more than the donations made. In turn, among the credit lines provided, the one extended to the Sicomines joint venture is a definite outlier in terms of monetary value.

As the agreement was announced in 2008, the Sino-Congolese relation was, in Curtis' words, "catapulted [...] to centre stage in China-Africa cooperation" (2008: 87). By means of the agreement, China Exim Bank will extend a US$3 billion credit line to the DRC towards infrastructure refurbishment. In exchange for the funding provided, the DRC has provided a consortium of Chinese companies with access to significant mining concessions[9] in the DRC's south-eastern parts.[10] The agreement, indeed one of the more prominent embodiments of Chinese state-level engagement seen to date on the entire African continent, thus has a dual identity as a debtor for a China Exim Bank credit line and as a state-level investment into the DRC's mining sector. The infrastructure projects are currently under implementation and the mining operation is slated to come into production in 2012-2013, reaching full capacity in 2016 (Jansson, 2011). As Table 1 indicates, the agents involved in bringing about the Sicomines agreement include not just the Chinese government and its policy bank China Exim. Whereas these stakeholders threw significant political weight behind the deal, it was actually initiated by the SOE China Railway Engineering Corporation (CREC) as it sought to implement its strategy to diversify into the extractive industries.[11]

Peace and Army Building Activities

Peace and army building activities also form part of the Chinese state-level engagement with the DRC. This facet has two components: bilateral exchanges and participation in the United Nation's (UN) peacekeeping operation (PKO) in the DRC. As indicated in Table 1, the two forms of activity have slightly different structural drivers. The activities within the bilateral framework are traditional foreign policy tools which date back to 1972 when Sino-Congolese bilateral relations stabilised.[12] Throughout 1972-2006, military exchanges featured prominently in Sino-Congolese ties. Many Congolese officers were trained in China, including the incumbent President Joseph Kabila Kabange prior to his ascendance to the presidency in 2001 (e.g. Melmot, 2009: 16). It is often argued (e.g. Curtis, 2008: 93) that President Kabila developed a political proximity with China during this period which became useful in the context of the Sicomines agreement. Today, Sino-Congolese bilateral military exchanges take the form of training of- and material support to FARDC[13], the Congolese army, the latter notably in the form of the supply of military vehicles (Hellström, 2010: 11, Xinhua, 2010). The technical training is provided in Kamina, eastern DRC by engineering troops from China's PLA.[14] The bilateral military exchanges thus have a fairly long history and as such, it represents continuity in the Sino-Congolese relation.

Conversely, China's active participation in the UNPKO in the DRC is driven by the recent changes in Chinese foreign policy. Generally, Beijing's participation in UNPKOs is one of the policy areas in which the growing Chinese sensitivity to international demands for the country to assume a more important role as a "responsible international actor" is most clearly reflected. In Taylor's words, China has gone "from an absolute refusal to support peace operations under any circumstances to a permanent commitment to doing so" (2009: 151). Until the end of the Cold War, there was little incentive for the Chinese government to reconsider its stance on what Carlson terms "the sovereignty-intervention nexus" (2004: 11), given that very few peacekeeping initiatives actually materialised during this period (Carlson, 2004: 12; Taylor, 2009: 140; Thompson, 2005). The 1990s' dramatic transformations in world politics incited change also in Beijing's stance on sovereignty, and its contributions to UN peacekeeping activities started to grow by the mid-1990s (Carlson, 2004: 13; Gill and Huang, 2009: 6). As of June 2011, China was the 15th largest out of the 115 contributors to UNPKOs (UN Peacekeeping, 2011). In similarity with the changes in Chinese foreign policy towards Africa, this quite radical change in Beijing's attitude towards PKOs is, as indicated in Table 1, largely propelled by the structural imperatives of a changed global order. China now needs to display that it is a responsible member of the international community (Carlson, 2004: 11, 14; Gill and Huang, 2009; Taylor, 2009; Thompson, 2005). Yet, even though the Chinese interpretation of sovereignty has undergone such significant changes over the past four decades, China continues to insist on participating only in PKOs that have host government consent (Carlson, 2004; Taylor, 2009: 143, 157-158).

The UNPKO in the DRC, MONUC[15], was initially deployed in 1999. China started contributing with troops to MONUC in 2003 and as of June 2011, China was the 13th largest contributor to the mission with a standing, rotating peacekeeping force consisting of a 175 member engineering unit, a 43 member strong medical team and 16 observers (Chinaview, 2008; Ekengard, 2009: 19-20; Sun and Wang, 2011; Taylor, 2009: 149; UN, 2011; UN Peacekeeping, 2011). The Congolese regime never opposed the deployment of MONUC and participation in the mission was therefore never considered problematic by Beijing (Taylor, 2009: 147). This stands in sharp contrast for example to the controversy and political manoeuvring around UNAMID, the AU/UN hybrid operation in Darfur, Sudan.[16] China's willing participation in the PKO in the DRC is thus a clear reflection of changes on agency level: in the Chinese government's stance on sovereignty and peacekeeping.

Mining Related Activities

Apart from the Sicomines agreement discussed in section 2, the Chinese presence in the DRC's mining sector is diverse. As indicated in Table 1, the structural driver for all these activities is the strong (albeit fluctuating) demand for raw materials in the world economy, largely driven by China (e.g. Farooki, 2011). In terms of agent drivers, three distinct groups can be identified: individual entrepreneurs and private companies; private companies partly owned by SOEs; and wholly SOE-owned ventures.

Individual Entrepreneurs and Private Companies in Katanga Province

Private Chinese entrepreneurs started coming to the DRC's south-eastern Katanga province in 2005-2006 as the mining sector began to take off after the 1998-2003 civil war. During the boom in 2006-2007, before the global economic crisis hit Katanga in 2008, around 30 Chinese companies were active in the province.[17] This was a rather heterogeneous group, ranging from individual entrepreneurs and micro-sized[18] companies to small- and medium-sized operations. They were largely involved in two forms of activity: mineral trading and processing.[19] The former group of actors, the traders, were largely part of a "gold rush"-type influx driven by the high metal prices on the world market. During the author's 2008 field work, Chinese respondents explained that the profits for mineral traders in Katanga had been very high around 2005 (see also Jansson et al., 2009: 36). These lucrative opportunities drove a great deal of more or less serious private Chinese entrepreneurs to "set up shop" in Katanga to make a quick profit without necessarily having any long-term ambitions. However, as stated by one Chinese respondent in 2008, the opportunity to make a good profit in the "wild west" of Katanga gradually decreased as more Chinese traders entered the market.[20] It was also established during the 2008 field work that both the processing and trading ventures were largely run by private-owned companies or individual actors that had very little contact with the Chinese Embassy in Kinshasa. Only a very limited part of them had any form of support from the Chinese government (see further in Jansson et al., 2009:38). These activities can, as indicated in Figure 1, thus be character-ised as pure private sector activities. Practically all of these operations came to a halt in late 2008 or early 2009 as a result of the global economic downturn, which hit Katanga province hard (Jansson, 2010). In November 2010, virtu-ally all individual Chinese entrepreneurs had left Katanga and only eight of the small- and medium sized companies were operating at limited capacity. A number of other factories remained dormant.[21]

Partly SOE-owned Private Companies in Katanga Province

As of the author's field work in Katanga in March 2011, a total of only six Chinese companies were still operating in Lubumbashi, Likasi and Kolwezi. The global economic downturn has had a concentration effect in the group of Chinese companies in Katanga, culling out the "fortune seekers" from those with long-term ambitions. The group of Chinese companies has been drasti-cally reduced and the few remaining are medium- and large-sized ventures. A number of these companies, which as shown above were operating purely on market-seeking logics with no state support when they established their opera-tions in the DRC, have now partly been purchased by SOEs. For example, the SOE China Nonferrous Metal Mining Corporation (CNMC) has recently purchased a share of a medium-sized Chinese company in Katanga which op-erates two mining concessions and a processing plant.[22] These companies are thus currently changing characteristics, moving from the private sector-end of the continuum illustrated in Figure 1 towards the state-level end.

Wholly SOE-owned Ventures in Katanga Province

Two mining ventures in Katanga are, beyond the parastatal[23] Gécamines' share of the joint ventures, fully owned by Chinese SOEs. The China Railway Group Limited (CRGL) subsidiary China Overseas Engineering Group Corporation Limited (COVEC) has been active in the DRC's mining sector since 2005 as party to two joint ventures: COMILU and COMMUS. COMILU (*Compagnie Minière de Luisha*) is a JV in which Gécamines holds 28%, COVEC 35.38% and CRGL 36.72%. Established in 2006, this JV mines the 26.1 million tonnes of Luisha copper and cobalt deposits, the 1.45 million tonnes of Kalumbwe and Myunga deposits, and has a fairly large smelting operation. COMMUS (*Com-pagnie Minière de Musonoï*) is a 73:27 JV between COVEC and Gécamines. Established in 2005, it holds the 30 million tonnes Musonoï copper and cobalt concession. (China Railway Resources Group 2011, *Interface Exécutif - Légis-latif* 2010, interviews[24], Huderek 2011, Minarco-MineConsult 2007, *Ministère des Mines* 2007) As illustrated by Figure 1, these are thus Chinese state-level activities in the DRC's mining sector.

Private Companies in North Kivu and South Kivu Provinces

While the largest group of Chinese entrepreneurs in the DRC's mining sector have sought opportunities in Katanga, the lucrative trade in minerals from the country's eastern parts has also attracted a small group of Chinese actors. Three Chinese companies currently operate *comptoirs* (the DRC's mineral trading houses) in Goma, North Kivu province, trading in cassiterite and coltan originating from the South Kivu, North Kivu and Maniema provinces. Two of these companies also operate *comptoirs* in neighbouring Bukavo, South Kivu province.[25] Beyond this basic information, little is known about these companies. For instance, I do not have any information regarding their ownership structures. They do not have explicit linkages to SOEs and they are currently the only economic actors that purchase minerals in Goma and Bukavu openly and officially despite the implementation of the Dodd-Frank legislation.[26] This would indicate that they are private, market-seeking actors that do not have to worry about their reputation. Yet, it is still possible that they are partly or wholly owned by Chinese SOEs.

Sino-Congolese Trade

Analysis of trade between China and Africa is a thorny task methodologically speaking, since an indefinite share of the commercial exchanges between the two countries is routed via trading hubs. As noted by Taylor, "Chinese estimates of trade with Africa need to be treated with caution. The part played by Hong Kong as a transit point for Chinese imports and exports makes the official bilateral figures very dubious" (2009: 19-20). These challenges are relevant also in terms of the existing data on Sino-Congolese trade. Given that this chapter uses these figures as basis for its discussion around the characteristics and drivers of the commercial exchanges between the two countries, it is necessary to consider these challenges in further depth.

I do not have access to any information pertaining to the routes by means of which Chinese goods are exported to the DRC. It is therefore not possible to evaluate whether the official data recorded upon the goods' exit from China (illustrated in Figure 3) corresponds to the data recorded upon its entry into the DRC. To my knowledge, the only existing study of how Chinese consumer goods are being traded in the DRC has been conducted by Vircoulon (2010b), a study which focuses specifically on Kinshasa. However, his work provides no data in terms of the trade routes by means of which these goods reach the DRC. The data gathered by the Congolese customs authorities[27] in terms of the country of origin of consumer goods imported to the DRC can only be accessed upon demand in Kinshasa and is not available online.[28] I did not gather this data whilst in the field and do therefore not have access to it at this point. Similar reliability challenges apply to the data on Chinese imports from the DRC which, as shown by Figure 4, largely comprise of cobalt and copper. The figures recorded upon the minerals' entry into China (upon which Figures 2 and 4 are based) are most likely not comprehensive. Contrary to what is often assumed, Congolese copper and cobalt does currently not reach China with the help of the Chinese companies operating in the DRC. These companies focus on their core activity, mineral processing, and sell their produce to mineral trading companies which in turn handle the export onto the world market. As of January 2011, most of the Chinese companies were selling their goods to Geneva-based mineral trading multinational Trafigura.[29] As a result, an uncertain amount of the DRC's minerals are exported to China via Switzerland.[30]

Figure 2: Sino-Congolse trade 1995-2010

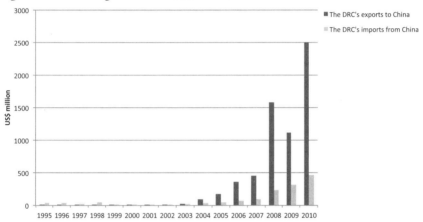

Source: World Trade Atlas data (for 1995-2009) and UN Comtrade database (for 2010).

With these methodological caveats in mind, the chapter now proceeds to the analysis of the characteristics and drivers of Sino-Congolese trade. As illustrated by Figure 3, trade volumes between the DRC and China began to grow in 2004, slightly earlier than the other Chinese impulses in the country and just after the end of the DRC's 1996-1997 and 1998-2003 civil wars.

Gu notes that the drivers for Chinese private companies operating in Africa can be understood both in terms of "push" factors (competition in China) and "pull" factors (opportunities in African countries) (2009: 577-578). These remarks are relevant also in terms of the exports of Chinese consumer goods to the DRC, which largely comprise of electrical appliances, vehicles and parts, foodstuffs, pharmaceutical products, machinery and footwear. As illustrated by Figure 2, Chinese exports to the DRC have increased over the past decade, albeit with a

Figure 3: Composition of China's top-20 exports to the DRC 1995-2009

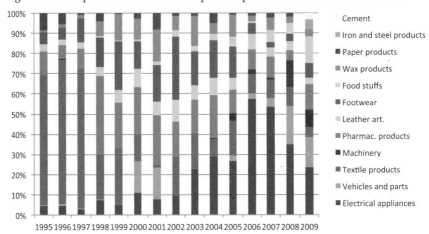

Source: World Trade Atlas data. Author's categorisation using HS commodity classification.

slower pace than the Chinese imports of Congolese raw materials. As listed in Table 1, the "push" factors for this form of Chinese activity in the DRC are surplus production and competition among wholesalers and retailers of consumer goods in China. The "pull" factor consists in the relatively unexploited Congolese market, which allows for Chinese traders to make a profit significantly easier than they would be able to do back in China. In interviews with the author in 2009, Chinese consumer goods retailers in one of Kinshasa's townships (*cité*) stated that that while competition is tough in the *cité*, profit margins are sufficient to motivate continued operations.[31] Agency is thus important in terms of understanding the "pull" factors at play. As noted by Gu: "the key is not the objective conditions of the African market, which are similar for all entrepreneurs [...] but the subjective element in the character of the Chinese entrepreneur [...] willing to go into areas where the profit margins are very low to begin with, and supply chains are weak" (ibid.: 574). Apart from Vircoulon (2010b), little research has been conducted on the import of Chinese consumer goods to the DRC. There is no comprehensive data over the size of this group or the exact nature of their activities. They enter the country in an uncoordinated fashion to set up business ventures where they identify market opportunities.[32] However, Vircoulon (2010b) shows that it is an activity run by private actors and not SOEs. According to him, a number of well-established Chinese business actors practically monopolise the procurement, import and wholesale part of the trading chain, while retail of the goods are made by a broader range of fairly newly arrived Chinese entrepreneurs. The Chinese actors involved in these activities are, just like the individual, small-scale entrepreneurs in the early days of Chinese presence in Katanga, operating on their own with little to no support from and contact with the Chinese embassy in Kinshasa (Vircoulon, 2010b). Chinese goods are certainly for sale also in other parts of the country, a retail phenomenon in which (at least as far as anecdotal evidence is concerned) Congolese traders are also involved. Yet, to my knowledge, no research has been conducted on this to date.

Figure 4: Composition of China's top-20 imports from the DRC 1995-200

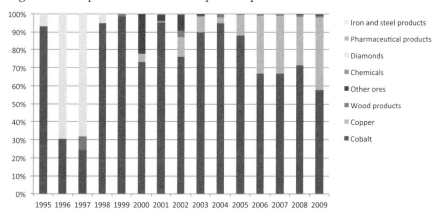

Source: World Trade Atlas data. Author's categorisation using HS commodity classification.

Congolese exports to China are, as is also the case for many other African countries, dominated by raw materials. As discussed above and as displayed in Figures 3 and 4, Chinese imports of Congolese copper and cobalt has been the main driver of the radical increase in Sino-Congolese trade volumes since 2004. The Chinese import of Congolese minerals reflects China's rise in a different way than the other state-level and private sector Chinese activities in the DRC. Structurally speaking, the Chinese demand for Congolese minerals is closely connected to the changes in China: the boom in the domestic construction industry as well as the country's importance in global value chains. Yet, in terms of agency, the "Chineseness" of the phenomenon is less direct. Of all Chinese activities in the DRC, this facet is the least tied to specific Chinese actors. As discussed above, business actors other than Chinese stakeholders are involved in the trading chain by means of which Congolese minerals reach the Chinese market. Besides Trafigura, these include a variety of actors involved in the complex networks, often informal and/or illicit, running the export of minerals from the DRC's eastern parts (e.g. Pole Institute, 2010; Vlassenroot and Raeymaekers, 2004).

As a representative for a Chinese company operating in Katanga stated succinctly: "Whatever is out there ends up in China anyway"[33]. Chinese foreign policy agency, formulated in its 2001 Going Global Strategy, *zou chuqu*[34] (Barboza, 2005; Brautigam 2009: 74; Zha and Hu, 2007: 109), has to date not played any important role in this facet of Chinese activity in the DRC. Yet, this will change as soon as the Sicomines joint venture (discussed in section 2 above) comes into production in 2012-2013.

The construction sector

The Chinese construction sector has been booming over the past decade. Foster et al note that it has seen an annual growth of 20 percent since 1999, "making China the largest construction market in the global economy" (2008:ix). This has provided a valuable training ground for China's construction companies, most of them SOEs (Broadman, 2007: 90, 267; Burke, 2007: 327). Over the past decade, Chinese construction companies have moved into African countries. As shown in Table 1, this development is a result of both structure- and agency-related factors. Gu's (2009: 577-578) remarks on the "push" and "pull" factors for Chinese private companies operating in Africa referred to above are useful also for understanding the structural drivers of Chinese state-owned construction companies operating in African countries. The "push" factor is here represented by domestic market saturation in China (Corkin, 2011: 11). The African continent's ability to "pull" Chinese construction companies is due both to the availability of tenders for projects funded by the Chinese government in Africa (e.g. Kaplinsky and Morris, 2009: 553, 561) but also the general opportunities in the African market with donor- as well as privately-funded projects available, and with less tough competition than in Europe or the United States (Corkin, 2011: 11). In terms of agency, two factors are at play: the SOEs search for lucrative markets and Beijing's political will to see Chinese companies operate in Africa (Taylor, 2009: 7-8). Chen et al note that "the Chinese government's involvement plays an important role in facilitating [Chinese construction firms'] market entries [in African countries]" (2007: 458). Chinese construction companies compete successfully in tenders for infrastructure projects in Africa, in the words of Gill and Reilly, "due primarily to their efficiency and low costs" (2007: 41). These Chinese companies work for a variety of principals. Chen et al's survey of 33 Chinese construction companies operating in Africa conducted show that 49 percent of the companies' projects came from international tenders, 40 percent from bidding among Chinese companies and 11 percent from sole source negotiations (2007: 458).

These dynamics are largely reflected in the DRC. Currently, seven[35] Chinese state-owned construction companies are active in that country, which in 2005-

2006 was the fourth most important African country in terms of tenders secured by Chinese companies on the African continent.[36] (Foster et al., 2008: 29). This strong Congolese "pull" factor is largely due to the significant emphasis placed by that country's development partners on infrastructure reconstruction. Tenders are being issued for a plethora of construction projects in the country, mostly funded by bi- and multilateral donors (Trefon, 2011: 53 *et seq*), but also to an extent by the Chinese government, as illustrated in Table 2. As the overview below shows, the DRC-based Chinese companies carry out work for several different principals: the Chinese government (development aid projects for which they win tenders back in China); international donor organisations (largely the African Development Bank and the World Bank, projects acquired through international tender processes); and private business interests, both Congolese and other.

Sinohydro (which is also party to the Sicomines JV discussed above) has been the most active of the Chinese construction companies in the DRC, notably as contractor for the World Bank.[37] It implemented three road- and one bridge project for that principal between 2002 and 2008, and was thus active in the DRC long before the Sicomines agreement was initiated. CREC, the other main party to the Sicomines JV, has also taken up such assignments, most well-known of which has been the refurbishment work the company did on Kinshasa's artery *le Boulevard du 30 juin*. While the final stages of work carried out by CREC on the *Boulevard* were indeed financed by means of the Sicomines agreement, the initial stages were actually funded by the City of Kinshasa and the Congolese government (Eyobie, 2009). Interestingly, even though the funds for that project was not extended by China, CREC's early work on the Boulevard is the example most often mentioned by *kinois* (Kinshasa residents) and expatriates living in Kinshasa when China's support to Congolese infrastructure reconstruction is discussed (e.g. Trefon, 2011: 35). This is a prominent example of how different forms of Chinese activity in the DRC are confused both with each other and with unrelated developments (such as this case of the DRC using its own funds for infrastructure rehabilitation). The chapter returns to this discussion further below.

The Congolese government also finances China Road and Bridge Corporation's US$52.6 million refurbishment undertaking on *Boulevard Lumumba* in Kinshasa, as well as China Guangdong Changda Highway Engineering Corporation's refurbishment of *l'Avenue de Libération*, also in Kinshasa.[38] In November 2009, China New Era International Engineering Corporation won a tender to refurbish the Lukaya water treatment plant in the Kinshasa area, a World Bank-financed project worth US$21 million (Kuediasala, 2009). As of September 2011, this project is still under implementation (Mobateli, 2011). China Jiangsu Construction Development Company is not working on any major donor-funded projects at the moment, but is instead implementing a few private projects: an apartment block for a Chinese business man and a villa for a Congolese private person.[39] China Jiangsu has earlier constructed the Sino-Congolese Friendship Hospital in N'Djili, Kinshasa, a donation from the Chinese government in 2004 (refer to Table 2), as well as the new offices of the Chinese Ministry of Commerce in Kinshasa. As of the 2011 field research, the company was also in negotiations for the construction of a hotel in Lubumbashi and a shopping centre in Kinshasa, both of which projects would be for Congolese business actors. Lastly, *Société Zhengwei Technique Coopération*[40] is currently implementing projects in Kinshasa for Huawei, the Congolese government, the World Bank and the African Development Bank.[41]

Telecommunications

The DRC's telecommunications sector is growing rapidly. Despite infrastructure constraints such as the lack of a national fibre optic cable network, the number of mobile phone users grew from 1.2 million in 2003 to 9.2 million in 2008 (Kiambu, 2006; Mthembu-Salter, 2008; Mvogo, 2009). Competition is currently tough between mobile network providers as well as between companies selling telecommunications equipment (interview[42], Mvogo, 2009). Two Chinese companies, ZTE and Huawei, are currently active in the DRC. ZTE is state-owned and its entry into the DRC in 2000 was driven by Chinese government's foreign policy ambitions: its will to facilitate its SOEs' expansion overseas and to strengthen bilateral ties with the DRC. ZTE entered by means of the formation of a joint venture, a mobile phone operating company called Congo-China Telecom (CCT), between ZTE and the Congolese telecommunications parastatal the Congolese Office of Post and Telecommunications[43] (Mthembu-Salter, 2008: 9-10). The total costs for the establishment of CCT was RMB 164 million, 80 million of which was, as indicated in Table 2 above, covered by a China Exim Bank credit line (*People's Daily*, 2000). Mthembu-Salter argues that this credit line was mostly used to purchase telecommunications equipment from ZTE (2008: 10). CCT is still active in the DRC[44], and is now the fourth largest among the mobile network operators in the country (*Reuters*, 2011). Whereas ZTE's entry into the DRC was facilitated by a Chinese government credit line, the company is now operating according to market-seeking logics (Mthembu-Salter, 2008: 13). Apart from its engagement in CCT, it is currently the fifth largest telecommunications equipment provider in the DRC, supplying equipment to Vodacom and CCT.[45]

Huawei is a privately owned company[46] (Mackie, 2011). As Huawei developed in China, a market which is dominated by a few large state-owned players (*Xinhua*, 2008, Yu et al., 2004), it found a competitive niche in the rural market, since "the main orders for the lucrative urban network systems went to either state-owned companies or foreign firms" (Mackie, 2011). From there, it developed into one of the world's largest telecommunication equipment providers. Huawei is present in the DRC since 2004, a market it entered without support from the Chinese government (Mthembu-Salter, 2008: 10). Today, it is the second largest player in the DRC after Stockholm-based Ericsson in terms of consolidated telecommunications sales.[47] It is currently supplying equipment to Luxemburg-based Tigo and CCT and is, according to a senior manager of a European telecommunications company, currently developing its capacities very fast.[48]

Even though there are significant differences in terms of these two companies' characteristics, ZTE being an SOE and Huawei a private company, their structural and agency related drivers seem to have converged over time, as indicated in Table 1. Structurally speaking, they are both "pushed" overseas by the competition in the Chinese market and "pulled" by the opportunities in the burgeoning Congolese market. In terms of agency, both companies remain in the DRC as a result of their market-seeking ambitions.

Concluding Discussion

It is often mistakenly assumed that all Chinese activities in the DRC emanate from the bilateral government-to-government ties between the two countries. This is prominently exemplified by the following quote from Trefon:

> When Laurent-Désiré Kabila became president, he developed an anti-imperialism and anti-Western discourse. This opened new opportunities for exchanges with China. Chinese companies invested in mobile phone services and infrastructure, hospitals and health clinics, and Congolese students received scholarships to study in China. Congolese businessmen started communicating between Congo and China, importing containers full of cheap products 'Made in China'. Today, China is the number-one recipient of Congolese exports and continues to intensify its activities. It is now the major foreign commercial partner to track in Congo. (2011: 35)

Trefon's portrayal of a uniform development emanating from strengthened bilateral ties in the late 1990s is misleading. As this chapter has shown, the activities he lists both differ and converge in terms of their characteristics and drivers. While some of the drivers are related to the bilateral relations between the two countries, others are not. It is this chapter's argument that the only two truly common denominators between the Chinese activities in the DRC are that they are all reflections of the past decades' changes in China, propelled by

China's rise. While some of them are related to the bilateral ties between Congo and China, others are not.

The donations and credit lines provided by the Chinese government to the DRC reflects the Chinese government's changing foreign policy ambitions in an era where the Chinese leadership needs to ensure the continued access to raw materials and where the ties to other developing countries are increasingly important as the power configurations of the global political economy change. The Sino-Congolese military exchanges taking place within the bilateral framework reflect Beijing's foreign policy ambition to maintain strong ties with the DRC. China's participation in the UN's peacekeeping operation in the DRC mirrors the growing Chinese sensitivity to international demands for the country to assume a more important role as a "responsible international actor". The strong (albeit fluctuating) demand for raw materials in the world economy, notably driven by China, is reflected in the DRC by means of the various Chinese activities taking place in the DRC's mining sector as well as by the export of Congolese raw materials towards China.

The import of Chinese consumer goods to the DRC echoes the tough competition among wholesalers and retailers of consumer goods in China, which pushes Chinese entrepreneurs to seek opportunities in less exploited markets like the DRC. Chinese construction companies' presence as contractors in the DRC furthermore mirrors several developments in China: the market saturation in the Chinese construction sector which "pushes" the companies to seek opportunities overseas; the Chinese government's financial support enabling the SOEs to compete successfully for tenders; and the Chinese companies' strong operational capacity, acquired through their experience of large-scale infrastructure construction projects domestically. Lastly, the presence of the Chinese telecommunications companies ZTE and Huawei in the DRC reflects the competitive environment in China's telecommunications sector where a few large SOEs dominate the market. The SOE ZTE's arrival in the DRC was also a result of the Chinese government's will to facilitate its SOEs' expansion overseas and its ambition to strengthen bilateral ties with the DRC.

These dynamics are crucial to take into account when analysing the Chinese presence in periphery countries like the DRC. Analyses which make the connection between Chinese activities overseas and the complex changes in China itself, and which goes beyond the portrayal of all Chinese activities as part of one uniform trend, have the potential to make an important contribution to our understanding how China's rise impacts on semi-periphery and periphery countries.

Notes

1   The author would like to thank the colleagues who provided comments on earlier drafts of this chapter.

2   The country has been renamed several times. Upon independence in 1960, it was named the Republic of the Congo-Léopoldville and in 1964, the name was changed to the Democratic Republic of the Congo-Léopoldville. The country was renamed Zaïre in 1971 and its current name was given to it in 1997.

3   The post-conflict, resource-rich Central African country had a GDP per capita of US$186 in 2010 (IMF, 2011). In 2009, subsistence agriculture and the extraction- and export of raw materials accounted for 47.4 percent and 7.1 percent of GDP respectively (African Economic Outlook 2011). The country could thus be labelled a 'periphery economy' in the traditional dependency theory-sense of the term.

4   I am well aware of the debates (*e.g.* Nest, 2011) around Autesserre's (2010) argument that the international community's determination to define the DRC as a 'post'-conflict country and push it to hold elections instead of attending to local-level conflicts has had devastating implications for long-term peace. However, I do not engage further with this matter here.

5   China Export-Import (Exim) Bank is now the only state-owned Chinese policy bank. China Development Bank (CDB) went commercial in 2008 and the Agricultural Development Bank of China in 2010 (Downs, 2011:20; Reuters 2010; Xu, 2008). The two latter banks now operate according to commercial logics, yet political considerations are, to some extent, still at play in terms of the decisions taken and the strategies pursued (thanks to Pak K. Lee and Charles C. L. Kwong for conveying insights in this regard). China Exim Bank is the only Chinese (policy) bank which has extended actual loans to the DRC to date. CDB has, however, shown interest in the DRC for almost as long as China Exim Bank. During 2008-2009, negotiations were at an advanced stage for the financing of a Sicomines-type barter deal, yet no agreement was ever signed (Jansson, 2011). As of 2011, relations between the CDB and the DRC seem reinvigorated. A framework agreement was signed by both parties in March 2011 to collaborate on a number of areas: roads and railways, mines, energy, oil, agriculture and manufacturing (Kavanagh, 2011). Yet again, no specific financing agreements have been signed. Refer to Jansson (2011) for a more in-depth analysis of CDB's ambitions in the DRC.

6   From independence in 1960, the DRC switched allegiances on a number of occasions between the People's Republic of China (PRC) and the Republic of China (Taiwan). In 1972, the DRC recognised the PRC, and bilateral ties have since been stable.

7   Whether or not a credit line is classified as ODA in OECD-DAC terms is determined by the grant element, which is essentially way of ensuring that the cost for the loan is low enough – that it is concessional. The IMF defines the grant element as 'the difference between the loan's nominal value (face value) and the sum of the discounted future debt-service payments to be made by the borrower (present value), expressed as a percentage of the loan's face value' (IMF, 2010). In other words, the grant element is the difference between the cost for a similar loan at market interest rates

(more specifically currency-specific 'commercial interest reference rates' or CIRRs) and a loan at discounted interest rates (*ibid.*). The interest rate, the grace period and the total repayment period are key variables for the calculation of the grant element.

8   Author's interviews in Kinshasa, 21.02.2011 and 07.03.2011.

9   The quantities involved are approximately 10.6 million tonnes of copper and 626 619 tonnes of cobalt. For further details, refer to the main agreement, 'la Convention de Collaboration', pp. 30–32. The agreement is available on Global Witness's homepage, http://www.globalwitness.org/sites/default/files/library/China-DRC%20April%202008%20contract%20French%20and%20Chinese_0.pdf

10 The Sicomines agreement is a very complex setup and this chapter does not fully account for the dynamics involved. The topic is treated at length in Marysse and Geenen 2009 and 2011, Jansson 2011 and Vircoulon 2010a. These publications also account for the 2008-2009 (geo) political controversy around the agreement. It is not discussed here given that it is not directly relevant for the chapter's argument that the Chinese activities in the DRC reflect the past decades' changes in China.

11 Author's interview with a well placed Chinese respondent, 14.03.2011, Kinshasa. See further in Jansson 2011.

12 Prior to this, during periods of non-recognition, Mao's government offered training, material supply and monetary support to rebels fighting the Congolese government. This form of support was, however, never very significant. (Curtis, 2008: 89 *et seq*)

13 *Forces Armées de la République Démocratique du Congo*

14 Thanks to Maria Eriksson Baaz for providing me with this information.

15 *Mission de l'Organisation des Nations Unies en République Démocratique du Congo.* On the 1st of July 2010, MONUC changed names to MONUSCO (*Mission de l'Organisation des Nations Unies pour la Stabilisation en République Démocratique du Congo*) (UNSC, 2010) "to reflect the new phase reached in the country" (UN, 2011).

16 In the case of UNAMID, the Chinese approach went through a remarkable change between 2004 and 2007 which was largely due to concerns for the reputational risks of being associated with Khartoum. Beijing went from refraining to vote on UNSC resolutions on Darfur – an abstention motivated by the lack of host government consent – to applying pressure on Khartoum to cooperate with the international community and accept a UN force in Darfur. UNAMID was finally deployed in November 2007 and China has continuously contributed with troops to the mission since December that year. (Large, 2008: 288-291; Taylor, 2009: 148-149; UN Peacekeeping, 2011)

17 The account of the activities of Chinese companies in Katanga draws on the following: field work conducted by the author in Lubumbashi and surrounds in September 2008 and March 2011; author's email exchanges and telephone interviews with Chinese respondents throughout 2008-2011; and the author's previous publications: Jansson et al (2009) and Jansson (2010). As mentioned, the 2008 and 2011 field work was conducted in collaboration with Professor Jiang Wenran of the University of Alberta, Canada, whose contribution is gratefully acknowledged.

18 This chapter defines companies with ten or less employees as micro sized enterprises, companies with up to 50 employees as small sized enterprises, companies

with less than 250 employees as medium sized and companies with more than 250 employees as large sized enterprises.

19 I do not consider mining as one of the core activities of the group of Chinese actors operating in Katanga at this time, since only a few of them had access to mining concessions. Those who did were involved in joint ventures with Congolese actors that may have had access to a mining permit but lacked the resources needed to start exploration on the concession. However, as of 2008, these ventures had only reached the exploration stage and had not yet begun extractive activities (Jansson, 2010).

20 Author's interview, 11.09.2008, Lubumbashi.

21 Author's telephone interviews with managers of two Chinese mining companies, 25.11.2010.

22 Interviews, 09.03.2011 and 11.03.2011, Lubumbashi. This acquisition is part of CNMC's broader move into the Central African copperbelt - the company is also a majority shareholder in the Chambishi Mine in Zambia (CNMC, 2011). I cannot provide the names of the companies discussed, given the commitment to keep the respondents anonymous.

23 Most mining ventures in the DRC take place in a joint venture (JV) with one of the country's mining parastatals. These are Gécamines and Sodimico (copper and cobalt), MIBA (diamonds), Okimo (gold), Sakima (cassiterite) and *l'Entreprise Minière de Kisenge* (manganese). Generally the JVs are set up with the foreign investor as a majority shareholder.

24 Author's interviews, 9-11 March 2011, Lubumbashi.

25 This data was partly acquired in an interview with a senior representative of the Congolese Ministry of Mines, 02.12.2010, Brussels; and partly kindly made available by Thierry Vircoulon.

26 The United States' Dodd-Frank Wall Street reform act, adopted in July 2010, requires that companies listed in the US account for the due diligence efforts they have undertaken to ensure that the minerals they use are 'conflict free' (meaning minerals "that [do not] directly or indirectly finance or benefit armed groups in the [DRC] or an adjoining country" (Verbruggen et al., 2011:10)). The minerals covered by the legislation are cassiterite, coltan, gold and wolframite and their derivatives tantalum, tin and tungsten (King & Spalding, 2011, Verbruggen et al., 2011). Many US-listed companies stopped purchasing minerals originating from the DRC already prior to the entry into force of the law on the 15th April 2011 for fear of damaging their reputation (Vircoulon 2011). This resulted in a *de facto* embargo which has been devastating for the livelihoods of the many thousand Congolese whose survival depends on different parts of the mineral trading chain (ITRI, 2011; Stearns, 2011). It is now only the Chinese actors in eastern DRC that buy the so called 'conflict minerals' openly and officially, according to the New York Times "at a steep discount" (Aronson, 2011).

27 *Direction générale des douanes et accises* (DGDA). However, most imports to the DRC are managed by BIVAC, a Kinshasa-based subsidiary of the Paris-based company *Bureau Veritas*. BIVAC is subcontracted by the Congolese government to manage all imports of goods worth more than US$2500 to the DRC. Source: Author's telephonic interviews with a civil servant at the statistics department of the DRC's

central bank; and with a representative of BIVAC, 06.10.2011.

28 More specifically, the data is available upon request from BIVAC in Kinshasa (see the endnote above). <u>Source:</u> Author's telephonic interviews with a representative of BIVAC, 06.10.2011.

29 Author's personal correspondence with a manager of a Chinese company, 13.01.2011. See also Trafigura (2011).

30 Thanks to Peter Kragelund for drawing my attention to this.

31 Author's interviews, 04.03.2009, Kinshasa.

32 Author's interviews in Kinshasa with Wu Zexian, then Chinese Ambassador to the DRC, 23.02.2009; and with the Director General of the Congolese National Agency for Investment Promotion (ANAPI), 02.10.2008 and 27.02.2009, Kinshasa.

33 Informal conversation, 09.03.2011, Lubumbashi.

34 While *zou chuqu* literally means 'go out', it is mostly translated as the 'Going Global strategy' in the literature.

35 I have data on the operations of seven Chinese construction companies in the DRC but have not been able to ascertain if the seventh company, *Société Zhengwei Technique Coopération*, is an SOE or a private company. Given that it is well-established in several African countries it is probably an SOE, but I have not been able to confirm this.

36 More specifically, 72 percent of tenders won by Chinese companies were issued in four African countries. The DRC's share was 12 percent, the other three being Ethiopia (31 percent), Mozambique (16 percent) and Tanzania (13 percent) (Foster et al., 2008: 29).

37 Author's interview with a well-placed Chinese respondent, 26.02.2009, Kinshasa.

38 Author's personal interview with a representative for the Congolese Agency for Major Construction Works, 09.02.2011, Kinshasa.

39 Author's interviews with a well-placed Chinese respondent, 24.02.2009, 09.02.2011 and 07.03.2011, Kinshasa.

40 Refer to my comment in endnote 35.

41 Author's interview with well-placed Chinese respondents, 14.03.2011, Kinshasa.

42 Author's interview with a senior manager of a European telecommunications company, 15.02.2011, Kinshasa.

43 *Office Congolais des Postes et des Télécommunications.*

44 CCT has been up for sale several times, both to Johannesburg-based MTN and to France Telecom, but no agreement has yet been reached in this regard (Africa-Asia Confidential 2009:5, Reuters 2011).

45 Author's interview with a senior manager of a European telecommunications company, 15.02.2011, Kinshasa.

46 Although it has no formal state involvement, allegations have been made that the company is secretly involved with the Chinese military, charges denied by Huawei (*e.g.* Mackie 2011).

47 Author's interview with a senior manager of a European telecommunications company, 15.02.2011, Kinshasa.

48 Ibid.

References

Africa-Asia Confidential (2009) "Big numbers on Congo's telecoms projects", 2(6). April. Page 5.

African Economic Outlook (2011) "Democratic Republic of Congo". Available at http://www.africaneconomicoutlook.org/en/countries/central-africa/congo-democratic-republic/

Alden, Chris and Alves, Ana Cristina (2008) "History and Identity in the Construction of China's Africa Policy", *Review of African Political Economy*, 35(115): 43-58.

Alden, Chris; Large, Daniel and Soares de Oliviera, Ricardo. (2008) "Introduction", in Alden, C.; Large, D. and Soares de Oliviera, R. (eds.) *China Returns to Africa. A Rising Power and a Continent Embrace*. London: Hurst.

Aronson, David (2011) "How Congress Devastated Congo", *New York Times*, August 7. Available at http://www.nytimes.com/2011/08/08/opinion/how-congress-devastated-congo.html

Autesserre, Séverine (2010) *The Trouble with the Congo. Local Violence and the Failure of International Peacebuilding*. Cambridge: Cambridge University Press.

Barboza, David (2005) "China seeks known brands to go global", *New York Times*, June 30. Available at http://www.nytimes.com/2005/06/29/business/worldbusiness/29iht-brands.html

Brautigam, Deborah (2011). "Chinese Development Aid in Africa: What, Where, Why and How Much?" in Golley, Jane and Song, Ligang (eds.) *China Update 2011*. Canberra: Australia National University.

Brautigam, Deborah (2009) *The Dragon's Gift: The Real Story of China in Africa*. Oxford: Oxford University Press.

Broadman, Harry G. (2007) *Africa's Silk Road: China and India's New Economic Frontier*. Washington: The World Bank.

Burke, Christopher (2007) "China's Entry into Construction Industries in Africa: Tanzania and Zambia as case studies", *China Report*, 43: 323-336.

Butts, Kent Hughes and Bankus, Brent (2009) "China's Pursuit of Africa's Natural Resources", *Collins Center Study*, 1-09. Center for Strategic Leadership, U.S. Army War College.

Carlson, Allen (2004) "Helping to Keep the Peace (Albeit Reluctantly): China's Recent Stance on Sovereignty and Multilateral Intervention", *Pacific Affairs*, 77(1): 9-27.

Chen, Chuan; Pi-Chu, Chiu; Orr, Ryan J.; Goldstein, Andrea (2007) "An empirical analysis of Chinese construction firms' entry into Africa". Paper presented at CRIOCM2007 International Symposium on Advancement of Construction Management and Real Estate, 8-13 August 2007, Sydney,

Australia. Available at http://crgp.stanford.edu/publications/conference_papers/Chen_Chiu_Orr_Goldstein_Emp_analysis_Chinese_Africa.pdf

China Railway Resources Group (2011) "绿纱矿业有限责任公司简介" (Member Companies: Luisha Mining). Avilable at http://www.crmrc.com.cn/news_view.asp?newsid=250

Chinaview (2008) "Chinese peacekeeping forces arrive in DR Congo", November 13. Available at http://news.xinhuanet.com/english/2008-11/13/content_10351900.htm

CNMC (China Nonferrous Metal Mining Corporation) homepage (2011) "Chambishi Copper Mine". Available at http://www.cnmc.com.cn/417-1102-1600.aspx

Corkin, Lucy (2011) "Chinese Construction Companies in Angola: A Local Linkages Perspective". Making the Most of Commodities Programme, Discussion Paper No. 2. Cape Town: University of Cape Town, Milton Keynes: Open University.

Curtis, Devon (2008) "Partner or Predator in the Heart of Africa? Chinese Engagement with the DRC", in Ampiah, Kweku and Naidu, Sanusha (eds.) *Crouching Tiger, Hidden Dragon? Africa and China*. Scottsville: University of KwaZulu-Natal Press and Cape Town: Centre for Conflict Resolution.

Downs, Erica (2011) *Inside China, Inc: China Development Bank's Cross-Border Energy Deals.* John L Thornton China Center Monograph Series, No. 3. Washington DC: Brookings Institution.

Ekengard, Arvid (2009) "Coordination and Coherence in the Peace Operation in the Democratic Republic of Congo". User Report. Stockholm: Swedish Defence Research Agency.

Eyobie, Victoire (2009) "Modernisation du Blvd du 30 Juin", *Entreprendre*. Available at http://www.entreprendre.cd/entreprendre/Actualite/Articles-phares/MODERNISATION-DU-BLVD-DU-30-JUIN

Farooki, Masuma (2011) "China's Structural Demand and the Commodity Super Cycle: Implications for Africa", in Dent, Christopher M. (ed.) *China and Africa development relations*. London: Routledge.

Foster, Vivien; Butterfield, William; Chen, Chuan; Pushak, Nataliya (2008) *Building Bridges: China's Growing Role as Infrastructure Financier for Sub-Saharan Africa*. Washington: World Bank.

Gill, Bates and Huang, Chin-Hao (2009) "China's expanding role in peacekeeping. Prospects and policy implications". SIPRI policy paper, no. 25. Solna: Stockholm International Peace Research Institute.

Gill, Bates and Reilly, James (2007) "The Tenuous Hold of China Inc. in Africa", *The Washington Quarterly*, 30(3): 37-52.

Gu, Jing (2009) "China's Private Enterprises in Africa and the Implications for African Development", *European Journal of Development Research*, 21(4): 570-587.

Hellström, Jerker (2010) "China's role in the Democratic Republic of Congo (DRC)", Unpublished briefing paper presented at the seminar "China's Response to Security Threats in Africa", Brussels Institute of Contemporary China Studies (BICCS), Brussels, 17-19 May 2010.

Huderek, Richard (2011) "Katangan Copperbelt. Who is Where in Katanga?" on Google Maps, available at http://maps.google.com/maps/ms?ie=UTF8&hl=e n&msa=0&msid=214623921724127971595.00044e1e24afa04af0cca&z=7

IMF (International Monetary Fund) (2010) "Concessionality and the Design of Debt Limits in IMF-Supported Programs in Low-Income Countries". Available at http://www.imf.org/external/np/pdr/conc/index.htm

IMF (2011) "Gross domestic product per capita, current prices. IMF staff estimates", World Economic Outlook Database, April 2011.

Interface Exécutif - Législatif (2010) "Gécamines et la stratégie des partenariats". Available at http://www.linterfacemag.com/Entreprises_pg63.php

ITRI (2011) "DR Congo miners request direct talks with US government on trade embargo", March 4. Available at http://www.itri.co.uk/pooled/articles/ BF_NEWSART/view.asp?Q=BF_NEWSART_322533

Jansson, Johanna (2009) "Patterns of Chinese investment, aid and trade in Central Africa (Cameroun, the DRC and Gabon)", Briefing paper prepared for World Wide Fund for Nature (WWF). Stellenbosch University: Centre for Chinese Studies.

Jansson, Johanna (2010) "DRC: Chinese investment in Katanga", in *Pambazuka News*, Issue 476.

Jansson, Johanna (2011) "The Sicomines agreement: continuity and change in the DRC's international relations". Occasional Paper No. 97. Johannesburg: South African Institute of International Affairs. Available at http://www. saiia.org.za/images/stories/pubs/occasional_papers/saia_sop_97_jansson _20111031.pdf

Jansson, Johanna; Burke, Christopher and Jiang, Wenran (2009) "Chinese Companies in the Extractive Industries of Gabon & the DRC: Perceptions of Transparency". Report from a research undertaking by the Centre for Chinese Studies, prepared for the Extractive Industries Transparency Initiative (EITI) & Revenue Watch Institute (RWI). Stellenbosch University: Centre for Chinese Studies.

Jiang, Wenran (2009) "Fuelling the Dragon: China's Rise and Its Energy and Resource Extraction in Africa", *China Quarterly*, 199: 585-609.

Kaplinsky, Raphael and Morris, Mike (2009) "Chinese FDI in Sub-Saharan Africa: engaging with large dragons", *European Journal of Development Research*, 21(4): 551–569.

Kavanagh, Michael J. (2011) "Congo and China Development Bank Sign Infrastructure Deal", Bloomberg. March 28.

Kiambu, Jacques (2006) "Télécommunications et politiques de développement dans la République Démocratique du Congo", *Afrique Contemporaine*, 2(218): 175-183.

King & Spalding (2011) "Client Alert. Dodd-Frank's "Conflict Minerals" Provision". April 27. Available at http://www.kslaw.com/imageserver/KSPublic/library/publication/ca042711.pdf

Kuediasala, Faustin (2009) "Congo-Kinshasa: Desserte en eau - Les travaux de l'usine de Lukaya confiés à la firme chinoise CNME", *Le Potentiel*. November 13. Available at http://fr.allafrica.com/stories/200911130316.html

Large, Daniel (2008) "From Non-Interference to Constructive Engagement? China's Evolving Relations with Sudan", in Alden, Chris; Large, Daniel and Soares de Oliviera, Ricardo. (eds.) *China Returns to Africa. A Rising Power and a Continent Embrace.* London: Hurst.

Mackie, Nick (2011) "Innovation in China: Huawei - the secretive tech giant", *BBC News*. July 25. Available at: http://www.bbc.co.uk/news/business-14238345

Marysse, Stefaan and Geenen, Sara (2009) "Win-win or unequal exchange? The case of the Sino-Congolese cooperation agreements", *Journal of Modern African Studies*, 47(3): 371-396.

Marysse, Stefaan and Geenen, Sara (2011). " 'If you control the railway, you command the wealth of a country': Chinese involvement in DRCongo", in Ansoms, An and Marysse, Stefan (eds.) *Natural Resources and Local Livelihoods in the Great Lakes Region of Africa. A Political Economy Perspective.* Houndmills, Basingstoke: Palgrave Macmillan.

Melmot, Sébastien (2009) "Candide in Congo. The Expected Failure of Security Sector Reform (SSR)". Focus Stratégique n° 9 bis. Paris, Brussels: Institut Français des Relations Internationales.

MFA (Ministry of Foreign Affairs of the People's Republic of China) (2006) "China's African Policy", January 12. Available at http://www.fmprc.gov.cn/eng/zxxx/t230615.htm

Minarco-MineConsult (2007) "Appendix V. Independent Technical Review Report". Available at http://main.ednews.hk/listedco/listconews/sehk/2007 1122/00390_252968/E133.pdf

Ministère des Mines (2007) "*Rapport des travaux 2. Partenariats conclus par la Gécamines*". Available at http://www.miningcongo.cd/pdf/tome2.pdf

Mobateli, Angelo (2011) "Congo-Kinshasa: Inauguration du module III de l'usine de la Regideso de N'Djili", *Le Potentiel*, September 15. Available at: http://fr.allafrica.com/stories/201109141420.html

Mohan, Giles and Power, Marcus (2008) "New African Choices? The Politics of Chinese Engagement", *Review of African Political Economy*, 35(1): 23-42.

Mthembu-Salter, Gregory (2008) "Price Power: China's role in the telecommunications sector of the Democratic Republic of Congo*", China-Africa Policy Report*, No. 6, South African Institute of International Affairs (SAIIA). Available at : http://www.saiia.org.za/images/stories/pubs/chap/chap_rep_06_mthembu_salter_200807.pdf

Mvogo, Jean-Paul (2009) "Dynamiques et perspectives du secteur des télécommunications en RDC". Paris : CapAfrique. Available at: http://www.capafrique.org/pdf/20090901%20Mvogo.pdf

Nest, Michael (2011) "From local-level violence to international relations theory: a journey through the trouble with the Congo", *African Security Review*, 20(2): 66-72.

OECD (2010). "DAC Statistical Reporting Directives", DCD/DAC(2010)40/REV1. Paris: OECD.

OECD (Organisation for Economic Cooperation and Development) (2008) "Is it ODA?" Factsheet. Available at: http://www.oecd.org/dataoecd/21/21/34086975.pdf

Okenda, Jean-Pierre. (2010) "Report on the violation of the rights of workers in the Chinese companies in Katanga and the imbalance in the DRC-China Consortium Agreement", in Marks, Stephen (ed.) *Strengthening the Civil Society Perspective. China's African Impact*. Cape Town, Nairobi and Oxford: Fahamu, Emerging Powers in Africa Programme. Available at http://www.fahamu.org/downloads/strengthening_the_civil_society_perspective.pdf

People's Daily (2000) "Eximbank Supports Congo (Kinshasa) Telecom Project". December 14. Available at http://english.peopledaily.com.cn/english/200012/14/eng20001214_57833.html

Pole Institute (2010) *Blood Minerals. The Criminalization of the Mining Industry in Eastern DRC*. Pole Institute: Goma. Available at http://www.pole-institute.org/documents/Minerais%20du%20sang%20VA%A0.pdf

RAID (Rights and Accountability in Development) (2009) "Chinese Mining Operations in Katanga Democratic Republic of Congo", September. Available at http://raid-uk.org/docs/ChinaAfrica/DRCCHINA%20report.pdf

Reuters (2010) "AgBank to pay $248mln in IPO fees, lowest of Big 4", July 14. Available at http://www.reuters.com/article/2010/07/14/agbank-fees-idUSHKU00007520100714

Reuters (2011) "France Telecom targets DR Congo mobile operator", July 17. Available at http://www.reuters.com/article/2011/07/17/francetele-com-idUSLDE76G05920110717

Snow, Philip (2008) "Foreword" in Alden, Chris; Large, Daniel and Soares de Oliviera, Ricardo. (eds.) *China Returns to Africa. A Rising Power and a Continent Embrace*. London: Hurst.

Stearns, Jason (2011) "Interview with Eric Kajemba on Conflict Minerals", *Congo Siasa*, August 3. Available at http://congosiasa.blogspot.com/2011/08/interview-with-eric-kajemba-on-conflict.html

Sun, Xingwei and Wang, Chuanfeng (2011) "13th Chinese peacekeeping force leaves for Congo (K)", *PLA Daily*, July 19. Available at http://eng.mod.gov.cn/Peacekeeping/2011-07/19/content_4263373.htm

Taylor, Ian (2009) *China's new role in Africa*. Boulder: Lynne Rienner.

Thompson, Drew (2005) "Beijing's participation in UN peacekeeping operations", *China Brief*, 5(11): 7-9

Trafigura homepage (2011) "About us". Available at http://www.trafigura.com/about_us.aspx

Trefon, Theodore (2011) *Congo Masquerade. The political culture of aid inefficiency and reform failure*. London, New York: Zed Books.

UN (United Nations) webpage (2011) "MONUC: Helping bring peace and stability in the DRC". Available at http://www.un.org/en/peacekeeping/missions/monuc/

UN Peacekeeping webpage (2011) "Troop and police contributors, 2011, June". Available at http://www.un.org/en/peacekeeping/resources/statistics/contributors.shtml

UNSC (UN Security Council) (2010) Resolution 1925 (2010), S/RES/1925 (2010).

Verbruggen, Didier; Francq, Evie and Cuvelier, Jeroen (2011) "Guide to Current Mining Reform Initiatives in Eastern DRC". Antwerp: International Peace Information Service. Available at http://www.ipisresearch.be/att/20110412_Guide_Mining_Reform_EDRC.pdf

Vircoulon, Thierry (2010a) "Autopsie d'une controverse internationale. Le partenariat sino-congolais sous le feu des critiques", *Temps Modernes*, January.

Vircoulon, Thierry (2010b) "Stratégies chinoises de survie à Kinshasa, République Démocratique du Congo" in *Repenser l'Indépendance : la RD Congo 50 ans plus tard - Actes du Colloque du cinquantenaire*. Goma : Pole Institute.

Vircoulon, Thierry (2011) "Derrière le problème des minerais des conflits, la gouvernance du Congo", *On the African Peacebuilding Agenda*, April 13. Available at http://www.crisisgroup.org/

Vlassenroot, Koen and Raeymaekers, Timothy (2004) "Conflict and Artisanal Mining in Kamituga (South Kivu)", in Vlassenroot, Koen and Raeymaekers, Timothy (eds.) *Conflict and Social Transformation in Eastern DR Congo.* Gent: Academia Press.

Xinhua (2008) "China Unicom unveils details of merger with China Netcom". June 2. Available at http://www.chinadaily.com.cn/china/2008-06/02/content_6729822.htm

Xinhua (2010) "President of DR Congo meets Chinese army official", March 13. Available at http://www.chinadaily.com.cn/china/2010-03/13/content_9585105.htm

Xu, Shenglan (2008) "China Development Bank goes commercial", *China Daily*, December 12. Available at http://www.chinadaily.com.cn/bizchina/2008-12/02/content_7261101.htm

Yu, Liangchun; Berg, Sanford V.; Qing, Guo (2004) "Market performance of Chinese telecommunications: new regulatory policies", *Telecommunications Policy*, 28: 715-732.

Zha, Daojiong and Hu, Weixing (2007) "Promoting Energy Partnership in Beijing and Washington", *Washington Quarterly*, 30(4): 105-115.

Chapter 7

Embracing the Dragon
African Policy Responses for Tying Down China and Enhancing Regional Integration

Introduction

With China determinedly asserting its dominance in economic relations with African countries, debate on the effects of the Chinese commercial onslaught on Africa has been fierce and Chinese rebuttals predictable. With particular regard to China's burgeoning development assistance and commercial relations, African countries have generally expressed a collective hurray of appreciation for their expanded range of alternatives in supply of investment and aid. This appeal is predicated on China's role as a countervailing force to both OECD conditionality and to the continent's reliance on Western sources for foreign investment and development assistance (Alden, 2008: 118). Expectedly, some segments of the so called "traditional donors" have erupted in collective dismay, not only at their increasingly weakened position in influencing Africa through aid, but also at China's audacity to ruffle the existing aid architecture. For many African states, Chinese development assistance and commercial aspirations offer a veritable foil to Western (traditional) economies. By offering alternatives to aid-receiving countries, emerging donors, particularly China, are introducing competitive pressures that constitute a serious challenge to the existing multilateral development regime (Woods, 2008). For Africa, it's a good time. The pressure on traditional donors (and economies) presents an opportunity for increased independence and leverage for African external economic relations.

Incidentally, the criticism of China coming out of the sidelines of the Fourth Ministerial Forum on China-Africa Cooperation (FOCAC) held in Egypt in November 2009, may signal diminishing goodwill on Africa's part over China. This was the first major meeting between African countries and China since the outbreak of the global economic crisis and its eventual containment. At the meeting, several high ranking African Ministers[1] censured China's style of economic relations with Africa. Africa's subtle dissatisfaction with the conduct of China-Africa relations was subsequently expressed in the African Union's post-FOCAC report[2]. The paper proposes that, rather than merely vacillating between loathing and excitement over China, Africa should "tie down Gulliver" while the goodwill between the two is high. This paper proposes concrete supranational policy action plans for responding to China's growing economic engagement with Africa. Although there has been much elucidation on the pros and cons of Chinese involvement in Africa, there has not been much in terms of developing a collective policy framework for engaging China outside of some policy proposals made by Raphael Kaplinsky and Masuma Farooki in (Kaplansky and Farooki, 2009: 42).

This paper seeks to contribute to the enhancement of Afro-Chinese economic relations by shifting focus from the debate on the pros and cons of Chinese involvement in Africa to arguing that time is ripe for Africa to develop unified policy measures to manage China and make provisional policy proposals on how this can be done. The hypothesis asserted in this paper is twofold. First, a nascent disenchantment over China provides a veritable prod to coalesce an African "China policy" to manage China-Africa relations. Second, that if widely adopted, an African "China policy" would not only refine a coordinated continental response to China but would also help consolidate regional convergence in key policy areas.

The paper is divided into four main parts. The immediate section deals with two key ideational opportunities provided by Chinese foray into Africa. Although many positive outcomes of Chinese involvement have been discussed, its ideational benefits to Africa's policymaking—as opposed to merely increased alternatives in capitalization and foreign direct investment (FDI)—have not been duly captured. The following section deals with the justifications for a unified African policy. In doing so, the paper first questions the accuracy of the now putative notion of generalized "Chinese-African" relations. This aggregation of African benefits from China is misleading, the paper argues. Chinese relations with African countries—in trade, investment and aid—are overwhelmingly bilateral and the paper argues that if not addressed early, this predominantly bilateral approach will likely stymie rather than aid regional integration processes. Second, the paper deals with the rising pitfalls of Chinese business practices at the national level in African countries and how increasingly robust Chinese involvement in the continent is ruffling local business communities. In spite of a seemingly widespread government approval of Chinese involvement, the growing vexation and alienation of local business entities is not sustainable, and thus must be addressed. Finally the paper will broach and discuss policy propositions for anticipating and regulating African states-Chinese economic relations.

China-Africa Economic Relations
A Psychological Boost for African Policymaking

Although the concept of Africa's aid dependency is axiomatic, little has been done to broach on the developmental effects of aid dependency and loss of "policy space" on African states' economic planning. Unlike commercial relationships which are mutually interdependent, the relationship between a donor country and a recipient country ineluctably points to one's position in relation to the other. The donor naturally occupies a better position in terms of material resources, prestige and influence relative to the recipient. Is such positioning entirely irrelevant to economic development? Apparently not. As psychologists have argued, dependence connotes a state of helplessness. Behavior described as dependent implies seeking not only proximity to other persons but also attention and *approval* (*italic* added, Ainsworth, 1969: 2). The very notion of seeking approval has been very present in African policymaking where almost every major national economic policy decision has had to have the backing of major multilateral donors. For instance, since the 1990s African countries' economic planning blueprints (the Poverty Reduction Strategy Papers - PRSPs) are closely managed and evaluated by the World Bank and the IMF. These institutions, in fact, proudly claim to have launched the PRS initiative. This calls into question the level of policy ownership by African governments. Development is not merely an increase in material resources but a growth in the collective psychological resources (confidence) of a country. Poverty fuels a psychological state of social helplessness while wealth stokes confidence by increasing choice and options. The essential question in the psychology of national development is what type and quality of national psyche is relatively more amenable to generating and sustaining development, at both personal and societal levels (Bhola, 1990)? As Inkeles (1974: 328) noted, two core psychological attributes are essential to development: (i) a basic threshold of individual responsibility and planning, and (ii) freedom from absolute submission to any received authority. In as far as it has stymied the development of these essential attributes, development assistance and received authority from traditional[3] donors has played a role in crippling the psychological independence of African policymaking. As it has been found, some governments have thus accepted their subordinate position and the inevitability of donor involvement in policymaking, and have thus given up on national ownership and responsibility (Whitfield and Maipose, 2008: 4). This constitutes a psychological dereliction of duty on some African governments' part; what has been called a state deficit syndrome.

China is breaking this psychological dependency. In terms of impact on policy making, the most important contribution that China is likely to bring will be to increase the independence of African states' policy making and diminish the idea of development cooperation as charity. By expanding the sources of FDI and aid available to poorer countries, China, like other emerging donors, is expanding poorer nations' alternatives in procuring capital. An increased range of alternatives (choice) has consequently diminished the value of traditional donors' assistance and boosted Africa's latent negotiation resources in its economic relations. The fact that China is not propositioning Africa to follow or imitate its development strategy is a reflection of Chinese flexibility on the heterodox nature of economic development. This is a departure from traditional donors' proclivity to instruct African countries on the right policy and the subsequent crippling "search of approval" mentality which has permeated African states' policymaking. As (Kabeberuka, 2007: 13) observed it is instructive to note that China is not only expanding the policy choices but also the responsibility of African governments by increasing the *premium put on the ability to choose* a set of optimal combinations" (*italic* added) in policy. Thus China is helping to boost the two psychological essentials of a development mindset - the freedom and responsibility- of African states in economic policy making. This in turn helps actualize Amartya Sen's idea of development as being the expansion of freedoms.

From Stipulation to Negotiation -
Chinese role in enhancing economic diplomacy

Learning to be effective negotiators with other economies is going to be an essential policy skill for Africa's overall economic development. One of the key aspects of any negotiation is to be strategically "armed" with an objective and some negotiation resources such as better knowledge or an indispensable link. However, as far as economic diplomacy goes, it has been persuasively argued that often, African countries lack the capacity to influence or set the agenda and pace of negotiations during bilateral or multilateral negotiations with other parties (Osakwe, 2004). The very idea that African states have a marginal influence on the agenda suggests that usually, African countries have little time to even crystallize their objectives in commercial negotiations. The question then to ask is why African countries often participate in negotiation processes where their objectives are not clearly evident. The answer lies in African countries' diminished confidence (psychological state) about "what they bring to the table" during a negotiation. Due to African countries' sense of dependence on traditional donors, these more developed donor-nations often use a strategic threat of suspending bilateral assistance programs to enforce compliance of African states. There has thus been an axiomatic notion that in any negotiation process involving an African country and an external party, the African country has very little to offer and thus the partner is only being generous in seeking the African country's partnership. This is demonstrated by (Oyejide and Njinken 2007: 2) who have pointed out that, African countries often go to the table with an erroneous belief that their best alternative to a negotiated Agreement (BATNA) would automatically be worse off than the status quo, even when the evidence in specific cases points to the contrary.[4]

By affirming the widespread demand for African commodities, China will increase some African countries' strategic resources for negotiation and thus boost Africa's economic diplomacy. Due to China's open demand for commodities, Africans can now see themselves as coming to the table to negotiate and not to be merely instructed. The premium on African resources represents a valuable negotiation resource. By empowering African economies and national agencies, China will help reduce an apathetic attitude to commercial negotiations by African countries and reduce African countries' disposition to concede too readily in economic negotiations.

Justifications for a Unified "African-Chinese" Policy
Chinese- African Economic Relations:
The Pitfalls of Aggregation

One of the paradoxical outcomes of the 2006 China-Africa (Forum for China-Africa Cooperation) FOCAC Summit was its role in cementing the idea of aggregated Afro-Chinese relations. This summit gave a misleading impression that African countries were engaging China as one political entity with unified interests. However, although African leaders gathered in large numbers in Beijing, it was also clear that each African country had gone there seeking its own interests rather than pursuing an aggregated continental objective. Notwithstanding, the summit cemented an erroneous putative view of Africa as a unified block in its external relations contrary to reality. Any talk of aggregate Sino-Africa relations without any actual collective continental projects is deceptive for a number of reasons.

First, it conceals the lopsided nature of African-Chinese economic relations, a lopsidedness that is often embraced by scholars of China-Africa relations. For instance (Cook and Lam 2008: 5) noted that "According to recent customs data, in 2008 trade between China and Africa increased by 45% to $107 billion. Exports increased 54% but *for the first time Africa has a trade surplus* of over $5 billion" (*italic* added). In similar fashion, (Oyejide *et al*, 2009: 7) observed that "bilateral

209

Table 1:
Country Specific Distribution of Africa- Chinese Economic Relations (2007/2008)

FDI			TRADE			ODA	
Country	amount	Percentage	Country	amount	Percentage	Country	amount
Total	211.199 USD billion	100%	Total	56 Billion			?
S.A	411.17 m	19.5%	Angola	20.60	24%	Angola	?
Nigeria	184.89 m	8.7%	S.A	7.93	17%	Sudan	?
Algeria	186.00 m	8.8%	Sudan	5.55	8%	Tanzania	?
Zambia	75.05.34 m	3.5%	Egypt	--	6%	Zambia	?
Niger	196.25 m	9.3%	Nigeria	0.48	7%	Ethiopia	?
Angola	101.11 m	4.8%	Zambia	0.5	0.9%		
Congo DR	236.19m	11.2%	Congo	3.40	6.0%		

Sources: Investment – 2010 Statistical Bulletin of China's Outward FDI: 60-61
Trade – From Sarah Cook and Wing Lam, 2008: 5-6
ODA: Penny Davies, 2007: 56-57

Africa-China trade has been fairly balanced in recent times. In *particular, during 2004–2007, Africa enjoyed a small trade surplus with China* (except in 2007), to the tune of about $2 billion per annum" (*Italic* added).

Such broad aggregations hide the huge trade deficits that most African countries have with China. The danger of an aggregated perception of Sino-African relations is that while Chinese interests are disproportionately centered on a few resource-rich countries, a generalized "African" aggregation hides the specific economic effects of Chinese firms' engagement in each individual African country. Although China may be principally only benefiting a few countries, an aggregated view gives the impression (and false comfort) of unified continental benefits.

This is of course to the disadvantage of resource-low countries in Africa as shown above in Table 1 which shows the country specific distribution of Chinese economic relations in trade, aid and investment. As the table shows, only seven countries account for more than 80% of Chinese investment in Africa, while similarly, seven countries account for more than 65% of trade with African countries.

The notion of an "African" trade surplus is therefore misleading as many African countries suffer huge trade deficits with China as Table 2 above shows. Since con-

Table 2: Country Specific trade deficit with China

Country	Trade deficit with China
Egypt	US$2.3b
South Africa	US$2.44b
Kenya	US$892.5m
Cameroon	US$75m
Nigeria	US$52m
Mauritius	US$439m
Zimbabwe	US$189

Sources: Egypt: The Daily News Egypt, South Africa: Chinese Ministry of Commerce, Kenya: the Embassy of Kenya in Beijing, Cameroon: Cameroon's Institut National de la Statistique: Quoted in Khan and Baye (2008: 23), Nigeria: Nigeria–China Business Council, Mauritius: Vinaye D. Ancharaz (2009: 9), Zimbabwe: China in Africa (2011).

tinued reference to aggregate terms shows Africa as having a trade surplus, there is little realization and likely less urgency among African countries with lesser trade and huge deficits with China to more exigently seek an address to this imbalance.

Second, although cloaked in generous language[5], the Chinese refusal to disclose specific figures for its development assistance to individual African countries is in fact a strategic decision based on the fear that giving specific figures on each country would raise accusations of favoritism among African countries and thereby potentially raise the demands or grievances of some African countries. Thus, the so called 53-country aid strategy reflects China's sensitivity against favoritism (Davies, 2007: 49-50). In essence, China is afraid of African countries' solidarity in coalescing around fixing standards for its aid frameworks.

Crafting an African "China Policy" would, therefore, compel individual states to examine the effects of China on their economy and lay a more emphatic claim to reciprocal relations as far as aggregated Africa-Chinese relations are concerned. To do this, an African "China Policy" would compel intra-African aggregation so that any generalized Africa-China relations would at least have agreeable economic components for each country or region. Additionally, African supra-national institutions (such as the African Development Bank or the African Union) would then have a standardized framework for dealing with China in developing partnership programs with an actual regional or even continental dimension rather than having China deal with African countries bilaterally or as just a conglomeration of countries. An African "China policy" would give each African country a veritable platform to claim demonstrable "win-win" outcomes from China–Africa economic relations as well as lock in intra-Africa agreements that would obviate or at least mitigate potential wars of incentives over Chinese investments.

Edging Out Domestic Business –
Rising Discontent and why it's Unsustainable

The continued march of Chinese firms in edging out African firms in domestic tenders, local import trade and major business sub-sectors is slowly rising as demonstrated by some recent examples from East, West and Southern Africa shown below in Box 1. While most governments have lauded China, and have thus readily awarded construction tenders to Chinese firms, most local African businesses, as shown in the box below are experiencing great pressure from Chinese competition.

The hidden cost of Chinese efficiency is twofold. First, Chinese domination of business will become politically unsustainable if not checked in time. Already there have been sporadic clashes in several African countries targeted at the Chinese. Second, if proper competition policies are not swiftly adopted, African countries will lose out on their abilities to catch-up on technological transfers from Chinese companies. A unified policy will help African countries' businesses to anticipate and prepare for China's formidable entry into business in Africa.

Efficiency vs Backlash –
China's Economic Success Stirs Domestic Politics

In the long-run, African countries cannot remain entirely unswayed by the effects and exigencies of domestic politics on trade policy.[6] Although African countries do widely accept the ineluctable utility of competition in global business, the sudden flood of Chinese firms will likely lead to a political backlash that will be politically difficult to ignore, as demonstrated by the 2009 FOCAC meeting. Rising frustration over China's political apathy may have finally been vented at the Fourth Ministerial Forum on China-Africa Cooperation (FOCAC) held in Egypt in November 2009. As evidence of political backlash against the Chinese, there have been sporadic politically motivated attacks on Chinese workers in Cameroon as well as deadly attacks in Ethiopia. More recently in Zambia, popular opposition to China has been particularly impetuous, and culminated in the election of a putative anti-China president in September 2011. Although most

"China Quietly Usurps African Textile Market" (Ghana – Textiles)

"Africa is going through a double whammy, as China has penetrated deeply into the African textile market, seriously dislocating the domestic textile companies in Africa. While Africa was hoping to cash in on the concessions being extended by both the US and the EU to promote its exports to both the countries, it is now facing a dilemma because of deluge of Chinese textiles. What China seems to be losing in the US market, appears to be made up in the African market. In Ghana, the textile industry continues to face challenges, amid growing competition from cheap imports from China. The Director General of Nigeria Textile Manufacturing Association (NTMA), Jolaoso Olarewaju, said between 1996 and 2006, the number of employees on the association's employment data had reduced from 250,000 to less than 30,000"

Originally published in The Stitch Times: January 2010

"China's march in Kenya upsets local firms" (Kenya – Construction)

"A report by 14 universities in Africa under the aegis of the African Economic Research Consortium (AERC) released two months ago warned that increasing investment, foreign aid and diplomatic ties with China would hurt Kenya. Fears have been raised about threats to engineering talent and skills and the collapse of local construction companies due to invasion of Chinese construction firms, says the report. The researchers feel that Chinese firms are undercutting local companies and that the latter may collapse. They estimate that more than 50 per cent of construction activities in Nairobi, both private and state-sponsored, have been captured by Chinese construction firms usually preferred for projects ranging from roads, water systems, power generation and hospitals. Increasingly, the structure of employment is changing, with an increasing proportion of foreign employees in Chinese enterprises, says the report by the University of Nairobi Institute for Development Studies."

Originally published in The Daily Nation: January 23rd 2010

"Cosatu lambasts 'Chinese tsunami" (South Africa - Textiles)

ANGER is mounting in Africa, particularly in SA, about what the Congress of South African Trade Unions (Cosatu) calls a "tsunami of cheap Chinese goods" stifling local industries and wiping out jobs. SA's textile union estimates 800 manufacturing units and 60000 jobs have disappeared in SA since 2001 because of unfair competition from China.

Originally published in the Johannesburg Business Day: January 21 2010

Box 1: Displacement of Domestic African Business by Chinese Firms

African governments have shrugged off the backlash thus far, this kind of backlash will become more attractive in populist democratic elections and thus more difficult to ignore or suitably manage with ad hoc solutions.

When the backlash against Chinese competition is taken up by trade unions, as in South Africa (and possibly supported) by local manufacturers and industrialists (as in Ghana and Kenya), governments' arguments for Chinese efficiency will increasingly become politically untenable. Any sudden economic backlash against Chinese goods could be injurious to both Chinese investors and even local manufacturers since (even in the event of sudden nationalistic consumption patterns), the domestic industries' capabilities in price and quality may be so badly eroded as to be unable to credibly substitute manufacturers of previously Chinese-supplied commodities. An African policy, therefore, ensures that governments suitably prepare both the consumer and the producer for the growing Chinese onslaught.

Chinese FDI, Employment and Technology – Compelling Linkages in Domestic Economies

In recent years African countries have been very active in courting FDI. Yet merely attracting FDI is not sufficient for the requisite long-term job creation in African countries that would cause a radical shift in the general population's perception of FDI in general, and Chinese business in particular. African countries should look at FDI and trade in a broader, long-term developmental perspective. Chinese aid, trade and FDI should not only be aimed at increasing government income, (through licenses or privatization for instance) but at improving the long-term productive capabilities of a wide section of the populace. This can only be effected by ensuring that Chinese economic activities have widened linkages in the local economy in terms of employment, technology transfer and skills enhancement. The managerial skills and advanced technology of the Chinese business should be tapped into early by inaugurating a policy that facilitates this transfer. Chinese FDI should not be left to fortify itself in FDI "enclaves" that have few linkages with the rest of the economy. Linkages with local enterprises would be instrumental in enhancing productivity growth of domestic firms.

Chinese Buy-outs and Acquisitions – The Next Headache

In addition, governments and businesses in Africa must get prepared for the next phase of the Chinese onslaught on Africa which is likely to be buyouts (either partial or whole) and mergers and acquisitions of profitable African companies. Finding themselves without time to organically build their brands, Chinese companies have now taken to brand buying as a shortcut to enhancing their local presence. A case in point is the purchase of 20% stake in Standard

Bank- South Africa's largest bank- by the Industrial and Commercial Bank of China (ICBC). Although Chinese businesses in Africa are not automatically supported by the Chinese State, for some companies, this acquisition is backed by the Chinese State with ample financial support as part of the Chinese "go-out" *(zou chu qu)* policy[7].

African governments should anticipate and define how they will react to such takeovers. Will African governments set aside some strategic companies that will be protected from potential acquisitions? If so, what would be the selection criteria for such "strategic" companies? Should African governments initiate preemptive negotiations for agreements with Chinese companies to obviate domestic anxiety about such takeovers?

Therefore, clear partnership mechanisms for creating dynamic learning, and fostering competitiveness for domestic firms should be conceived and embraced within an African "China Policy". Since such mechanisms (such as compulsory requirements on employment and training of domestic staff), are not necessarily benign to FDI, Chinese investors could resist their implementation and thus a need for a unified front by African countries. While many countries may have the intent of creating such linkages, pinning down the Chinese to adopt such domestic industry augmenting measures would require the combined muscle of the entire continent. Obviously, it is not easy for African states to agree on such measures for tying down China, because such an agreement would spell out and regulate some aspects of intra-Africa competition on FDI. However, if agreed, they would constitute a giant leap in intra-Africa convergence in policy. Thus an African "China policy" provides a means of not only managing China but forging intra-African convergence on key policy areas such as competition in FDI.

Policy Action for "Tying Down" China
From "CADFund" to a Chinese targeted Trust-fund at the AfDB

As part of its *zou chu qu* policy China already has the China-Africa Development Fund (CADFund). The fund is a US$1 billion facility provided by the China Development Bank whose objective is to support Chinese companies who wish to invest in Africa. According to the Chinese, this fund is meant "to build up bridge linking and connection of the economic and trade cooperation between China and Africa, enhance the self-development capability of Africa as well as to promote mutually beneficial and win-win between China and Africa by market-oriented operation" (CADFund, see the reference list).

While this fund has potentially immense benefits for Africa in terms of enhancing FDI, for all intents and purposes, this fund is completely China-centric and primarily intended to achieve the interests of Chinese firms with very little, if any, African input in its administration. African countries cannot determine their interests and priorities since the fund is fully administered by the Chinese Development Bank. Thus while the Chinese "win" is assured, the African "win" is only implied. In addition, this is a fund aimed at assisting the Chinese private sector as opposed to African states' public or private sector. As an exigent measure for developing projects with a veritable African (continental) ownership, African countries should establish a special trust fund administered by the AfDB. This would ensure that all African countries who are members of the AfDB would have a fair shot in promoting their interest with regard to Chinese FDI.

As a counterpart to the CADFund, African countries should set up a fund at the African Development Bank to deal with collective economic issues regarding China. Primary to the objective of this fund would be the collective promotion of African economic interests in China. Establishment of such a fund would also goad the establishment of a minimal formal agreement on what such "collective African economic" issues would comprise. Once agreed, the fund would go into funding collective projects with a veritable regional or continental dimension. Similarly, the fund could be used by individual countries to either enhance its economic interests in China or mitigate injurious effects of Chinese commercial onslaught on the country.

A Chinese targeted trust fund, administered by the AfDB, would have two benefits. One, it would facilitate convergence of the continent in determining minimal collective interest with regard to China. Two, African countries, through such a fund, would have greater financial capabilities over how to embrace China. This could include facilitating further entry of Chinese firms into targeted sectors in any given country, helping domestic firms to readjust to the Chinese onslaught with cheaper imports or even helping promote a given country's exports in China.

Maximize Capacity Enhancement for African Firms and Workers

African countries have a lot to learn from the Chinese trade and FDI policy of the 1980s, in terms of contents, pace and sequencing. One of the most pressing challenges for any developing country is how to stem unemployment. FDI is thus seen as key in alleviating unemployment. However, as jobs trickle in, the utility of FDI should similarly be focused on the improvement of workers' skills and technological transfers to local companies. Chinese FDI should be used to reignite – not stymie – African industrialization. In China for instance, it was not until after 1986 that wholly foreign foreign-owned enterprises were permitted in areas outside of special economic zones (Tseng and Zebregs 2002: 12). Before 1986 most FDI consisted of equity joint ventures or cooperative joint venture companies. The motivation for this requirement was simply to enhance local entrepreneurs' business skills as well as technological transfer to Chinese companies. To the Chinese, international joint ventures presented an ideal form for securing rapid access to capital, technology and export markets within an economy in transition (Dolles and Wimking, 2005: 6).

African governments should take heed and implement a similar policy with the intent of enhancing technological transfer to domestic firms. Since African countries have by this time a good idea of the main target industries for Chinese FDI in their countries, focus should shift from mere volume of FDI to the effects of Chinese FDI on employment creation and technological transfer. In addition, a vigilant policy on joint ventures[8] would propitiate domestic firms into a state where foreign competition will be more readily acceptable. In anticipating external competition domestic companies will have an option of getting into a joint venture or going it alone. Some policies for enhancing transfer of capabilities would include the following:

Set Standards on Equity Joint-Ventures

- Set clear minimum requirements on equity joint ventures and cooperative joint ventures for Chinese companies investing in certain strategic target sectors for the enhancement of technology transfer. This will have the incidental effect of precipitating governments to ponder the question of the relevance of, and aspirations for any strategic industry or industries.

Make Unambiguous Stipulations on Curbing Foreign Workers

- Enact strict limits on the number of foreign workers that each Chinese company can bring into African countries. This should be particularly pertinent for unskilled workers in construction or mining jobs. This would have the effect of not only raising local employment (in cases where the Chinese have brought their own workers), but also exposing and improving working relations between the Chinese and local workers.

Push China to Consider a Voluntary Export Restraint (VER)

Across the continent the textile industry has been worst hit by the influx of cheaper Chinese textiles. This hit has lead to major losses in manufacturing jobs for most African countries. Similarly, African manufacturing has been hit by Chinese competition abroad. Kenya, Lesotho and Swaziland all saw their exports of clothing under the African Growth and Opportunities Act (AGOA) drop sharply when the end of the Multi-Fiber Agreement (MFA) allowed Chinese garments unlimited entry into the US market (Kaplinsky, et al 2007: 25). Under the WTO regulations, African countries have little recourse. One such available recourse, however, would be to seek a voluntary export restraint on the part of Chinese manufactured textiles. For almost all major industrial economies today (Korea, Taiwan and now China and Bangladesh), the textiles industry has been an important massive employer of semi-skilled labor and a launching pad to industrial sophistication both in terms of knowledge and technology. Due to the assured demand for clothing, the textile industry is one that can still be salvaged in African countries.

It is instructive that South Africa was able to negotiate a Voluntary Export Restraint (VER) for textiles with China in 2006. African countries could tap into South Africa's experiences and angle for a continental extension of the VER. A VER by China could also potentially have the incidental and propitious effect of encouraging Chinese firms to set their factories in Africa in order to circumvent the VER. This would in turn increase FDI, technology transfer and employment in African countries.

Issue a Calibrated Convergence Policy on Reduction of Aid Dependency

Aid is not necessary debt, but concern has been raised that Chinese aid might have the effect of exacerbating African countries' debt[9] and aid dependency. As old debts are being cleared, there is growing concern among traditional donors of the possible future debt burden on African countries given the heavy concessionary loans being provided by China (Kaplinsky and Farooki, 2009: 17). The fear is that China could re-indebt poor African nations by lending loosely and unconditionally. In fact the US, the G7 and other traditional creditors have been vociferously trying to tie China down under traditional lending practices.[10] The average amount of aid to Sub-Saharan Africa as a percentage of the total national income is actually rather low at 4%. Yet, aid dependency should be an immensely valid issue of concern to African countries because to a certain extent, the level of aid dependency does influence the level of national ownership of the entire policy-making agenda. In addition, as shown below, in spite of the low continental average, many African countries still do rely on aid for substantial portions of their national income.

Just as the EU has set up caps on the percentage of fiscal deficits in its member Euro-zone states in a bid to reduce aid dependency (as well as manage China's lending), African states should set up a policy for maximum limits on aid as a percentage of the GNI – provisionally below 10% and possibly a further 1-2 % annual reduction for those countries already below 10%.

At the least, such a policy would deter countries from reckless "over borrowing" from China. More fundamentally however, if such a policy were adopted it would open the door for enhanced regional convergence in African fiscal

Table 3: Aid as a Percentage of Gross National Income in Select African countries

Country	Aid (as % of GNI)	Country	Aid (as % of GNI)
Burundi	47.9%	Burkina Faso	13.8%
Sierra Leone	32.7%	Mali	13.8%
Mozambique	24.4%	DR Congo	13.1%
Malawi	20.6%	Niger	12.8%
Tanzania	17.4%	Madagascar	12.2%
Uganda	14.8%	Zambia/CAR	10.4%

Source: World Development Indicators, 2007: 348

policy. Such a policy would open up each economy to enhanced scrutiny from a supranational monitoring institution (the AU or AfDB perhaps) to ensure compliance to healthy fiscal environment in African economies. At a time when economies are ever closely intertwined, such a policy would be a step towards reaching Africa's regionalization aspirations. An attempt at the regionalization of fiscal policy is already happening in Africa with various distinct schemes for regionalization by different regional economic blocs[11]. Mitigation against escalation of debt due to Chinese lending could accelerate this fiscal convergence. However, there is little headway in terms of vigilant scrutiny or penalties for defaulting. The entry of Chinese aid into the fray should enhance this convergence.

Conclusion

Much of the debate on the rapidly developing economic relations between Africa and China so far has tended to focus on the pros and cons of these economic ties. As this paper proposes, however, rather than merely vacillating between excitement and loathing of China, African states should embrace an African "China Policy" in order to reap constructively from Chinese-African economic ties. In moving beyond the pro vs. con debate, this paper thus seeks to provide policy proposals for a collective African framework for engaging China.

In the past, African criticism of China has been reticent. However, this reticence was broken in the follow-up to the Forum on China-Africa Cooperation (FOCAC) held in Egypt in November 2009. This nascent disenchantment was similarly expressed (though in a muted manner) by the post-FOCAC AU Report (EX.CL/544, XVI) in January 2010. Any further strident disagreements on economic relations between Africa and China would be injurious to both parties. Thus, an African "China policy" should be crafted promptly, while goodwill between Africa and China is still high. This paper argues that China should be pragmatically embraced, not with criticism or praise, but with policy.

Some policy proposals discussed in this paper include: the creation of a Chinese targeted fund for, among other things, African countries to mitigate any disenfranchisement of domestic business due to entry of Chinese businesses. Such a fund would also be useful in funding the development of a collective institutional framework for dealing with China. The fund would also be aimed at fostering minimum veritable intra-Africa agreements on collective interests with regard to China. Also discussed is the viability of negotiating a Voluntary Export Restrain (VER) for Chinese exports to Africa - especially for certain massively affected subsectors such as textiles. In addition the paper discusses a set of policies that would be aimed at ensuring that Chinese FDI, technology, and managerial skills have linkages to the local economy and finally, an intra-Africa policy for placing caps on loans (debt) as a percentage of the national income. This would ensure that African countries do not borrow recklessly from China and thus obviate any sharp increases in African countries debt as a result of "generous" Chinese aid. African policies for embracing China would not only be useful in Africa's continental economic diplomacy with China, but would also fundamentally enhance regional policy convergence within Africa. Thus, the entry of China does present opportunities for regional convergence.

Notes

1   Notable were the Nigerian and Libyan Foreign Ministers. The two countries strong leverage using oil resources grants them the political independence to criticize China but its unlikely that disaffection is limited to these two only.

2   Among other things the AU expressed dissatisfaction and urged China to the following: Simply the lending procedures of its financial institutions advocate for and support African courses in ASEAN, G20 and other fora, allow preferential entry of semi-finished African goods into the Chinese market and to allow greater technology transfer to firms in Africa. For more see Report of the AU Commission on Africa's Strategic Relationships (EX.CL/544 (XVI) January 2010.

3   In this paper "traditional donors", proximally, refers to the founder member of the OECD.

4   This is best illustrated by (Oyejide and Njinken, 2007) in "African Preparation for Trade Negotiations in the Context of the ACP-EU Cotonou Partnership Agreement" who for instance show that in the on going EPA negotiations between ACP and EU,

African Least Developed Countries (LDCs) would have been best placed in keeping the status quo of their preferential treatment as LDCs. Yet, these LDCs too opted to enter the EPA negotiations and thus open themselves up for European goods which would be a worse of outcome than the existing arrangement.

5   For the language and justifications used by China about this, see the report written by Penny Davies (2007) *China and the End of Poverty in Africa*, published by the Swedish development aid organization Diakonia in collaboration with European Network on Debt and Development (Eurodad): 49-50.

6   The political economy trade policy is often tolerated even when it's not economically efficient. For example as a 1980s Cato Institute paper indicated European Agricultural Policy costs European consumers some US$20 billion per year, for every US$20,000 per year job protected in Swedish shipyards, Swedish taxpayers pay an estimated US$50,000 annual subsidy. When Japanese consumers pay eight times the world price for beef, Japanese farmers are not eight times better off. See, J. Michael Fingers "The Political Economy of Trade Policy", *Cato Journal* 3(3): 1.

7   Specific to Africa, China has the China-Africa Development Fund (CADFund), a US$1 billion facility provided by the China Development Bank, whose objective is to support Chinese companies who wish to invest in Africa.

8   This policy suggestion is made within an understanding the GATS article XVI stipulations and limitations. Article XVI makes reference to (i) prohibiting measures which restrict or require specific types of legal entity or joint venture, and (ii) prohibiting measures which require maximum percentage limit on foreign shareholding or the total value of individual or aggregate foreign investment. However since as of 2006 (post WTO entry) China still did require a minimum of 25% of the capital must from the foreign partner(s), this suggests that if pursued collectively, African states could find a way of using joint ventures. http://www.chinadaily.com.cn/bizchina/2006-04/17/content_569167.htm

9   Debt is only a proportion of aid that mainly arises from bilateral or multilateral lending as opposed to grants. The OECD reports that in 2009 net ODA rose 0.7% in real terms and while grants grew by 4.6% bilateral lending grew by 20.6%. As lending is growing faster than grants this implies that the question of debt sustainability is still very relevant for African countries. For more see http://www.oecd.org/document/11/0,3343, en_2649_34487_44981579_1_1_1_1,00.html

10 For more on the debate on Chinese aid and the G7-efforts at trying down China, see Ngaire Woods paper, "Whose aid, Whose Influence? Emerging Donors and the Silent Revolution in Development Assistance."

11 SADC for instance has some of the more ambitious standards for fiscal convergence where by it has set the regional targets for inflation stability (6–9 percent range.), budget deficits ratio to GDP (± 3 percent range.), ratio of public and publicly guaranteed debt to GDP (no larger than 40%) and the balance and structure of the Current Account (no larger than 6 percent).

References

Accenture (2007) "China Spreads its Wings; Chinese Companies Go Global". Accenture Consulting Policy and Corporate Affairs Report. Available at http://www.accenture.com/SiteCollectionDocuments/PDF/6341_chn_spreads_wings_final8.pdf.

Agencies, (2009) "Gun men seize 5 Chinese Fishermen off Cameroon", *China Times,* July 8. Available at http://www2.chinadaily.com.cn/world/2009-07/08/content_8398201.htm

Ainsworth, Mary Slater (1990) "Object Relations, Dependency, and Attachment: A Theoretical

Review of the Infant-Mother Relationship", *Child Development,* 1969, 40: 969-1025.

Ancharaz, Vinaye Day (2009) "David V. Goliath: Mauritius facing up to China", *European Journal of Development Research*, 21(4): 622–643.

African Union Commission (2010) "Report of the AU Commission on Africa's Strategic Relationships" (EX.CL/544 (XVI). An African Union Executive Council Report.

Ajakaye, Olu et al. (2009) "China-Africa Trade Relations; Insights from AERC Scoping Studies", *European Journal of Development Research,* 21(4): 485–505

Alden, Chris (2008) "Africa Turns East: The Role of Political Regimes in Shaping Responses to China", in Chris Alden's *China in Africa*. Claremont: Zed Books Ltd.

Bayne, Nicholas and Woolcock, Stephen (eds.) (2007): *The New Economic Diplomacy: Decision-Making and Negotiation in International Economic Relations.* Hamshire: Ashgate Publishing Company.

BBC News (2007) "Scores Die in Ethiopia Oil Attack", April 24. Available at http://news.bbc.co.uk/2/hi/africa/6588055.stm.

Berger, Bernt and Wissenbach, Uwe (2007) "EU-China- Africa Trilateral Development

Cooperation; Common Challenges and New Directions", *DIE Discussion Papers, 21/2007.* German Development Institute.

Bhola, Harbans S. (1990) "The Psychology of Development and the Psychology of Literacy: A point of interscetion", *Psychology and Developing Societies,* 2(1): 53-65

Chifamba, T. Tadeous (2007) "Multilateral Trade Negotiations: How sensibly must African countries and trade negotiators stand? - Some lessons from WTO experience", *Occasional Paper, No.7*, African Capacity Building Foundation.

China-Africa Development Fund, "About us", Available at http://www.cadfund.com/en/NewsInfo.aspx?NId=153

China Daily, (2006) "How to Establish a Joint Venture in China?" April 17. Available at http://www.chinadaily.com.cn/bizchina/2006-04/17/content_569167.htm.

China In Africa (2011) "People's Republic of China- Zimbabwe Relations", June 10. Available at http://www.zhong-fei.org/en/node/751.

Cook, Sarah and Lam, Wing (2008) "The Financial Crisis and China: What are the Implications for Low Income Countries?" Institute of Development Studies, University of Sussex. Available at http://www.ids.ac.uk/files/dm-file/FinancialCrisisChinaandlowincomecountries.pdf.

Davies, Penny (2007) "China and the End of Poverty in Africa: Towards Mutual Benefit?" Diakonia and European Network on Debt and Development (Eurodad) Report. Available at http://www.diakonia.se/Documents/public/NEWS/China_and_the_end_of_poverty_in_Africa_2.pdf

Dollar, David (2008) "Lesson from China for Africa", *Policy Research Working Paper 4531*. World Bank.

Dolles, Harald and Wilmking, Niklas (2005) "International Joint Ventures in China After the WTO Accession; Will trust Relations Change?", *Working Paper, 05/7*, Deutsches Institut für Japanstudien. Available at http://www.dijtokyo.org/doc/WP05_7Dolles_Wilmking_IJVsChinaTrust.pdf.

Gabriel, Tony Gamal (2011) "HSBC report sees bright trade future for Egypt as deficit narrows", *The Daily News Egypt,* October 17. Available at http://thedailynewsegypt.com/trade/hsbc-report-sees-bright-trade-future-for-egypt-as-deficit-narrows.html

Inkeles, Alex (1975) "Becoming Modern: Individual Change in Six Developing Countries", *Ethos*, 3(2): 323-342

Johannesburg Business Day (2009) "Cosatu Lambasts Chinese Tsunami", August 24. Available at http://www.businessday.co.za/articles/Content.aspx?id=79332 .

Kabeberuka, David (2007) "The African Economy: Fifty Years after Independence", October 8, President Donald Kaberuka delivered a memorial lecture at the Bank of Uganda on "The African Economy: Fifty Years after Independence", in honor of Mr. Joseph Mubiru, the first Governor of the (Central) Bank of Uganda.

Kaplinsky, Raphael (2008) "China and the Terms of Trade: The Challenge to Development Strategy in SSA", paper prepared for Rise of China: Global Opportunities and Challenges Conference. The Open University, United Kingdom.

Kaplinsky, Raphael and Farooki Masuma (2009) "Africa's Cooperation with New and Emerging Development Partners. Options for Africa's Development", New York: Report by Office of Special Advisor on Africa, United Nations. Avilable at http://asiandrivers.open.ac.uk/Kaplinsky%20Emerging%20Economies%20and%20SSA%20final%20March%202009.pdf.

Kaplinsky, Raphael, McCormick Dorothy and Morris, Mike, (2007) "The Impact of China on Sub-Saharan Africa" Institute of Development Studies *Working Paper 29*. Viewed 1ˢᵗ November 2011. http://www.hubrural.org/pdf/ids_wp291_impact_china_on_ssa.pdf

Kenyan Embassy (2011) "Kenya-China Relations: Bilateral economy and trade relations and economic and technological cooperation". Available at http://www.kenyaembassy.cn/content/content.aspx?kid=64

Khan, Sunday Aninpah and Baye, Francis Menjo, (2008) "China-Africa Economic Relations: The Case of Cameroon." Report Submitted to the African Economic Research Consortium (AERC). Available at http://www.aercafrica.org/documents/asian_drivers_working_papers/Cameroon-China.pdf

Korniyenko, Yevgeniya and Sakatsume, Toshiaki (2009) "Chinese Investment in the Transition Countries", *Working Paper No. 107*. European Bank for Reconstruction and Development.

Li, Weijian, et al. (2010) *"Toward a New Decade: Research on the Sustainable Development of FOCAC"*, Report of Shanghai Institute for International Studies. Available at http://www.siis.org.cn/Sh_Yj_CMS/uploads/towardeng.pdf.

Lönnqvist, Linda (2008) "China's Aid to Africa: Implications for Civil Society", *Policy Briefing Paper 17,* International NGO Training and Research Centre.

Ministry of Commerce, China, (2010) "2010 Statistical Bulletin of China's Outward Foreign Direct Investment", Annual Report of China's Ministry of Commerce.

Ministry of Commerce, China, (2011) "South Africa Trade Statistics in August of 2010", Available at http://english.mofcom.gov.cn/aarticle/subject/minister/lanmub/201102/20110207420819.html

Mullainathan, Sendhil (2004) "Psychology and Development Economics", MIT and NBER. Annual Bank Conference on Development Economics at the World Bank.

Naudé, *William* A. (2005) "Evolutionary Psychology and Development Economics", Paper prepared for the UNU-WIDER Jubilee Conference on the Future of Development Economics, Helsinki, Finland, 17 – 18 June 2005. Available at http://www.rrojasdatabank.info/unurp05/Naude.pdf.

OECD (2009) "Development Aid rose in 2009 and most donors will meet 2010 aid targets", Development Co-operation Directorate (DCD-DAC). Available at http://www.oecd.org/document/11/0,3746, en_2649_34447_44981579_1_1_1_1,00.html.

Office of Fair Trading (2009) *Governments in Markets: Why Competition Matters - A Guide for Policymakers*. OFT, United Kingdom. Available at http://www.oft.gov.uk/shared_oft/business_leaflets/general/OFT1113.pdf.

Okemba, David (2010) "China's march in Kenya upsets local firms", *Daily Nation*, January 23. Available at http://mobile.nation.co.ke/News/-/1290/848224/-/format/xhtml/item/1/-/4w4kx5z/-/index.html.

Osakwe, Patrick (2004) "African Research Networking in Trade Policy and Multilateral Negotiations", Paper prepared for presentation at the OECD-DAC/WTO Meeting on Trade Capacity Building. Available at http://www.oecd.org/dataoecd/47/26/30231298.pdf

Oyejide, Ademola and Njinken, Dominique (2007) "African Preparation for Trade Negotiations in the Context of the ACP-EU Cotonou Partnership Agreement", Special *Paper 39* African Economic Research Consortium.

Renknakamp, Britta (ed.) (2010) "Special Issue on Innovation for Sustainability", *African Journal of Science Technology, Innovation & Development*, 2(1).

Tseng, Wanda and Zebregs Harms (2002) "Foreign Direct Investments in China. Some Lessons for Other Countries", IMF Policy *Discussion paper PDP 02/03*.

Whitfield, Lindsey and Maipose, Gervase (2008) "Managing Aid Dependence: How African Governments Lost Ownership and how they can regain it", *GEG Briefing Paper*. University College Oxford. Available at http://www.teol.ku.dk/cas/past_events/2009/whitfield/Aid_dependence_paper.pdf/.

Wissenbach, Uwe (2008) "The Renaissance or the End of Geopolitics? Towards Trilateral Cooperation in Africa", Shanghai: Shanghai Institutes for International Studies. Available at http://library.fes.de/pdf-files/bueros/china/05958.pdf Accessed 16th September 2011.

World Bank (2004) "The Poverty Reduction Strategy Initiative: An Independent Evaluation of the World Bank's Support Through 2003", World Bank Operations Evaluation Department. Available at http://www.worldbank.org/ieg/prsp/.

World Bank (2007) "World Development Indicators: Aid Dependency", *Annual World Bank Report*. Available at http://siteresources.worldbank.org/DATASTATISTICS/Resources/table6_11.pdf